WORK & YOUR FUTURE

WORK & YOUR FUTURE:
Living Poorer, Working Harder

by William T. Morris

RESTON PUBLISHING COMPANY, INC.
A Prentice-Hall Company
Reston, Virginia 22090

Library of Congress Cataloging in Publication Data

Morris, William Thomas, 1928-
    Work & your future: living poorer, working harder.

    Includes bibliographies.
    1. Industrial productivity. I. Title.
HD56.M67   658.5   75-1323
ISBN 0-87909-892-9

© 1975 by Reston Publishing Company, Inc. / *A Prentice-Hall Company*
Reston, Virginia 22090

10 9 8 7 6 5 4 3 2 1   Printed in the United States of America

To Mim

CONTENTS

PREFACE

Not a few thinkers, some calling themselves futurologists, have read in the trends of our material living the clear possibility of a declining level of real income. To them, there seems a fair chance that we may be headed for a period of working harder and living poorer. This prediction causes a great astonishment to those of us who have been nourished for years on the shorter work week, earlier retirement, the gradual disappearance of the dangerous, dull, drudgery in our working lives, and who have known, at least on average, the steady increase in material wealth. An irrational assault on that sanctified concept, the American Standard of Living. But inflation and shortages have made the classically dismal science of economics more dismal than ever. The notion of productivity, what you get for what you put in, output per man-hour, miles per gallon, has become a lot less abstract.

The recent "Phases" of economic intervention and the temporary closing of the neighborhood gas station have brought considerable attention to this vague yet powerful notion of productivity. The confluence of high inflation, unemployment, foreign competition, and dollar devaluation has brought an official response from the government that productivity is *the* solution to these problems. Productivity, indeed, is the solution to almost all of our problems, since without it, funds for attacking the great social problems of our time cannot be made available.

Time, Newsweek, and the business press are devoting extensive space to discussions of whether or not productivity is *the* problem and what we can do if it is. The government has established a National Commission on Productivity, has required major business enterprises to measure it, and through HEW, has issued a controversial study entitled, "Work in America." Even the Smithsonian has produced a major exhibit attempting to make the concept of productivity tangible for all.

There is broad public discussion of the decline of the work ethic, the blue collar blues, the white collar blues, and the failure of financial incentives for the younger members of our work force. Foreign workers are thought to be outworking us. Lordstown is explained in terms of boredom and frustration. The Swedes are reported to be using small teams to build entire automobiles. Absenteeism has become a serious challenge to management and human relations experts.

With a service-dominated economy, productivity is seen as not only hard to measure, but harder to achieve. Health care costs go up and somehow the question of becoming more productive in the delivery of health care seems like the wrong question to raise. Productivity in government is being measured, standards for the productivity of lawyers are being successfully used, and even the National Council of Churches is raising some questions about its own productivity.

This book has three objectives:

1. To provide a clear, non-technical introduction to the problem of productivity and its social, political, and economic implications. To deal with the myths, conventional wisdom, traditions, research findings, and actual experiences which surround productivity.

2. To provide ways of understanding some of the many curious experiments and unexpected developments which we have seen in the past. To help one make some sense out of what has happened and what is being said about productivity and how it may be changed.

3. To suggest some new and different hypotheses about the sources of productivity improvements and their personal and cultural impacts in the future.

Not many statistics, not much jargon. We are attempting to present for the reader, whatever may be his role in our economy, the old ideas and some new ideas about understanding and coping with what these times have inevitably labeled "our productivity crisis."

WILLIAM T. MORRIS

1
Living Poorer, Working Harder

THE WORLD TURNED UPSIDE DOWN

It was a time of surprises, of half told stories with low probability endings, a time when even hindsight seemed poorly informed. It was, like all times, a time when the persistent occurrence of the unforeseen made us wonder about the effort we had invested in attempts to learn from the past. As always, our great problem was to distinguish the great new trends from the small interruptions in the old ones. Social commentators, examining us from afar, called the time "the age of management." Management was widely taught to young people as the relevant profession, as the way to change the system from the inside. Management was taught as if management was possible, as if, in fact, things could somehow actually be managed. It was the beginning of the Seventies.

In Britain a few years earlier, a professor had completed a long and careful study of the attitudes of people working in a large automobile plant. A competent sociologist, he found the workers well integrated into the system, not holding any serious grudges, and rather satisfied with their wages. They saw their work as neither likeable nor distasteful, but as a necessary part of life to be done and dispensed with as quickly as possible so that they might turn their attention to the other aspects of their lives. Their working lives were not something they wanted to dwell on because their real interests were in their homes, their hobbies, their gardens, and their families. They were resigned to working and to a degree reconciled with their work situations.

1

Several hundred copies of the professor's report found their way into the hands of his subjects. A few days later, the automobile firm published its profit figures for the year, profits which happened to amount to some 900 pounds per employee. The following day rioting and violence broke out among the work force, and for two days the management of the firm was besieged in its offices.

In the United States, an earlier period of high investment in modern production equipment gave managements the justifiable expectation that the anticipated gains in productivity were about to appear. In the steel industry, for example, careful studies had shown that major investments in new equipment would clearly lead to important gains in productivity which would amply repay the necessary outlays. The gains, however, did not appear at the appointed time. Worse still, no really plausible explanation or persuasive excuse seemed to appear which would make the mystery any more acceptable.

The new General Motors Assembly Division plant at Lordstown in northern Ohio became a veritable fountain of sociological evidence, the import of which was to be felt, it was said, in drastic social changes. The Lordstown situation foretold wholly different work attitudes of a new generation, the need to abandon the assembly line, and the final death of a persistent anachronism call "Taylorism." It was virtually impossible to find any reference in all of this to what had in fact happened at Lordstown. Because of a corporate reorganization, two plants formerly managed by two separate GM divisions were now under a single division. Correspondingly, it followed that two union locals would now have to be combined into a single local. It was obvious and predictable that the two local leadership groups would make increasingly strident claims and demands on the company in order to demonstrate that each could do more, get more, and raise wages more than the other. The two union leadership groups were fighting each other for survival.

Working people, to their small comfort, became once again, as in 1870, 1917, and 1933, the leading characters in the dramas of the popular social critics. What it was really like to work in a basic steel mill or on the fastest automobile assembly line in the world was revealed in the most personal terms. The rush to generalize these experiences filled the air with ideas about alienation, the meaninglessness of work, its dehumanizing character, and the "blue-collar blues." The rhetoric of popular sociology dwelt upon the need for restructuring work to make it self-actualizing and to give it a new "meaningfulness." When serious studies of these phenomena got under way, it was more than usually difficult to identify the large numbers of alienated and blue-collar working people who were expected to personify the decline of the work ethic. It seemed more than usually difficult to go beyond the basic data of instant sociology. The day in the life of the steel worker or the auto worker, although doubtless reasonably factual, seemed to have been too carefully selected in the search for drama. These accounts tended to show working people being treated like children and responding like children. They persuasively supported the famous "Theory X" of the late Douglas McGregor. Managements were pictured as frustrated in their attempts to manage, devoid of understanding, and perhaps even lacking concern for their production people. For good measure, a healthy dose of unsafe and unsanitary working conditions was usually thrown in, along with drugs, loan sharking, organized crime, disorganized crime, peer pressure to restrict output, union corruption, and the final eruption of frustration in sabotage. We saw once again the traditional exposé of the passionate reformer.

Absenteeism, of all things, became the perplexing problem of those whose profession it was to manage and motivate working people. Recession, inflation, and unemployment which are traditionally supposed to help when motivation and management fail, simply did not prevent folks from just taking Mondays and Fridays off. Managers everywhere comforted each other with their lack of a "handle" on the absenteeism problem. Lectures, point systems, and free dishes for good attendance, failed to influence the 15 to 20 percent of the work force who took long weekends when they felt like it.

Surprises like these are the clay from which extrapolators sculpt new eras. Proclaiming the suspension of all hitherto reliable historical tendencies, nasty surprises are seen as the foreshadows of unprecedented changes. People, attitudes, and conditions, we are excitedly told, are now so changed that what we thought we knew about the nature of work, working people, managers, technology, and productivity is all out the window. We have finally gone too far, presumed too much, and the result of such immoderation is discontinuity.

THE NEW DOOMSDAY HYPOTHESIS

The signs which foretell a sustained decline in the real income, in the material standard of American life, are present. Since the beginning of our recorded economic data, real personal income has gone up more or less steadily, accompanied along the way by a similar rise in productivity. Per capita real income and output per man-hour have also moved up together —a nice, mutually reinforcing relationship. Increasing real income has provided us what we needed to invest in good health, good education, and capital equipment. These benefits, in turn, have made us more productive and led to still more real income, some of which we have consistently chosen to invest in still more health care, more education, and more tools of production. Along the way we have been sufficiently fascinated with the material wonders of such a productive economy as to devote considerable effort to enhancing this mutually reinforcing relationship between real income and productivity. As long as we looked at the relationship somewhat abstractly, we seemed to understand that this feedback effect was what had permitted us to become the most productive people in the world, and to enjoy the highest levels of necessities, toys, and pleasures.

This basic equation of our economy is always, of course, stated in terms of averages, suppressing that troublesome fact that there are not only wide variations in individual levels of income, but wide variations in the levels of productivity per man-hour. The relationship was a little less fascinating when it indicated the possibility of increasing one person's productivity in order to permit laying off another. One real income might increase as a result, but the other seemed inevitably to go down to the level of unemployment compensation. The relationship evident in the averages once again masked the fact that not everybody could be or was average.

Still, one who presumes to suggest that this productivity-real income relationship is about to fail clearly takes on the burden of proof. With few exceptions, national economies everywhere are deeply involved in efforts to make this relationship work for them as it has for us. Some are trying it our way, some in their own way, but many see it as the great national priority. If productivity and real income are going to decline in the United States, our citizens will not be the only ones who are intensely interested, radically skeptical, and wanting very much to believe that there is a "quick fix" somewhere near at hand.

Many of us will simply not entertain the idea that real wealth and productivity could, on the average, go anywhere but up. Some of us, conditioned by the seemingly unheralded arrival of the environmental crisis, the energy crisis, two digit inflation, and a new work ethic, will try to make a friend of change. These days, anything is possible. What next? To others, a decline in real income is not only anticipated but actually welcomed, if that is necessary to mend what they see as the evils of our present ways. Productivity and wealth are doubtless a mixed blessing. To those of us who value material advancement as a high priority, the possibility that our efforts may now be frustrated will provoke anxiety, in the least, and perhaps even aggression. To those whose priorities have led them somewhat away from ever more glorious cars, boats, and second homes, there are such enticing possibilities as a decline in the rates at which we pave the landscape, pollute the air, and invade our wild lands with motor homes. To those who are action oriented, any suggestion that the expected increases in productivity and income are not forthcoming is a challenge to do something about it right away.

SCENARIO X AND SCENARIO Y

We will be taking these two economic pulses, real income per capita and output per man-hour, as central descriptions of what is happening to our social enterprise. We should not, however, assume that these more measurable and more material aspects are the expressed or implied objectives of most of us as participants. It has always been said of real income that its chief import is in the freedom of choice it brings. To choose not just material things, but ideas, arts, experiences, or social systems. The essence of what is correctly called the "quality of life" and what we are attempting to assess with social indicators, is this opportunity to make decisions. Similarly, we wish to encourage no narrow definition of the impact of work on our processes of personal growth. It is not simply the result or the product of our working time, but very much the process, the nature of the work itself, which bears heavily on our personal growth and self-realization. To these things we will return, but for the present they must remain as simply implications of income and productivity.

To bring the situation into somewhat sharper focus, we will look at two simplified models or scenarios of our future economic life. Scenario X we have known, loved, and sought to enhance. Scenario Y roughly sketches the results we might expect if today's surprises turn out to be not mere disturbances, but rather the forerunners of persistent trends. Economists may find these models a little simple-minded, yet they may be rich enough to usefully focus a pair of partially revealed visions.

Scenario X

Suppose we were to maintain our characteristic economic momentum much the same in nearly all respects as it has been over the past ten to twenty years. Suppose we were to extrapolate our experience over this period into the future ten to twenty years. What would be our situation? Scenario X is the easier scenario to envision and the one most often discussed by economic studies and computer models designed to make long-range forecasts. What do the futurologists see if things are assumed to continue fairly much as they have?

Clearly we will have more people, and more goods and services will be produced. Our Gross National Product would almost double by 1985, but what would happen to the average individual and the average household? Productivity has grown at roughly three percent per year in the non-governmental sector of the economy in the recent past; if it were to continue at this rate, our productivity would become truly remarkable. Output per man would be doubling about every 24 years. If the 1985 GNP will be double its present level (measured in constant dollars), about 70 percent of this growth would be in pro-

ductivity alone. If the marvelous relationship between productivity and real income stays with us, our real income will double
about every 24 years. To appreciate what this would mean may
require a little reflection. Since 1950 both real compensation
per man-hour and output per man-hour have moved closely
together and have just about doubled. In this sense, we are, on
the average, earning twice as much as we did in 1950. If things
continue this way, our income would be doubling again in the
next 24 years. Economists and their forecasting models have a
pretty good record concerning long-range forecasts like this
one, because they can ignore or average the minor cyclical
swings. (We assume, of course, that they can distinguish what is
and what is not a minor cyclical swing.)

With this great increase in productivity, many things would
be possible. By 1985, for example, most households would have
an average income of about $10,000. (In 1974 most were in the
$7,000 bracket.) Households would by 1985 be buying about 50
percent more than they do now. Industrial production would
double by 1985, the work force would expand by 28 percent,
but the man-hours worked would rise by only 22 percent. The
shorter work week would, for most of us, be a happy way to
take advantage of this level of income.

Most likely, this kind of productivity would prove the key
to achieving modest rates of inflation and a more stable growth
of the economy. It would surely help to give us favorable foreign trade balances, assuming of course that our trading partners do not somehow become even more productive than we
ourselves. In addition, perhaps unemployment could be brought
down to a level of 4.5 percent, surely more tolerable than the
six percent we have experienced from time to time.

Where would all of this productivity gain come from in the
future? There would be more people in the 22 to 64 age group,
the most productive years on the average. We would be spending as much or more on research and development as we had in
the past. Productivity would rise as a result of continuing very
substantial investments in new plants and new equipment.
Industries like chemicals, electric utilities, rubber and plastics,
instruments, and machinery would see substantial and outstanding growth in output and productivity as a result of the
discovery and application of new technologies.

We would, on the average, be much more productive because we would be healthier, and our investments in health care systems would continue to grow as they would succeed. We would be better educated, better trained, and perhaps more highly motivated to be productive. Perhaps our increasing wealth would be accompanied by an increasing desire for more wealth and we would work more effectively, although not harder, as a result.

Automation, computers, and new technological breakthroughs would produce temporary dislocations and short run unemployment, but we would find more effective ways to cope with these problems. This would in turn, increase our willingness to search for and utilize all sorts of ways to increase productivity. Indeed, we would continue to accumulate knowledge of how our economic system really works and thus become more skillful in achieving the proper balance of "hands on" and "hands off" management of the economy. It would become more reliable in its conformance to our long run economic goals.

There have been a great number of careful studies of our economic future which have made the general assumption that the economy will continue much as before. They seem to generally agree in their scenarios with the rough picture we have outlined here. Scenario X is the classical graduation address about faith in our future. It is the easy extrapolation of what we have known and know to be possible, and for most of us who habitually suppress our uncertainty about the future, it *is* the future. But lately experts here and abroad have speculated otherwise. Clearly the probability of a genuine Scenario X taking place is not 100 percent. What other scenarios are possible, and what probabilities might we reasonably associate with them? For our purposes, it is sufficient to look at one alternative future, Scenario Y.

Scenario Y

Suppose over the next ten to twenty years the economy does change. Suppose, for example that:
* productivity increases are small, and for some periods in some industries they are absent altogether
* shortages of energy and raw materials contribute to declining increases in output

* rapid and continuing increases in the productivity of the Common Market countries and Japan contribute to our deteriorating foreign trade position
* inflation attacks intermittently, sometimes in the form of "cost push" and sometimes as a result of "demand pull"
* serious unemployment occurs in sectors hardest hit by energy and material shortages and by foreign competition
* unions become even more determined in the pursuit of job security and wage increases to match the pace of inflation
* union tactics increasingly take the form of restricting the supply of labor and opposing productivity-enhancing policies
* population growth and wider participation by women and minorities tend to increase the supply of labor
* industry, experiencing high interest rates and excess capacities, finds less and less motivation to invest in renewed capital equipment
* disenchantment with research and development continues to restrict investments in new products and new production technologies
* the traditional sources of productivity improvement, capital investment, new technologies, incentives to work harder, and so on, seem to have little or no effect
* seeking to preserve our customary increases in real income, we turn away from the shorter work week and seek opportunities to work overtime, to moonlight, and to strive for advancement
* the resulting increase in the supply of labor only tends to stabilize or reduce real wages, and this is self-defeating
* in our frustration, we turn to ever more government "interference" in the workings of the economy, some of which helps, but much of which does not
* taxes rise

If one is willing to suppose these things, then it is not too difficult to predict the inevitable conclusion of Scenario Y. As measured by the averages, the decline in real income that we have experienced only for the briefest periods in the past could become a trend extending over a number of years. The failure of the traditional methods of increasing our income and productivity (which is certainly a central consideration) would very likely lead us into self-defeating behavior that would only make things worse. Determined to increase our real income, we would try working harder. This would be, at best, only partially effective, and we would indeed be, as the prophets of Scenario Y ultimately see us, working harder and experiencing a decline in income. Thus, working harder and living poorer.

CHANCE AND SOCIAL CHANGE

There is a substantial body of opinion which sees us as strongly and safely involved in the momentum of Scenario X. Deviations from this model are seen as temporary aberrations which will shortly be corrected, and the future of our social system is best modeled by extrapolation of what we have known. The burden of proof is, in this view, very much upon those who would suggest that anything like Scenario Y has even the slimmest chances of occurring. Futurologists wisely urge that it is less than reasonable to assume that any single future is certain to occur; therefore, we should not regulate our behavior on the assumption that any one scenario will eventuate. Rather, we would more honestly reflect our uncertainties by attaching probabilities to various scenarios and by explicitly considering the chances of various possible futures. It is upon these probabilities that beliefs, plans, and actions can best be founded by those who want to have some explicit appreciation of why they are doing what they are doing.

The question is thus not one of trying to form an opinion about which possible future is going to occur, but rather one of expressing explicitly a more subtle, more sophisticated, and more realistic point of view. Which futures are very likely, or very unlikely, and which have sufficient probability of occurrence are the questions which warrant consideration in our planning. The function of anticipating social change is to prepare for it, and these preparations must sensibly recognize that social change is less than perfectly predictable. It is very much a matter of uncertainty, probability, or chance. The question is, then, what are the signs which support an upward revision in the probability which reasonable people associate with Scenario

Y, the "working harder, living poorer" future? If, indeed, Scenario Y seems reasonably probable, what should we do about it? In the spring of 1974 Scenario Y occurred in Italy. The average Italian factory worker is already finding himself working harder and living poorer. High inflation and productivity problems have done it.

Evidence For Scenario Y

These indications say to some that Scenario Y is not only possible but quite likely. Indeed, it already may be well under way. If this view is accepted, the next step is to consider reactions and responses. If the function of anticipating social change is really to prepare for it, many will see the chances of Scenario Y as amply justifying some preparation at this point. Washington, D.C., seems to be taking this view. Management is at least expressing this view. A few major union leaders are gradually moving toward it.

Even those who do not ascribe a high probability to Scenario Y are beginning to acknowledge the existence of a serious productivity problem. Even if we continue with Scenario X with a steady three percent annual increase, we will not be able to make up the difference between the resources available to the nation and what the nation wants to achieve with those resources. This increment will not cover the increases in wages and fringe benefits that working people are determined to get. It will not meet the competition of the other industrial nations. It will not provide the resources for the improvements we are demanding in education, in health care, in crime control, in the rehabilitation of our cities, or in the elimination of hunger. It will not bring equality to minorities, nor substantially reduce unemployment. It will not control inflation, nor permit a growing real income. It will not bring us closer to the thirty hour week, nor will it eliminate the dull, unsafe, and unhealthy jobs that persist in our economy.

In exploring these effects we have concentrated mainly on the qualitative indications and made limited use of statistics. Where statistics have been used, they are based on the data of the Bureau of Labor Statistics in order to preserve some semblance of consistency. Again in an attempt at consistency, we have largely used the future projections of the University of Maryland's econometric model.

Attitudes

One of the most disturbing, most difficult to effectively document, and most widely publicized hypotheses suggests that there is a fundamental change under way in the attitudes of working people. In particular, younger members of the work force are seen as suffering from "alienation," widespread dissatisfaction with work, and a general feeling that working hard is just not going to pay off. These new attitudes are used to explain the symptoms of declining productivity. Tardiness, absenteeism, wasteful work practices, the use of drugs and alcohol on the job, and high turnover are all specified as the result of the new attitudes of young people. Surveys continue to suggest that "discontent" is growing among younger working people who do not have college degrees, that fewer and fewer of these people are willing to work "as hard as their parents did," and that increasing numbers of them have concluded that hard work does not always get rewarded. These young people do not respond to monetary incentives, nor do they react productively to traditional authoritarian management efforts. There appears to be less and less willingness to work at the routinized, repetitive, highly productive jobs that have been basic to our system of high levels of output at low unit labor costs.

While people who have looked into the relationship between attitudes and productivity caution that the data is weak and often quite primitive, there is certainly evidence in some quarters that we have productivity problems which can be very appealingly explained in terms of attitudes. However unsophisticated may have been the methods used to establish the relationship between growing job dissatisfaction and declining productivity, there are many managers who feel that the problem has reached such a magnitude and appeared in such clarity that sophisticated methods are beside the point. The explanations are readily provided by the popular sociologists.

Over the years, the work week has gone down steadily. Each generation has in fact not worked as hard as its predecessors, and there is no reason to suspect that the generation now entering the work force is not aware of this and intent upon continuing the trend. "Today's youth" are relatively better educated, have had little experience with hard times, are interested in work with some social meaningfulness; and, seeing jobs as neither as important nor as hard to find as their parents, they are just not willing to put up with the working conditions, supervisory styles, and low intrinsic job rewards of the past. The simple, powerful, time-honored incentive of money as the key to material fulfillment is seen as having a seriously reduced appeal.

"Behaviorists" who study the attitudes of working people feel one of the explanations is the broad consensus which has developed around the relationship between educational levels and the nature of work. Those entering the work force are clearly better educated on the average and thus, quite naturally, seek jobs which are meaningful, intrinsically rewarding, and somewhat more challenging than many traditional entry level jobs. Those who design jobs have gone right on taking advantage of the productive possibilities of the division of labor, the standardization of tasks, and the very close measurement and control of highly repetitive work assignments. Clearly, it is suggested, the character and quality of work simply has not changed to match the changes in attitude resulting from these advances in educational levels.

Survey after survey has produced the finding that what working people say they want is a greater measure of independence, self-direction, and freedom in the design and conduct of their work. There are fewer and fewer opportunities to be one's own boss it seems. A century ago, only half of the work force was on wages and salaries, but this has now risen to over 86 percent. The desire to work the way one wants, at the pace one wants, and with clearly useful results still strongly exists. The fulfillment of these needs has been steadily reduced by the prevailing trends in job design. Pride of craftsmanship, pride of accomplishment, and the feeling of service are all declining because there are so many jobs where these seem to have been totally eliminated as possible responses. Surveys indicating that working people say they would work harder if they had more to say about the nature of their work and more independence in doing it are now widely seen as explaining a decline in productivity and as leading indicators of more serious declines to come.

THE SERVICE SECTOR

Two-thirds of people who work now produce services. Over the past two hundred years of our economic development, nothing has been more fundamental than the steady flow of people from agriculture into manufacturing and from manufacturing into the service sector. Agriculture, once a low productivity enterprise, has grown dramatically more productive and released people for industry. As industry has grown more productive, it has released people (relatively speaking) for the production of services. As our level of real income has advanced, we have desired more services, both personal services and services to business. The unhappy aspect of all this is that the service sector is characterized not only by low productivity, but by low rates of productivity increase. The traditional strategies of capital investment, new technology, and automation have little room to work out their consequences in the service fields. To make matters worse, most establishments that render services are small, economically inefficient units, and the aggregation of them into larger units seems out of the question. A General Motors just cannot be created in the barber shop business. Still worse, we cannot even measure the productivity of doctors, beauticians, or TV repairmen. If we cannot measure their productivity, then it almost seems futile to even contemplate possibilities for improving it.

For a long time, our increases in productivity have been closely associated with this flow of people from low productivity jobs on the farm to higher productivity jobs in manufacturing. The flow now toward low productivity jobs in the services will not only deprive us of this traditional productivity increment, but also will see us facing decrements as more and more people produce not goods, but services. Even if industry continues to grow more productive, as we produce and consume more services, our real income must be seen as exposed to a strong downward pressure. Perhaps the greatest element of pessimism here stems from the observation that the grand old ways of increasing productivity just don't seem applicable when it comes to doing something about the service sector. The Bureau of Labor Statistics has attracted considerable attention with its estimates that our annual productivity increase of about three percent will be reduced by 0.2 percent by the reduction in the flow of people away from the farm and by another 0.2 percent by the flow of people into the service industries.

Technology

Many of the basic technologies on which our productivity depends seem to "have run their course" and have little potential for productivity improvements. Like many technological forecasts, this one is a matter of considerable uncertainty in many opinions. Yet there is evidence which seems persuasive to others. Our steel mills are old, technologically obsolete, and cannot be made more productive without massive investments in replacement. The conditions which would warrant the necessary investment in modern replacements are now highly uncertain. Many basic industries such as steel, shoes, and motor vehicles have achieved only the most modest productivity gains in recent years. The railroads which are essential to our economy gained a productivity increase when they got rid of the passenger service, but little more can be done. The railroads are a good example of a "mature" technology in which we have a huge investment, on which we rely heavily, and which exhibits little opportunity for the application of productivity increasing strategies.

Likewise the internal combustion engine is a mature technology that has reached the final leveling off point in its productivity curve. Turbines, rotary engines, and so on represent only marginal improvements in productive potential. In so many of the most productive segments of manufacturing, the strategies of standardization, high volume line production, and automation have been taken to their foreseeable limits. Little more can be expected. Our technologies, at least the very important ones, are thus characterized as being in a final state of development. Maturity is the inevitable fate of all production processes; they become "perfected" and seem to have little further potential. This forecast does not imply that great new advances in productivity will require huge investments of research, time, and money. If there are to be "quantum jumps" they are not to be forthcoming in the immediate future.

Unions

Labor unions have been the obvious, traditional target for those who sought to explain productivity difficulties. Their history has been heavily characterized by goals and achievements antithetical to productivity. Continuous wage increases, restrictive work practices, and a militancy which has seen productivity growth as a threat to job security give the unions a strong, determining hand in the emergence of Scenario Y. Many see union power as on the rise, militancy increasing, and labor agreements reaching new heights in the complexity of work rules which serve to limit productivity. Most unions are seen as quite unable to accept the relationship between productivity increases and increases in real income. Union leaders are characterized as totally devoted to short run wage increases and measures which will enhance job security, and quite unconcerned with the ultimate effects of these things.

The picture is, however, mixed. Unions which will participate in the construction of the Alaska pipeline have agreed to a no-strike clause and a productivity provision which will limit many of the restrictive work practices typical of the construction industry. Work rules and featherbedding in their most wasteful forms are fading in many industries. The United Steel Workers and the United Rubber Workers have publicly advised their members that future wage increases and future job security will depend significantly upon productivity increases. The president of the Steel Workers has said, "Workers cannot get anything by dropping the bargaining bucket into an empty well."

Just what the result of these new public positions will be is not yet clear. Complex grievance processes and large numbers of grievances continue to typify union activities in many plants. The notion that productivity means speedups, working harder, and fewer jobs remains firmly entrenched. Long strikes continue to be the weapon for resisting automation and technological advances of major impact, in spite of the leadership of the mine workers and the longshoremen in learning to live with technological change. The New York printers' fourteen month strike against the Daily News which was settled in the spring of 1974 reflects the persistent nature of these attitudes. Even those who feel that union viewpoints may be swinging toward a more general appreciation of the importance of productivity to the membership, see this as happening far too slowly to be of much immediate help in actually preventing the productivity declines anticipated in Scenario Y.

Perceptions

There is the strong possibility, given our propensity for socially shared perceptions, that Scenario Y may seem to happen without actually doing so. A recent survey indicated that during a period when people experienced an advance in real income of five percent, most people surveyed felt they had actually grown poorer. Apparently a high level of publicity about inflation which seemed to have gone out of control and about productivity which seemed to be in incurable difficulty, served to make people think they were worse off than they really were. But, of course, the effect if one feels poorer is about the same if one is poorer. Clearly, a general discouragement over rapidly rising prices and a considerable volume of commentary on declining productivity can give large numbers of us the impression we are working harder and living poorer, whether or not this is actually the case.

It is a sociological commonplace fact that our absolute wealth is far less important than our wealth relative to that of the neighbors. How we are doing can only be answered in terms of a comparison. It is particularly a phenomenon of our society that when our neighbors shift their consumption patterns in the face of rising prices, that we notice more readily what they are consuming more of than what they are consuming less of. Thus, it is especially easy to get the impression that we are getting poorer than they, when in fact it is only their pattern which is changing. In similar fashion, the common phenomenon felt by people who reach middle age and the height of their earning capability, is that their expenses seem also to rise so they feel as if they had never earned more nor been able to save less. As the composition of our population shifts and there are more of us who are middle-aged, this perception will become even more common. The impact of rising prices is, of course, amplified for persons in this position of finding their solvency threatened at a time when they had expected to achieve some measure of financial independence.

DECLINING PRODUCTIVITY INCREMENTS

To many, the best, most persuasive, and most direct evidence that Scenario Y is here is the data on our productivity itself. Output per man-hour in the private, nonfarm economy actually declined during four different periods in the past four years. During the first quarter of 1974 this productivity measure declined at an annual rate of 3.5 percent. We seemed to be getting poorer in a hurry. Whether or not this could be fully explained by the decline in auto production resulting from the energy crisis, and whether or not this could be seen as the beginning of a trend were of course the key questions. However one answered them, the phenomenon of an actual decline in productivity of this magnitude was a matter that drew much attention. One's reaction is not helped by the fact that during the entire year of 1973, our productivity performance was distinctly worse than most other industrialized nations.

Since 1889, the output per man-hour in the private economy has been extremely well-behaved — until quite recently. From 1889 until about 1945, productivity rose dependably at an annual rate of about 2.1 percent. From 1945 up to 1965 the annual rate of increase jumped to around three percent. Not unreasonably, economists, managers and legislators began to assume that three percent was normal and dependable. The path of stable growth seemed comfortably certain. However, between 1965 and 1970 our productivity increases slowed down to a level of less than two percent per year. To some, this brought a gnawing uncertainty about our economic future. To others, it was a productivity crisis, and reinforced by the spotty performance since 1970, was heavy evidence for Scenario Y. To the economists making long-range forecasts, it was a signal for an important revision in their assumptions. Some began projecting ten year productivity increases as low as 2.5 percent per year and busied themselves with translating this into changes in our GNP.

The University of Maryland's economic forecasting model is one of the most sophisticated, computer-based prediction systems which regularly looks at our economic future. In late 1973 the creator of the Maryland econometric model felt a need to change its basic assumptions about social, technological, political and economic conditions. Working with its new assumptions, the model predicted productivity increases through 1985 averaging only 1.5 percent per year, or less than half of the rate to which we have become accustomed. "The sedate seventies," the creator of the model said, "and the aging eighties will follow the soaring sixties." The model foresaw the steepest productivity declines in industrial chemicals, petroleum refining, steel, nonferrous metals, household appliances and motor vehicles. Clearly this is a substantial segment of our manufacturing sector.

Government officials have passed through a phase of talking about these numbers as the crisis in productivity, but productivity figures are still carefully watched. Many people, apparently from the President on down, are giving credence to the notion that there is a trend in the direction of Scenario Y.

Measurement

During the 1971–73 multi-phase economic stabilization program, it became evident that productivity was a concept central to the achievement of our economic objectives; yet, it was a concept around which a good deal of disquieting uncertainty seemed to appear. It was widely remarked that many managements did not understand the notion of productivity measurement, did not engage in any such measuring activities, and did not have much of an idea about how productivity might be improved. Some people were disturbed that there was much ambiguity about such an important economic factor as output per man-hour. It became a matter of public concern that there seemed to be no way of measuring the productivity of the government itself, or of policemen, pilots, teachers, or symphony conductors. Even the productivity measures in the manufacturing sector failed to take into account such obvious considerations as changes in the quality of the products whose physical volume alone was being measured. All of this led to a generalized conclusion that we were not very well-informed about a highly important aspect of our economic system.

Many other industrial nations have productivity institutes which are supported by the government and are dedicated to measuring productivity, helping find ways to improve it, and furnishing factual bases for the establishment of national policies aimed at influencing productivity. We have none. Worse still, our National Commission on Productivity, judged by some to have been ineffectual, was downgraded in 1974 to an Office of Productivity with much reduced staff and resources. As the economic controls program wore on toward its largely ineffective end, it seemed quite reasonable to conclude that whatever it was we knew or did not know about measuring productivity was quite useless as a basis for achieving our economic goals through governmental policy and action. This finding left many of us with a substantial degree of pessimism about the future of our achievements in productivity, and a strong feeling that nothing good was in store for us in the near future. We seemed to be caught completely off base in an area that was obviously of major significance.

Foreign Productivity

We have always been proud of the fact that the American worker was the most productive in the world. Based on the 1970 Bureau of Labor Statistics Data, we took great comfort in the fact that for every $100 worth of goods and services we produced, the German worker produced $74, the British worker $59, and the Japanese worker $56. But trade deficits and dollar devaluations have made us wonder. In 1970 the rest of the industrial world was catching up and very rapidly indeed while our productivity increment seemed to be in trouble. In the 1965 to 1970 period when our annual increase in output per man-hour was less than 2 percent, Japan achieved 14.3 percent, Germany .7 percent, and Britain 3.8 percent. The average for the Common Market countries was well over three times the average of the U.S.

While the relationship between productivity and foreign trade may be complicated, it seems clear that trade means jobs and growth beyond that which we can achieve by serving our own markets. There is little question that we are experiencing serious difficulties as the result of imports in such areas as steel and automobiles, difficulties which will hardly improve if foreign productivity continues to catch up and ultimately to overtake ours. Certainly, if we are not to live poorer we must be attentive to foreign productivity advances.

The reasons for foreign productivity increases which significantly exceed our own are fairly well understood. Europe and Japan are now reaping the harvest of the major rebuilding and modernizing of industry which followed the destruction of World War II. The other industrial nations have continued since that time to invest a far larger percentage of their GNP in new plants and equipment, and in research and development. The rate of investment in plants and equipment in Japan between 1965 and 1970 was a phenomenal 30 percent of their GNP per year on the average. During the same years, our investment was at the rate of about 10 percent. If this continues, it seems quite likely that American products made by American workers will be increasingly priced out of world markets.

Our foreign competitors are seeing greater productivity increases because they are somewhat behind us in the process of moving people from the low productivity jobs in agriculture to the higher productivity work in manufacturing. While our agricultural work force is down to only 4.5 percent, Germany has 9.6 percent of its workers in agriculture and Japan, 16.9 percent. Japan is also famous for its life tenure system provided for some employees and for its heavy reliance on debt financing. Thus both labor costs and financing costs tend to be seen by Japanese managers as essentially fixed costs. Therefore, they find it reasonable to operate at very high levels of production as long as the price received is sufficient to cover the variable or out-of-pocket costs of production. The result may show up in very low export prices.

Japan is also known for its "quality control circles," the groups of six or seven workers who meet regularly on their own time to work out ways of improving their own productivity. The quality control circles compete with each other for special badges to wear on their hats and cash awards for productivity improvements. Such an alignment of employee and management interests is rare in American industry, and the prospect of so many clever Japanese busily improving productivity is awe-some.

Capital Investment

To many, the most basic indication of the onset of Scenario Y is the low level of our investment in plants and equipment, one of the really basic sources of productivity increases. This lack of new and modernized capacity has shown up in productivity lags in the railroads, in steel, and in other industries. We have, as we have noted, invested the smallest portion of our GNP in modernizing our production systems of any of the leading industrial nations. To a great degree this is understandable. Managers have in recent years faced high interest rates and a severe series of credit crunches. The stock market has been of little use as a source of capital. Profits have been squeezed by rising costs and less has been available in the way of retained earnings. The result is that the average age of plants and equipment in many American industries is significantly higher than in those same industries in Japan, Germany and other industrialized countries. And of course, productivity is correspondingly impaired. Our lower investments in research and development mean that there are fewer technological advances embodied in new equipment and thus fewer attractive opportunities for modernization and expansion.

The Maryland econometric model forecasts further declines in our investment in plants and equipment. Between 1971 and 1975 real capital spending is expected to increase each year by an average 7.4 percent. From 1975 to 1985, however, the annual increase is seen as falling to a level below 2 percent. If these forecasts prove reasonably accurate, we face a period of growing obsolescence in our productive system and a growing neglect of what has traditionally been a fundamental source of productivity improvement.

The Government Sector

Scenario Y is prominently characterized by a continued rise in the importance of the government sector, the public sector of our economy. The seemingly limitless proliferation of government agencies is a relentlessly growing part of our economic life. Whatever one thinks of their worth as social institutions, these agencies suffer from severe and obvious difficulties. The incentive to productivity is often weak, the possibilities for measuring it extremely limited, and the methods for improving it not very obvious. The Social Security Administration, the Department of Defense, and even the Post Office present considerable challenges to those who would measure and try to enhance government productivity. The Bureau of Labor Statistics, admitting the very great difficulty of saying anything at all about government productivity, reports that the rate of productivity increase for the public sector has always been significantly lower than the rate of increase for the private sector.

As the government grows, not only do we commit more of our GNP to activities where productivity measurement is a serious problem, but we promote two other obvious effects. Taxes rise, removing funds from private investments. Government agencies control, regulate, and monitor private sector operations in ways which seldom increase their productivity. This is not to say for a moment that the results may not be socially very advantageous, but one must recognize that the social advances are bought at a cost, part of which is in declining private sector productivity.

GOVERNMENT REGULATIONS New federal mine safety regulations have probably had an adverse effect on productivity increases in mining over the past two or three years. Pollution control devices are clearly having a downward effect on the productivity of the automobile engine. The Occupational Safety and Health Act has required a diversion of investment funds and a reduction in productivity in a vast number of instances. Federal, state, and local governments are very active in imposing reporting requirements, equal employment opportunity requirements, environmental protection requirements, and product safety requirements on the private sector. This upsurge of government "intervention" in our production system culminated in the 1971–74 economic controls on wages and prices which inevitably tended to distort resource allocation and perhaps reduce incentives. Now all of these things may be socially beneficial or not, according to one's own economic and social inclinations. But nearly all of them come to us at the price of some reduction in productivity as it is conventionally measured.

Of course these are, to a degree, two-way streets. Air and water pollution, thermal pollution, traffic congestion, work accidents, and health hazards themselves have negative effects on productivity. But efforts to abate pollution and to hire the hard-core unemployed likewise have negative effects on our abilities to increase productivity. There are not many "laissez faire" nineteenth century capitalists left, but it is not at all unreasonable to note that in some senses these governmental actions make us richer while in other senses they make us poorer. Carried recklessly forward, many see the government's growing array of programs as a stimulus to Scenario Y.

Management Attention

Productivity improvements actually occur at the working level in the form of modifications and improvements of production systems. They occur largely as the result of management attention, management initiative, and management decisions to undertake innovations. It is argued by some that the complexity of the management task is gradually increasing to the point where management attention is being seriously distracted from productivity improving activities. Managers are spending so much of their time dealing with other problems that this aspect of their traditional functioning is suffering. The energy crisis, foreign competition, changing work attitudes, government regulations, and "consumerism" are placing demands on key decision makers which can only be met through neglect of their basic innovative decision making role. Managers are so distracted by the symptoms that they fail to deal with fundamental effects. The validity of this argument is, of course, hard to judge in general, but the business press furnishes anecdotes which support the basic hypothesis with increasing frequency.

Shortages

Our present rash of shortages, both of materials and of energy, has clearly cut deeply into our productivity growth. In the first quarter of 1974, productivity declined rapidly, largely as a result of the cutback in the production of large cars. Those who look ahead, those who were not surprised by the present shortages, say that world demand is beginning to press hard on the available world supply of fuels, materials, and basic commodities. These shortages are expected to persist and to continue to have adverse effects on our productivity. We will have to devote much more of our attention to economizing these scarce inputs, to holding down scrap rates, and to finding substitutes. More and more effort will go into the exploration of efficient recycling systems. Even the materials which may not be scarce will be more expensive. As the Mesabi iron runs out and we no longer have ready access to high grade, cheaply mined ores, we will turn to far more expensive foreign sources. Shortages, we are reliably told, are not an aberration, but a continuing problem which will create productivity problems not only in the manufacturing sector but in our own households. In fact, the productivity of a household has become one of the more interesting problems of the time. It is a problem to which we will shortly return.

RESEARCH AND DEVELOPMENT

Government support of research and development peaked in 1964, when measured as a percent of GNP. Since that time it has leveled off at three percent and then dropped to about 2.6 percent. Our stock of knowledge, the output of research and development, is the inventory on which applied research, technological advance, and productivity increasing innovations draw. As our stock of knowledge goes down, so in the subsequent years one may expect our innovation rate to go down and the productivity increment from this source to be correspondingly impaired. Some part of the post 1965 declines in productivity are thought by experts to be directly associated with this declining support of research and development.

Company supported research and development amounted to about 1.1 percent of our GNP in 1972. It is projected to remain at this level through 1980. During the same period, company sponsored research and development in Japan, starting at the same level, will increase by 23 percent to a level of 1.7

percent of their GNP. During the period from 1969 to 1972, five industries — aerospace, electrical equipment, chemicals and drugs, machinery, and motor vehicles — accounted for 75 percent of all company sponsored research and development. The service sector and other nonmanufacturing activities accounted for 60 percent of the GNP, but employed less than one-sixth of the research and development scientists and engineers.

While there has been considerable talk about and money expended on the problem of transferring the benefits of military research to private production, it is not clear that this has been at all successful. What is now called the problem of "technology transfer" has itself become a matter of research expenditures, a sure sign that all is not going as well as could be expected.

Research which directly attacks the problem of productivity itself, the costs of which often appear to exceed the benefits to the individual firm, has not been a matter of interest to the administrators of government research funds. Our failure to establish a national productivity institute and the very modest government outlays in this area, suggest the strong possibility of underinvestment in this particularly relevant field of investigation.

Coupled with these effects, some see a reduction in management's willingness to innovate, to make the decision which will translate developments into practice. The heavy burden of sunk costs into old facilities weighs heavily, if irrationally, on some managers. Growth and innovation seem to go together. Innovations make for growth, and growth provides opportunities to innovate. As growth slows down, so will innovation, which will in turn reinforce the further slowdown of our growth rates. Just how managers are currently looking at decisions to innovate is difficult to document, but there is evidence that they may be becoming somewhat less willing to take these kinds of risks.

The First Derivative Hypothesis

There are several important and related hypotheses about our sense of being poorer, our dissatisfaction with our incomes, and our tendency to demand more of our economy:

a) the steady rise in real wages which we have always experienced leads us not only to expect further increases, but to aspire to augmenting increases;

b) the Joneses spend their income differently and thus always have more of something than we do; there are too many Joneses for us to keep up with all of them;

c) we have grown used to being the country with the highest standard of living; we feel threatened when we learn that productivity in Russia or Japan is rising faster than our own; others are gaining on us and, if this continues, they will surely pass us;

d) as long as we were an expanding population and a growing economy, new needs and new demands could be met with new resources; if growth slows, new needs cannot be met without taking something away from somebody;

e) we discover that more cars, TV sets, and such things do not make us as happy as we thought they would, yet we fixate on "more" as the solution to our problems; we can't quite come to grips with the notion that less, or at least a stable level of material consumption, might give us the opportunity to discover more enduring satisfactions.

Thus, even if one believes that our historically reliable increase in real wages will continue, we are less than content with it.

The considerations which lend credence to Scenario Y must be spun out still further.

* Attitude surveys reveal that people do not even think productivity benefits them. Productivity is seen as benefiting big corporations.

* Teenagers and women are entering the work force in increasing numbers. Teenagers are less productive because they have less experience. Women are less productive than the average member of the work force because they tend to enter low productivity, clerical occupations.

* While long run projections of population (assuming re-replacement level fertility) indicate higher productivity due to an older work force and higher real incomes, these effects are not really going to be felt until the year 2000.

* We have been encouraged and habituated into a pattern of consumer preferences which are directly opposed to high productivity. We prefer variety, fashion, short service, lavish uses of energy, and excesses in cars, homes, and appliances.
* We are at a stage in our development when we are passing from economies of scale to diseconomies. Corporations, institutions, government agencies all are getting too big. For a while being bigger meant being more productive, but we have outrun this effect and now being bigger means being less productive.

New Approaches

Our basic hypotheses are twofold:

With Scenario X or Scenario Y we have a serious productivity problem. The problem is bigger in the latter case, but either way it should have some attention immediately.

Our present approaches to productivity improvement are not going to be adequate. It is not that they are ineffective so much as that they are too feeble, too slow in their diffusion, too limited in their scope, and too mild in their impact.

Our problem then is to look for the new approaches to productivity improvement, to search for ways of improving the effectiveness of our efforts to improve productivity.

Notes

The most useful key to the recent literature is *Productivity: A Selected Annotated Bibliography 1965–71*. U.S. Department of Labor, Bureau of Labor Statistics Bulletin 1776. U.S. Government Printing Office, 1973.

One of the best quick introductions to the subject consists of two works:

Work in America. Report of the Special Task Force to The Secretary of Health, Education, and Welfare. Cambridge: The MIT Press, 1973.

Fabricant, Solomon. *A Primer on Productivity*. New York: Random House, 1969.

The British study of attitudes in an automobile plant is described in *Workers' Control — A Reader on Labor and Social Change.* Edited by Gerry Hunnius, G. David Garson, and John Case. Random House: New York, 1973, pp. 332–35.

For a good look at the problem and future of productivity, see *Productivity. Second Annual Report of the National Productivity Commission.* U.S. Government Printing Office, 1973.

The Maryland econometric forecasting model's projections are reported in *Business Week*, September 22, 1973, pp. 93–4.

For those wishing to make further investigations into Scenario X and Scenario Y, there is a very large literature on the past and future of economic growth. The following are interesting starting points:

Almon, Clopper, Jr. *The American Economy to 1975.* New York: Harper & Row, 1966.

Kuznets, Simon. *Economic Growth of Nations: Total Output and Production Structure.* Cambridge, Mass.: Harvard University Press, 1971.

U.S. Department of Labor, Bureau of Labor Statistics. "The U.S. Economy in 1980: A Preview of BLS Projections." *Monthly Labor Review*, Vol. 93, No. 4, April, 1970, pp. 3–34.

2
Revolutions:
Past and Future

LOOKING BACKWARD

The history of our devotion to productivity is essentially the history of the human race. There have always been efforts to increase the ratio of output to input, to get more for less, although at times these efforts seemed slow and implicit. At other times, in eras marked out by historians as eras of progress, these efforts seemed to produce rapid results which tended, in turn, to reinforce further efforts to do something about productivity. Understanding what is going on today is somewhat easier if we look for some of the threads with which to make sense of the recent history of productivity and glance quickly at one or two of the interesting characters who had their hands in it.

The study sponsored by the Department of Health, Education, and Welfare, "Work in America," was intended to focus public concern on the supposed basic changes in the nature of work and working people. It might have done so more effectively if it had not failed so completely to square with the ideology of the Nixon administration. "Work in America," looking around for the villan, fixed, not surprisingly, on Frederick Winslow Taylor. The study labeled most of what it saw as the deplorable state of the art of productivity enhancement as "Taylorism." Anyone with an idea to offer on the subject of work and productivity can establish some kind of legitimacy these days by opening a few free shots at Taylor and "Taylorism."

THE SCIENCE OF SHOVELING

The industrial climate of the 1870's was evidently ready for someone to propose a science of shoveling. The War Between the States had demonstrated the ultimate power of the Northern industrial complex. The major engineering adventure of the century, the transcontinental railroad, had received its golden spike in 1869. We could make steel reliably and at a cost which permitted its use to grow dramatically. Inside factories, the synergy of the machine tool and the steam engine was being exploited to the fullest. Steam power made the use of fast, accurate machine tools possible, and the possibility of these tools enhanced the production of better steam engines. Large-scale production was beginning its impact on our material needs and passions. Hard-headed businessmen, with plenty to think about, had little time to challenge the easy presumption that science was an affair of the laboratory and had little to contribute to the "real" problems of practical affairs. Indeed the strength of their easy distinction between what was "practical" and what was "theoretical" had sufficient vigor and strength to survive all too often in their successors of today.

The science of shoveling burst with a thud on the Bethlehem Steel mill of the 1870's, the creature of a well-born, self-educated engineer named Frederick Winslow Taylor. He could see from the mill a "yard" two miles long and half a mile wide, containing endless piles of sand, coal, and ore. On a given day he could see between 400 and 600 men going at these piles with shovels. Each man had his own shovel and worked under the hard-nosed supervision of the traditional "gang boss." Taylor was made uneasy by all this human effort which was going into shovels of all sizes and descriptions. This uneasiness led him to bring the methods of science, although not its white-coat trappings, to bear on the need to rationalize the "yard" which he alone seemed to feel. First a hypothesis: there must be an optimum shovel size, one which will maximize the shoveler's productivity. Then a controlled experiment: one must actually measure the tons shoveled with various sizes of shovels. Not a casual experience, but a deliberate experiment. It turned out that the optimum shovel size was one designed to hold 21.5 pounds per load. This was a fact worth knowing when there were several hundred shovelers at work each day. Yet it had not been known, nor perhaps even wondered about. The consequences of applying science to work were evolving in Taylor's mind, but much more difficult experiments would be needed to suggest these consequences to many others.

The science of shoveling, when applied, raised the average man's productivity from a few tons to as much as 30 tons per day. Three very important precedents were set at this point. The shovelers themselves benefited to the tune of 60 percent higher wages. Bethlehem Steel found its cost per ton moved cut in half. Taylor followed with a crude but direct inquiry into the non-financial consequences. Most shovelers now found greater satisfaction in their work.

Other hypotheses, other experiments, and other applications of science to work followed with various attendant difficulties. One of the more or less typical jobs of the day involved picking up 92-pound pigs of iron, carrying them up a plank and dropping them in a railroad car. Taylor selected an experimental subject, known ever since by the name of Schmidt, who was suited for the project by reason of his willingness to do exactly what he was told without troublesome questions. The project of systematizing Schmidt undertook to find the "best" way to load pig iron. After a great deal of frustration with energy calculations, Taylor finally came upon the key variable: daily production was a strong function of the pattern of rest and work. Indeed Schmidt's output was maximized when he spent 47 percent of the time under load and 53 percent of the time unloaded. Apparently, Schmidt's docility permitted his work pattern to be regulated in this way, and his production rose from 12.5 tons per day to 47 tons. Schmidt's wages were raised from $1.15 per day to $1.85 and Bethlehem enjoyed the remaining benefit. It is not clear what happened to Schmidt's level of job satisfaction.

Wage Incentives

Somewhat later Taylor undertook his adventures in science in a machine shop, where "soldiering" was the norm, as it will always be in many work situations. "Soldiering" simply refers to the deliberate restriction of output by the workers who saw no reason to approach anything near their potential productivity. If they were on "day work," then they received the same wage as the least productive of their fellow operators and saw no sense in doing any more than he. If they were on piece work, they were well schooled in the "rate busting" policies of shortsighted employers. Hard work under a piece rate plan could lead to high earnings, but the company inevitably responded to high earnings by cutting the rate per piece. Thus, one was almost sure to end up worse off than before. Into this situation came Taylor with a brute force attack. He was a skilled machinist himself, so he went to the production floor to show the men how to do "a fair day's work." They failed to respond in any lasting fashion, so Taylor undertook to fire them. Their replacements proved to be men of the very same sort, and this approach quickly proved self-defeating. Taylor next began his own program of training the "culturally disadvantaged." He selected men who had the ability to become machinists but not had the opportunity to learn the skill. Taylor trained them in return for their agreement to work as he directed. Even these men, however, found the social pressure for soldiering too strong and went the way of their predecessors. Taylor's full support by management permitted him to release his frustration by simply cutting all the rates in the shop in half. The shock of this coupled with Taylor's demonstration that a "fair day's work" would actually permit an increase in earnings finally overcame the traditions of the shop. This, however, is hardly a series of experiments likely to be repeated today.

TAYLORISM Out of such applications of science Taylor began to evolve a "system." Nothing was clearer to him than the need for objectifying the concept of a fair day's work. This concept had to be removed from the realm of speculation and dispute and given the imprimatur of science. He developed the idea of motion study, which is the detailed observation and analysis of the elements of a job. Out of this came a "best way" of doing the job, followed by a careful measurement of the time required. Time study unhappily required a step which survives today as the least satisfying part of Taylor's system. The time study man had to make an explicit judgment of the relation of the pace and effort of the man being timed to something called a "normal" pace by a qualified operator. Taylor almost succeeded in replacing the subjectivity of a "fair day's work" with the subjectivity of a "normal" pace, by adding some very precise stopwatch readings along the way. Yet, the effect of what he did was greater than this.

Taylor's approach today would be called "interdisciplinary" because he saw the production situation as requiring the attention of a variety of sciences. He himself did some 40,000 cutting tool experiments and captured them in a tool-life equation which has only recently been improved upon. He developed a superior cutting tool material which increased the productivity of the metal working industries by several' fold. He worked his way up to the job of the foreman and indeed into the task of rationalizing the work of top management. All this was eventually gathered under the rubric, "The Taylor System of Scientific Management."

Taylor's youth was a time for innovations introduced without attendant diplomatic subtleties. He created a specially balanced putter, a tennis racquet with a curved handle which could give the ball a vigorous spin, and one afternoon he walked to the pitcher's mound to introduce the overhand pitch to baseball. He was a driven, self-confident type, who could comfortably be the first to bring science to change the rough and ill-considered traditions of American production. He became known, quite willingly, as the "Father of Scientific Management" and the head of the Taylor Society.

His own view of his work he often stated with simple imperatives. Science must determine the method of performing each element of work, not tradition or rule of thumb. There must be scientific selection and training of workers. The scientifically designed work must then be brought together with the scientifically trained men. Planning, he insisted, was too important to be left to those who did the work. Planning must be separated, specialized, and professionalized. His theory of the management of men was threefold: there must be a "plum" for them to strive after, an occasional "touch of the lash" to keep them striving, and a benevolent management which was continually pushing, teaching, guiding, and helping. Management, he concluded, was an art, based however on scientific principles. It remained for his successors, still plagued by the need for objectification, to pervert this into the notion that management was a science. In doing this they not only inter-preted Taylor falsely, but started one of the least productive disputes of the present century.

Taylor's Impact

History has viewed Taylor's work in somewhat curious ways. In 1915, the year of his death, the United States Con-gress made time study illegal at government installations. Three years later at the close of the Russian Revolution, Lenin urged the adoption of all of Taylor's ideas in the building of the new Soviet society. Taylor's concept spread and became institution-alized with considerable conflict and controversy throughout the quarter century following his death. World War II gave a new urgency to the notion that data, models, prediction, and optimization could play a role in productivity enhancement. Scientists, motivated by the national emergency, again em-braced the idea that these things could be done not only in the laboratory, but also in the world of work and operations. Op-erations Research brought models and experiments to military undertakings, and with the end of the war it left industry with a new, higher level of science with a strong influence on the art of management.

We are now 25 years beyond the emergence of Operations Research. Phase II in 1973 found us plagued with inflation and foreign competition. The governmental response was to deal with prices and wages, but the ultimate response must be to make significant increases in productivity. We can bring about productivity increases by automating, by getting people to work harder, and by methods and operations improvements. The second strategy is perhaps the least plausible. Careful studies suggest that the order of magnitude of productivity increase which is possible from automation is about the same as that from methods and operations improvement. Thus, Tay-lor's thrusting of science into operations and the possibility of a science of operations are likely to be of continuing interest to managers. We are now in the process of working out the con-sequences of Taylor's ideas in the service industries, in trans-portation, in banking, in health care, and in the public sector. Police operations, city management, and natural resources management are now subjected to ideas which Taylor began, but no longer are associated with his name.

Taylor's importance today is not so much what he accomplished, but the great questions he made explicit for us. There is the criterion problem: what is a fair day's work, what is the measure of effectiveness for an educational institution, and how does one measure the productivity of a system of criminal justice? There is the persistent, sometimes researched, endlessly disputed question of how to motivate people to be productive. There is the wonderfully curious hypothesis that science might help illuminate some of the dark corners of working, planning, and managing. Taylor was undoubtedly a genius; much of the evidence for this lies in the fact that he remains such an active target for those who currently deplore the "quality of work." He did things which were clearly effective in his time. Whether or not they continue to be effective is not really the point. We still discuss Taylorism because he was a great innovator whose ideas have persisted and are continuing a slow process of diffusion. Many of his subtle insights have been lost by the low resolution communication process that tends to neglect the original sources. Taylor's successors have made far less progress in this century than have others in most other fields. The behavioral sciences have not produced useful knowledge at anything like the rate achieved by the physical sciences.

This curious lack of progress in the development and diffusion of knowledge about productivity becomes even clearer if we go back a century before the time of the science of shoveling.

THE EIGHTEENTH CENTURY
AND BEFORE

The problems of productivity in something like the form we now understand them must have been on the minds of managers at least by the middle of the eighteenth century. Coal, iron, and the steam engine created the conditions for large-scale manufacturing. The manager who could bring together the necessary capital and the labor force could find himself master of a plant which employed several hundred people.

It is likely, however, that these men viewed their problems with a rather different emphasis than is now the case. After all, as the factory system began, a major problem was to keep the machines running and to get the product out the door. Machines were probably better cared for than the people who ran them. People at that time, especially children and women, were easier to replace than machines and were far less expensive. The manager owned the machine and was thus responsible for its care and maintenance, but he bought only the labor of his employees and thus their maintenance and their working conditions were no concern of his. Labor unions were not yet in existence to trouble him, and he found in the wisdom of his time every justification for his attitudes. As long as wages were sufficiently low, he need not trouble about the niceties of management. If motivation and productivity needed his attention, it was the stick and not the carrot which seemed most useful. But there were exceptions—exceptional plants run by exceptional managers. The year 1800 marked the retirement of one of these men and the assumption of major managerial responsibility by another.

The Soho Foundry

The man who retired from active management of his firm in that year was a mechanical engineer who is usually remembered for his inventiveness in improving Newcomen's steam engine. Mr. James Watt, partner in Boulton, Watt and Company who were operators of the famous Soho foundry, was also a dabbler in some theoryless experiments in industrial management which led to techniques far ahead of his time.

There is no reason to suppose that Watt was any more inclined to acquire his knowledge from books than managers before or since, but it is useful to see what he would have had to work with if this had been the case. Accounting, the most fundamental of all productivity measuring tools, was ancient by 1800. In twelfth-century Venice, sophisticated accounting devices were already at the service of merchants. By 1494, Pacioli had written a treatise called *Summa de Arithmetica* which marked the literary beginning of the history of modern accounting. In Germany in 1549, the first book in that language explaining double entry bookkeeping appeared. *Zweifach Buchhalten* by a certain Herr Schweicker was the first of many such accounting texts which came out in the sixteenth and seventeenth centuries. The great Goethe himself was impressed by the subtlety and effectiveness of this management device and called it "one of the finest inventions of the human mind." By 1800, double entry books were common practice for merchants and manufacturers alike. Characteristically, Watt developed for his firm the improvement which made the device vastly more useful to managers. Boulton, Watt and Company had a cost accounting system.

Books on management up to this time had concerned themselves with recipes for success in commerce. Little had been written about industrial productivity. One of the great classics of the business literature was *Le Parfait Negociant*, written by Jacques Savary in 1675. Classical is the proper term for this work because it reappeared in the last of many editions in the very year of James Watt's retirement. Education for success in business management appeared in the form of Thomas Watt's work of 1776 which he titled *An Essay on the Proper Method of Forming the Man of Business*. A number of handbooks for managers appeared in the eighteenth century which claimed to reveal all the knowledge of commercial operations then known. Typical of these is the *Universal Dictionary of Trade and Commerce*, the work of Malachy Postlewayt in 1755.

Division of Labor

Watt may have been acquainted with Adam Smith's great passage describing the division of labor in the pin factory, but it is interesting to note that it was some time before the Soho foundry evolved to an organization in which extensive division of labor was practiced. Certainly Watt, who had visited many plants as a consulting engineer on steam engines, was aware of the extent job specialization in manufacturing had developed at the time. He was, however, basically an experimentalist who worked things out for himself in his own plant.

Division of labor did, nevertheless, reach a high degree of

development in Watt's factory; the catalog of management techniques which went with it reads much like an outline of the ideas that were to occupy industrial engineers a hundred years later. To begin with, the plant was not arranged just by whim or expedient. Careful attention was given to plant layout, and a sensible scheme of departmentalization was the result. The products and the methods of production were standardized through management planning. A scheme we would now call a routing system controlled the flow of material through the shop. Most of the workers eventually were put on piece rates, which again was the result of management attention. Records of production were kept in elaborate fashion; these forerunners of time study were even used to develop mathematical formulas relating various aspects of the task to the performance time. All the problems of piece rates based on time standards were evidently a part of Watt's experience because in 1791 some of his men had gone on strike in a dispute over rates.

Delegation of authority was worked out in a well-organized plan and, as already noted, a cost accounting system was devised as a means of controlling the resulting management hierarchy. Watt already knew that cost accounting could be the basis for pricing the product and even more useful for detecting "waste and inefficiency." When new policies or reforms seemed necessary, elaborate statistical reports were prepared, which must surely have some claim to marking the earliest utilization of the staff industrial engineer.

The Soho foundry was, of course, an exception. But the important things to note about it are these:

1. It marks an early discovery of the immense importance of separating the planning of production from the work of production. Here was the key to modern staff organization.

2. The twin problems of motivation and control of the manufacturing organization were put on a rational basis.

3. There was no theory on which Watt could draw. He was a typical cut and try empiricist; however, it does not seem to have occurred to him that these experiments could be conducted in any way except the most expensive possible way. He experimented with the plant it-

self. This is not surprising, for the idea that staff advisers could reduce the need for and enhance the success of such costly tests is a very modern one indeed.

New Lanark

Also in the year 1800, another bright young man bought himself a cotton mill employing roughly 2,000 people in the little town of New Lanark in Scotland. This man was hardly likely to be admired by managers of his time, or by those who have prospered under free enterprise since, because he formed utopian socialist communities and was eventually to have a major part in the rise of the British trade union movement. He was, however, like Watt, an experimenter with the courage to try his ideas in practice at the risk of his own capital. His name was Robert Owen.

When Owen took charge of the New Lanark mills, the working and living conditions were as bad as anywhere else. Of his work force, some 400 to 500 were children between the ages of five and ten. They worked a thirteen hour day, after which they slept through what passed for their education. The adults who worked at New Lanark did so as a last resort. One went to work in the mills only when all other means of livelihood seemed to have failed. Drunkenness was a common occurrence in the mill. Owen, like Watt, made some changes in the machines and their arrangement, but his great experiments ran in another direction. He set out on a great program of social reform which centered around his mills but extended into the community to include education, religion, and public health. He wanted to change not only the material existence of his employees, but their habits and character as well. And, of course, they systematically opposed him. It was not until the company continued to pay wages through a long period of unemployment that Owen began to gain their confidence.

Owen clearly understood his program of reform in the mills could not be a sudden revolution. Over a period of twenty-five years he got the children out of the mills and into schools, shortened the work day, and made extensive improvements in working and living conditions. His biographer, Cole, said, "He meant to make New Lanark not merely a success as a factory, but the laboratory for a great series of social experiments in education and moral and physical reform."

Owen saw himself as an experimenter, too, for he remarked on taking over the mills, "I had now, by a course of events not under my control, the groundwork on which to try an experiment long wished for, but little expected to be in my power to carry into execution."

Owen saw, perhaps for the first time, that after certain minimum material needs had been taken care of other incentives began to emerge alongside the financial one. His system of "silent monitors" was a marvel of simplicity and directness. Over each machine hung a piece of wood painted a different color on each of four sides. The shop foremen rated the conduct of each employee, and his block of wood revealed for all to see his deportment on the previous day. The black side signified bad behavior; the white side, excellent behavior; blue and yellow fell in between. Owen could tell much about how things were going in the mills by a glance at the colors which met his eye.

What was the result of this great experiment in industrial productivity? Owen's mills prospered and provided him with a substantial fortune. Indeed they might have continued to enrich him for a lifetime if he had not eventually taken his wealth and lost it in his far less successful experiments in socialist communities. Interestingly enough, the experiments at New Lanark were widely known and his fellow industrialists came to see the secret of his prosperity. He had no imitators among them, however. Facts alone do not change people's minds.

Robert Owen, then, made the first industrial experiment in human relations. He demonstrated two astounding facts which were perhaps unbelievable to the managers of his day.

1. Men are not machines.
2. The simple, brute-force minimization of costs does not necessarily result in the maximization of profits.

Like others of his time, Owen experienced the difficulties which played a part in the rise of the modern corporation. He could not himself raise the capital to buy the New Lanark mills, so he had partners. His partners were few in number and, of course, did not at first accept his novel schemes for management. In 1812 he had to form a new partnership which included Jeremy Bentham. The larger and the more mechanized industry became, the greater grew its need for capital. Eventually the corporation as a mechanism for capitalization evolved. One of its most important aspects, for our purposes, was the separation of ownership from management. The division of labor in production was the first great specialization which began the industrial revolution, and the division of ownership and management was the second.

TO THE TWENTIETH CENTURY

After the experiments of Watt, Owen and Taylor, the history of fundamental experiments in productivity enhancement jumped to the automobile industry. What appears most remarkable is not the drama of rapid progress but quite the opposite. Basic experiments are few; their results diffuse in a very deliberate fashion, and the old ideas hang on doggedly. Henry Ford was the great demonstrator, the great popularizer, of the basic principles of modern productivity at dramatically high levels. His philosophy was to standardize the product, turn out hundreds of thousands of Model T's, and make a virtue of their uniformity even to the single color of black. He paid working people, not the minimum that the market would bear, but a wage which made some attempt to recognize their dignity, their contribution, and their productivity potential. He announced the $5.00 day and accompanied it with a liberal explanation of the underlying philosophy. Ford grasped the notion that specialization might be carried to some sort of human limit; and having done so, he realized the complex of men and machines which produce must be seen as a carefully integrated system. The automobile assembly line represented some sort of a high point in the "working smarter, not harder" movement. Ford was one of the last American managers who had the power and the control which made it possible for him to immediately translate into experiments his ideas about radically new productive systems.

Mr. Sloan and General Motors

The second great experiment of the same period was also developed in the automotive industry. It had long been an intriguing hypothesis that if one could assemble a really large production complex and find a way to coordinate its operations, there were possibilities for really astonishing levels of productivity. The problem was that nobody knew the secrets of managing large organizations in order to prevent confusion, duplication, competition, and the low levels of motivation and productivity often associated with "bureaucracy." The entrepreneurial experiments which have so much leverage on productivity needed to be directed at information flow and coordination in large organizations.

William C. Durant, founder of the General Motors Corporation, was confident of the great potential market for the automobile, and he was convinced that the way to exploit this potential was to bring together a group of existing companies already producing and marketing in the automotive field. He was most successful in carrying out this plan, and by 1919 he had built General Motors into the fifth largest industrial enterprise in the United States. Trouble lay ahead, however, Durant, the great builder, had little interest in the problem of making explicit the organizational structure of his firm or in developing administrative processes by which to operate it. The excitement of rapid growth for the company combined with the increasing revenues from automobile sales diverted his attention from these problems and suppressed the need to face them.

The General Motors Corporation, riding the postwar boom, entered 1920 as a highly decentralized collection of operating companies or divisions. The managers of these divisions, who were swept along by increasing demand and rising prices for cars, were aggressively expanding their inventories and their plant capacities. Each manager, concerned exclusively with his own division, wanted to protect himself against inflation and shortages by means of a strong inventory position. Continued inability to meet the demand for automobiles impelled each one toward larger and larger capital-investment programs. Although the division managers together constituted the executive committee of the corporation, none of them was concerned with the corporation's problems or with the possibilities of long-term economic movements. Nor was Durant in any better position to take the large view.

The major decisions for each division were made in several ways. Plant expansion, capital investment, production schedules, and prices were sometimes decided by Durant after informal talks with the division managers. Sometimes, the division managers took these things into their own hands, with only the most limited coordination with Durant's office. Durant would sometimes authorize a particular capital expenditure during a plant visit without any record of the decision being made. At other times, the executive committee would make capital appropriations; also, the members did consider "horse trading" of the form, "I'll vote for your project if you'll vote for mine." Thus, there were no standardized financial procedures, nor was there any method of controlling expenditures. Large overruns on capital authorizations were the rule. Furthermore, there was virtually nothing in the way of standardized accounting procedures, leaving Durant without any means of measuring and comparing the performance of his divisions.

In the spring of 1920, the divisions became increasingly demanding in their requests for capital. Their inventories continued upward. The corporation sought new capital both by borrowing and by the sale of additional common stock. Then, in September, the automobile market collapsed, the postwar recession began, and the General Motors Corporation very nearly ceased production. The firm's stock fell; it became more and more difficult for the divisions to meet payrolls and short-term debts; and Durant resigned as president. The new president, Pierre Du Pont, sometime before had seen an organization plan for the corporation worked out by Alfred Sloan, head of the parts and accessories division. Almost immediately after becoming president, Du Pont began to implement the Sloan plan. It was perhaps the first lucid design for what we now refer to as a decentralized organization.

Decentralization

Sloan recognized that there was much to be gained by permitting the divisions to have great responsibility for their own operations. On the other hand, there was clearly some need for central control and coordination of their operations if the firm was to realize the potential strengths of being large. In the area of capital budgeting, for example, Sloan clearly saw the message of the crisis of 1920. His response was to produce a design in which some smaller investments could be authorized by the division managers, but larger investments had to be submitted to corporate headquarters. At that point, a check needed to be made on that data submitted by the divisions in support of their proposals, and a common basis for comparison among proposals was necessary. The headquarters group would have to review each proposal both in the view of the long-term objectives of the corporation and long-term economic outlook. From the vantage point, an effective allocation of the corporation's available capital could be made among the divisions. This allocation was to be followed by controls on the expenditures of funds and by a method of measuring and comparing the overall financial performance of the divisions. In this way Sloan sought to leave the day-to-day operating responsibilities at the divisional level, whereas long-term decisions and problems of coordination among divisions were handled at headquarters. Pervading the whole design were the concepts of clear definition of authority and responsibility and carefully designed systems of information flow to permit effective coordination and control.

Sloan's design may best be viewed as an experimental response to a crisis in the evolutionary development of an organization. Other firms approached similar organizational forms from different starting points and by slower evolutionary processes. Of course, the Sloan design itself was only the beginning of an extended period of experimentation in organizational plans, but it did represent a rather complete and well-developed set of hypotheses on which to base such experiments. One might generally characterize the General Motors crisis as the result of excessive decentralization. Other firms, of which Du Pont is a good example, found themselves in difficulty for exactly the opposite reasons. They suffered from excessive centralization. Top managers in these highly centralized, functionally organized firms were unable to meet the twin stimuli of growing national markets and the dramatic enrichment of production and product technologies. Sloan's experiment showed the way toward a subtlety which is still under active exploration. Somewhere between a high degree of centralization and a high degree of decentralization lies the point at which the productivity potential of the large system is likely to be most fully realized. Here one can have some of the advantages of being large and some of the advantages of being small and not too many of the disadvantages of either. Somewhere between having no management information system and the burdensome military notion of unity of command, one finds the management information systems of the more successful of our modern conglomerates.

Systems Analysis

The auto industry was not only the field of operation for Ford and Sloan, but also later provided President Kennedy with his Secretary of Defense—a tough-minded innovator who must receive the major share of credit for contemporary productivity innovations. Robert McNamara, plagued by the professional military men and intensely frustrated by the Vietnam war, was another in the line of managers who had the courage to experiment in the face of a challenge to manage the unmanageable. McNamara surrounded himself with people trained in economics, mathematics, physics, and operations research. These people undertook to be clear about the options from which the Secretary had to choose. They tried to be more explicit than ever about the objectives of various programs; they made full use of the power of mathematical analysis and the digital computer to become as explicit as seemed reasonably possible about the costs, benefits, and trade-offs associated with major military undertakings. They demonstrated that modern systems analysis was more than an academic plaything; it could in fact make a substantial contribution, however controversial, to management problems of the highest order of complexity. President Johnson, a man seldom accused of being overly fascinated by things theoretical, was sufficiently impressed to direct that systems analysis should be used throughout the other major agencies of the Federal government.

Here was repeated a phenomenon which explains much of the diffusion of productivity innovation throughout the

American economy. Statistical quality control, emerging from the work of Dr. Walter Shewhart in the Department of Agriculture in 1928, was soon adopted as a part of the procurement process for major government purchases. Suppliers who wished to do business with Washington, D.C., were quickly and forcefully introduced to this powerful set of ideas. The sheer weight of Federal participation in the economy spread these concepts more quickly than could any other mechanism. The same process happened with systems analysis. Government agencies showed how to do it, supported its further development and application, and insisted on using it in major programs. In this sense, Secretary McNamara was the crucial figure in the diffusion of what may turn out to be *the* productivity innovation of the latter half of this century.

Historical Threads

Even a cursory glance at the last several decades of our concern for productivity would involve a great deal more than our brief look at these few men. We have said nothing at all of the great Hawthorne experiments and the resulting human relations movement. We have not mentioned the more recent experiments in participative management, organizational development, and the restructuring of work. We will return to these experiments in subsequent chapters where we will take special note of the recent increase in the rate at which they are being carried on. So rapid has this rate of experimentation become, that the techniques for productivity enhancement now seem to come and go much in the way of fads and fashions.

For those who have the inclination to explore the history of productivity experiments, there are some fascinating threads to look for. Basic advances in our knowledge of productivity phenomena have come largely as the result of experiments conducted without the benefit of much theory. We seem still to lack anything like a coherent theory to guide our next experiments, and it is clear that the next significant advances will come when there are people who combine the courage and power to make radically different experiments.

Many of those who have been concerned for productivity have been "one strategy" people. Others have been the "working harder" people who dealt primarily in terms of schemes for motivation. Also, there have been the machinery and technology people who saw capital investment as the single great secret of productivity improvement. Finally, there have been the "working smarter" people who believed primarily in methods, in management, and in the careful design of producing systems. Almost no examples exist of people who made significant attempts to experiment with more than one of these single approach strategies. This is a matter which will occupy our attention in subsequent discussions.

There is some evidence to support the notion that ideas about motivation and ideas about "working smarter" seem to have a much slower rate of diffusion than do technological advances. We will have occasion later to consider the importance of this phenomenon and speculate on some of the reasons for it. Ideas about "soft" approaches to improving productivity have emerged very early and found wide application only quite slowly until the recent emergence of academics and consultants who have a vested interest in marketing these ideas. All of this may, of course, be related to the relatively slow progress achieved by the behavioral sciences as compared with the drama of the physical sciences. This may explain in part the dominant belief that investment is *the* key to productivity improvement. The resulting imbalance between our application of the physical sciences and our knowledge of human behavior is seen by some as the basis for the current phenomenon called the "blue-collar blues" and the current popular concern with work attitudes. Perhaps the most subtle and yet potentially the most significant thread is the "measurement revolution," which began in the field of productivity with the experiments of Taylor and was given its great impetus by McNamara and the operations research profession. Measurement is the basis for much of the progress now being made, as we shall see in some detail in the next section. The measurement revolution is bringing within our grasp whole areas of productive activity which have formerly seemed totally out of reach. It has long been concluded as completely self-evident that little could be done about the productivity of doctors, lawyers, teachers, or barbers because there was simply no obvious and uniform way to measure their output.

THE BASIC MACRO FACTS
OF PRODUCTIVITY CHANGE

All productivity measures share the concept of a ratio of some measure of output or product to some measure of input or resources used in production. Miles per gallon is a common and useful measure of automobile productivity. Passenger-miles per gallon makes a useful measure for comparing the productivity of buses and aircraft. The most widely used measure is labor productivity or output per man-hour. This is not to imply that the output is exclusively the product of the labor involved, but rather the result of the labor in conjunction with the tools, machines, materials, and management skills which compose the entire work situation. In the case of manufacturing, one seeks a measure of physical output, such as the number of pieces produced. In the case of services, the problem of measuring output is likely to be much more difficult, as no such obvious possibility may present itself.

The purpose of productivity measurement is to make comparisons—comparisons of the efficiency of a production system over time or comparisons among alternative systems. The function of these comparisons in turn is to direct attention to the need or the opportunity for action. It is important to be clear at the outset that the indicated action may be more measurement. Many of our productivity measures are designed to perform just this function. Admittedly, these measures are not conclusive in themselves; however, they are good enough to indicate when and where more careful and more expensive input-output measurements should be made. These comparisons are intended to stimulate and evaluate management actions, but they must be used with care and discretion, and with deliberate interpretation. If, for example, labor productivity or output per man-hour goes up for a production system, this does not necessarily mean that the people are working harder. A change in labor productivity may be due to: the tools and machines available; the technology and methods of production; the materials employed; the size of the production system and the volume of output; the effectiveness of management in planning, scheduling, and controlling production; the design of the product and the product mix; the elimination of some jobs, with or without the addition of others; and training, education, and experience.

Synergy

All of the above factors are interrelated. Productivity is a synergistic phenomenon resulting from the interaction of many such considerations. A higher level of education is necessary for the introduction of new technologies and sophisticated capital improvements. Advanced management techniques can be used to get the most out of big, complex production systems; big systems in turn create the opportunity to employ advanced techniques. Productivity grows from the mutual interaction of such complementary effects. Thus if labor productivity changes, the indicated action may be more measurement to try to discover why it has changed. Labor productivity may be a good enough indicator that attention is warranted, but it is not subtle enough nor sufficiently explanatory to indicate what sort of action might be appropriate. To increase the explanatory power, total factor productivity is sometimes calculated by dividing output by the sum of man-hours and machine-hours. This process eliminates the quantity of capital equipment used as an explanation of differences. In still more subtle attempts to reduce explanatory uncertainty, different types of labor and equipment are sometimes weighted before they are added to form the divisor. Weights might be developed, for example, to take account of differing levels of skill, education, and experience among members of the work force.

Sometimes input and output are measured in terms of wage dollars and sales dollars. When this is done, it is usually the practice to use "constant dollar" measures in order to eliminate the effects of changes in wage rates and prices.

Labor Productivity

For our purposes, however, it will be both simple and useful to concentrate on changes in labor productivity and think of these changes as the result of three broad classes of interacting effects:

1. Changes in the amount of capital equipment, machines, and tools available—the tangible capital input.

2. Changes in the "quality of labor" including the skill, education, training, experience, health, energy, and attitudes of the working people—the intangible or "labor embodied" capital.
3. Better management of the operations, methods, and technology of production, the efficiency or effectiveness with which the other two factors are employed—the "soft" sources of productivity improvement.

The third factor involves many aspects such as new materials, new processes, the substitution of mechanical energy and skill for human energy and skill, and the use of special jigs and fixtures. But it involves much more than hardware. It also involves computer-based management information systems, new job designs, new methods of scheduling and coordinating people, equipment and materials, better predictions of demand, and better quality control.

Put another way, labor productivity, or output per man-hour, is a conventional way of measuring how a complex set of effects influence one aspect of the output of a production system. Labor, capital, and management interact to form the system, and the behavior of each is influenced by the presence of the others. This is, in fact, precisely what one means by the term "system."

TRENDS

We have already briefly reviewed the trends in private, nonfarm productivity since 1889. This productivity rose steadily until 1945, then rose at an even higher rate of about three percent until 1965 when it dropped to a disturbingly low level of annual increase. Part of the problem of separating the trends from the temporary distortions is the variation of productivity with the expansion and contraction of business activity. Productivity is importantly related to the business cycle. During a contraction in the volume of production, output per man-hour falls because the inputs to the production system cannot be (and sensibly, should not be) immediately reduced in proportion. Similarly, productivity rises during an expansion of production, both because there is some slack in the system and because it takes some time to increase the inputs.

A great part of the perplexity over recent productivity data is, of course, whether or not it is indicating a long term decline or simply a cyclical movement. Each time the Bureau of Labor Statistics announces the new figures, there are immediate attempts to read the long run implications, a very difficult feat indeed. The recent figures have lent considerable credence to Scenario Y and have enhanced the fascination of looking for broad social explanations rather than business cycle relationships.

Sources of Productivity Gains

Where have our past productivity increases come from? Careful statistical analyses of the long run data have made it possible to roughly separate the portion of the annual productivity increment which is explained by each of our three broad contributing factors. Curiously, the great and obvious explanation of massive increases in plants and equipment, coupled with persistent improvements in the health and education of the work force—the things which seem so important to developing nations—are not the major factors which explain our experience.

Nearly 70 percent of our productivity increases can be explained otherwise. Greater efficiency in combining capital and labor is the dominant explanation. New technology, and new management techniques and skills are responsible for most of what we have achieved. Viewed in slightly more detail, the data from 1889 suggests that for most industries the big source of productivity gains was technological change, new knowledge applied to the methods of production, management skills and tools, and so on. The "soft" factors have been the most significant.

The remaining 30 percent of the annual increase in output per man-hour can be explained by our other two factors. The increase in tangible capital—machines and tools—thought by many to be the basic source of productivity enhancement, accounts for roughly 18 percent of the gains. The remaining 12 percent may be seen as the economic result of our progress in education, nutrition, and health care—improvements in what economists like to call the quality of labor. The quality of labor includes such personal characteristics as strength, energy, persistence, intelligence, knowledge, skill, and flexibility. The quality of labor is seen, by economists at least, as a generally increasing function of age and education.

Some Conclusions

From this data, we may squeeze a few tentative conclusions to guide us in our further analysis of the "living poorer—working harder" hypothesis.

1. In spite of all the excitement about technology, scientific breakthroughs, and savings and investment, the figures certainly do not support the notion that our productivity increases are accelerating. The weight of evidence is, in fact, to the contrary.

2. All of the basic effects, tangible capital, intangible capital, and management improvements do operate in significant ways to increase productivity. None can be dismissed as unimportant.

3. Management skills and technological change, our third factor, are the largest contributors to productivity increases. If one is interested in the potential for further increases, this poses an interesting question. Does this predominance of the third factor suggest it should receive most of our attention in the future? Does it suggest, alternatively, that the first two factors have somehow been neglected in the past and should now receive special attention as having the greatest untapped potential? Or does it mean that effort to increase productivity in the future ought somehow to be allocated among each of the three factors in order to produce the greatest return?

   There is of course a further hypothesis. The way in which labor and capital are combined in a production system, for all of its importance, may have been seriously neglected both by managers and government policy analysts. In spite of this neglect the combination of labor and capital has been the major force in productivity gains and may remain the greatest source of future gains.

4. While these facts may be of some use to government policy analysts, they do not tell us directly what to do if we become concerned about Scenario Y. Actual changes in productivity occur in individual plants and at individual work places.

5. It is reasonable to wonder what we are going to do about measuring and improving productivity in the growing service sector. How can we approach the difficult problems of the hospitals, banks, insurance companies, and gas stations?

6. Our system, viewed in the long run, has a special and very important synergy, or equity effect. Real income has moved up steadily with productivity. All three of our basic factors—labor quality, tangible capital, and efficiency—have contributed. In the long run, working people have usually received their due, such as a real wage increase justified by their contribution. Labor, roughly speaking, in the long run gets paid what it is worth. Clearly these three factors do not operate in the short term without delays, interruptions, and imperfection. However, people who are more productive will realize real wage increases. The data confirms this basic and marvelous effect.

THE MEASUREMENT REVOLUTION

The Bureau of Labor Statistics has adequate measures of productivity for only about a third of the people who work in our economy. At the macroscopic level, there are almost no productivity measures for state and local government, construction, trade, finance, insurances and medical services— production systems that are the bulk of our economy. At the microscopic level, the level of the individual plant and the individual job, nobody knows how serious the problem is, but it is clearly not any better. Fortunately, we now see these problems in a new light, in more sophisticated terms which we have called the measurement revolution. The advances in our abilities to measure inputs and outputs of production systems, given such a tremendous push by the McNamara era, come at a very fortunate time.

It seems simple enough to measure the output of a production system which is making a single type of physical product, uniform in quality and stable in production rate. As we move away from this situation, all sorts of measurement complexities arise, complexities which must be plainly acknowledged at the outset.

A bank typically provides a variety of services to both borrowers and depositors. All sorts of measures suggest themselves such as: number of loans, amount of loans, proportion of loans repaid, number and size of deposit accounts, check clearances, statements rendered, banking lobby transactions, and so on. The quality of the services rendered by the bank may vary markedly. Some banks restrict themselves to very conventional low risk loans, while others actively seek to play a role in the financial development of their localities. In some banks, depositors fill out the slips themselves, while other banks have tellers perform this function. If a bank decides that check clearance is the measure of its productivity, then like most banks, it will feel that it has become markedly more productive in recent years, in spite of the fact that its loan activity may have declined. If check clearance is the measure of productivity, then efforts should be turned toward luring more depositors and further computerizing the process of check handling. The severe competition in this area may mean low earnings for the bank and, coupled with the neglect of its borrowers, bank profits may decline. One may, of course, construct similar analyses of the difficulties to be expected in military units, law firms, police departments, or households.

It is easy to make the case that productivity in a bank is impossible to measure in a meaningful way. When one sees such a variety of activities—varieties in volume, quality, timeliness, price, and degrees of satisfaction to those served—it is easy to accept the notion that no measure exists which would be an acceptable, objective and reasonably inexpensive indicator of output. Consequently, it follows that these kinds of production systems are somehow wholly and fundamentally different in character from industrial systems.

By taking Sir Isaac Newton very seriously indeed, one may say that if it can't be measured, it doesn't exist. If it doesn't exist, nothing can be done about it. It is, therefore, futile to be even concerned about the productivity of such operations.

Since one obviously cannot measure the productivity of a library, a legislature, a university, or a department store, the whole concept of the design management and evaluation of such systems is nonexistent. If not actually nonexistent, the concept is at least unique and not a proper topic of discussion for laymen. In these situations, the ways people work, the nature of accountability, and the relationships between activities and objectives simply cannot be made explicit. To measure the productivity of a hospital, a welfare agency, or an insurance company is somehow to act in a way which is antithetical to the very purposes of these organizations.

The measurement revolution, which has been gathering momentum since 1945, does not reduce these problems to trivialities. They are difficult problems which are time consuming and expensive, but not futile. Progress is underway and the first useful and exciting results are in. The measurement revolution has taken more sophisticated approaches to the problem, not necessarily more complex or more subtle, but the sophistication of returning to basic and surprisingly simple measurement strategies. The new approach has been quite simply to try first to be very clear about the problem and then to find ways of sidestepping those aspects which would not yield to direct attack.

The Measurement Problem

One of the characteristics of a "good" or "meaningful" productivity measure is that maximizing the measure is widely regarded as consistent with the objectives of the production system. Maximizing the tons per man-hour in a steel mill may not be a good measure in this sense because it may involve big increases in pollution from other mill outputs, and increased danger to the health of the employees. The railroads became more productive when they eliminated the passenger business, if one measured output in ton-miles; however, the former passengers may not have thought so. Soft drink manufacturers became more productive when they converted to disposable containers, but many states have not agreed. Maximizing the student-credit-hours taught per full-time faculty member is not likely to be consistent with the objectives of a university.

Thus, one aspect of the measurement problem is that there is usually a difference between maximizing a productivity measure and maximizing the attainment of the goals of a company, institution, community, or social system.

A second characteristic of a good productivity measure is that it is "objective." It is independent of the person making the measurement and not subjected to judgment, personal bias, or perceptual distortion. Good productivity measures are purported to be based on what is lovingly called "hard data."

Single Numbers

When outputs vary in their number, quality, satisfaction to client or customer, and so on, in order to make a good productivity measure, one must somehow aggregate these multiple outputs into a single number. Similarly, the variety of the inputs must be suppressed into a single number so there can be one measure of productivity. Almost all of the science most of us have been taught is thought to be successful only if measures can be reduced to such single numbers so that we are able to make simple, direct comparisons and decisions.

Finally, a good productivity measure must be without imperfection in the view of all those concerned. If it has any taint of uncertainty, any taint of subjectivity, any indication that it is not completely consistent with one's goals, then the tendency is to reject it as useless. Imperfect productivity measures are almost never used for what they are worth. If a measure is to any degree uncertain or ambiguous, it is rejected as totally useless, for to do otherwise would expose one to obvious criticism.

Productivity in Social Service—An Example

The easiest way to see how the measurement revolution has approached these problems is by means of an example. Arnold Riesman and Burton Dean in a classic practical example of revolutionary measurement at work, have quantified in an especially useful way the outputs of seventeen social service agencies. The agencies, supported by the Jewish Community Federation of Cleveland, were involved in a set of activities so diverse and seemingly so difficult to measure in any constructive way, that we have listed them all on page 58.

Activities of Seventeen Social Service Agencies:

1. Individual Counseling (Vocational-Educational)
2. Group Counseling (Vocational-Educational)
3. Individual Counseling (Psycho-Social)
4. Group Counseling (Psycho-Social)
5. Family Counseling (Psycho-Social)
6. Family Life Education
7. Intake and Referral
8. Formal Education (Primary Jewish Focus)
9. Jewish Day School Education
10. Registered Activities (Primary Jewish Focus)
11. Registered Activities
12. Unregistered Activities (Primary Jewish Focus)
13. Unregistered Activities
14. Social Action
15. Adoptive Service
16. Foster Care
17. Group Foster Care
18. Institutional Health and Living
19. Temporary Shelter
20. Homebound Services
21. Day Care
22. Day Camp
23. Residential Camp
24. Resettlement
25. Job Placement
26. Religious Activities
27. Institutional Health Services (Short-Term)
28. Institutional Health Services (Long-Term)
29. Non-Institutional Health Services
30. Sheltered Workshop

The problem was to provide the Jewish Community Federation with some measures of the quality, quantity, and value of the outputs of the various agencies so that more reasonable decisions could be made about the allocation of funds. A method was sought that would permit measurement of the productivity of each agency encompassing all of the services it rendered and all of the client groups it served. The method also needed to permit an evaluation of the effectiveness of each service across agencies and clients, and the evaluation of how well each client group was being served in all agencies and types of services. This was hardly a trivial productivity measurement problem.

The first tactic was to simplify the view of the outputs of these agencies. A "package" was defined as a particular service rendered by a particular agency to a particular client group. The service-client-agency package, or unit of output, was then defined or described in terms of four dimensions:

1. the number of clients served by the package during a given time period,
2. the amount of direct contact time given to the clients in rendering the service during the given time period,
3. the value of the package, and
4. the quality of the package.

The first two dimensions represented the physical throughput of the system, the traditional productivity measures which are relatively easy to obtain but almost totally meaningless if considered by themselves.

The value of a package was interpreted by its relative importance to the community. The most difficult problem in this situation was to decide whose values were to be considered. It was clear that judgments would be involved and that some systematic and explicit method for expressing these judgments would be important. It was decided to obtain the value judgments of four different groups: the Jewish community at large, community leaders, social agency professionals, and the study team itself. Participants making judgments were asked simply to rate each client-agency-service package at one of five levels of value ranging from very high to very low. For purposes of scoring, these levels were given values from five to one.

The judgments were obtained by an interesting iterative process called the Delphi Method. In the case of the sixteen community leaders, each person was asked to provide his value ratings on the packages anonymously. The other participants did not know his ratings, nor did they have a chance to influence him directly. The research team then fed back to each participant a summary of the ratings furnished by the group as a whole. On the basis of this information, participants were asked to revise their ratings and the process was repeated again. Successive iterations continued until a sort of consensus was reached—approximately 80 percent of the group had evaluated each package in two contiguous categories. The Delphi Method has been thoroughly investigated and is known to have some interesting properties. In forecasting problems, Delphi panels have been shown to produce consistently better results than individuals, and consistently better results than face-to-face groups where a single dominant personality may sway the entire group.

When these results were obtained for each of the four groups, the problem of whose values were to be considered solved itself. It turned out there was an extremely high degree of agreement among the four groups. Although this is not always the case, there is more and more evidence that the values of well-informed and responsible people are likely to be in closer agreement than one might suspect.

Quality

The concept of the quality of a package was similarly broken down into a series of components:

* accessibility to the community,
* capability of meeting expressed needs,
* degree to which client-oriented goals are achieved,
* efficiency, hours of service per staff dollar,
* cooperation with other agencies, and
* degree to which community-oriented goals are achieved.

Next, each of these components was further broken down into elements, some of which involved the collection of readily available data and some of which required judgments. The Delphi process was again used to obtain judgments; the results were quantified and carefully aggregated into a quality measure for each package. The aggregation process took into account the concept that some components of quality were more important than others and that some judgments were necessary in combining measures of efficiency—for example, judgments about the achievement of client-oriented goals. Out of this complex and clearly expensive process came three measures for each package, agency, client group, and service: the service time received by clients, the value of the services, and the quality of the services. No attempt was made to combine these three numbers into a single number; instead, planners and decision makers were asked to consider all three. Several interesting things happened at this point.

1. All persons involved agreed that the measures developed were not unique; however, after considerable self-criticism and analysis, all groups agreed that the measures were highly indicative of the quality and value of the services offered. Just as important, the measures

and the methods for obtaining them were acceptable to both the social agencies and the Jewish Community Federation. In fact, the JCF board committed itself to use these measures in future planning and budgeting.

2. It became clear to everyone involved that the measures would have to be carefully interpreted. Comparing service time for an agency which offered twenty-four hour service to residents, to service time for an ambulatory clinic would necessitate some cautious interpretation.

3. Most important, the measures were actually used by planners, agency professionals, and budget makers throughout the system. Data on a given service-client package could be compared over time and between agencies offering the same package. Data could be compared for different service-client packages either over time or among agencies, and so on.

Sophisticated Measurement

In this interesting sense, the problem of measuring the productivity of these social service agencies was "solved." This result is typical of an increasing number of cases of sophisticated measurements in which we are more courageous in what we are willing to attempt, take a broader view of the methods of measurement we are willing to use, and find it possible to make practical use of measures which are not complete nor perfect in everyone's view. Sophisticated measurement is characterized by: multiple measures, clear acknowledgement of errors, biases, and uncertainties, explicit statements of assumptions, the wide use of explicit judgments by individuals and groups, the use of mathematical models to combine basic judgments and objective data into aggregate indicators. This process does not achieve the "objectivity," perfect reliability, or demonstrated validity to which we may have unrealistically aspired; however, it does have the significant virtue of being useful and permitting better-informed decisions to be made about the improvement of productivity. This process may not produce results that are obviously supported by a broad consensus; however, the more people who participate in the measurement process, the clearer they become about their judgments, and the better their chances of reaching a consensus. This process may be expensive, but as we learn more about it, we are finding an increasing number of situations in which the potential for productivity improvement appears to more than justify the measurement effort involved. In this sense, sophisticated measurement begins to make sense about measurement. As we move forward in our examination of possible responses to the onset of Scenario Y, we will have occasion to return from time to time to applications of revolutionary measurement methods.

The real problem—the action-oriented problem—is to discover those methods of measurement which give us a good indication of where the best potentials for productivity improvement are to be found. The sort of process indicated by the Riesman-Dean study seems to be an important move in this direction.

The Behavioral Consequences
of Measurement

Before we leave the subject of measuring productivity, we need to reflect on that important scientific subtlety: when you measure something, you often change it in the process. Measurement of productive behavior has consequences which are reflected in that behavior. To measure productivity is to influence it. As soon as people find that their behavior is being measured, they are very likely to do something about it. Just finding that someone is paying attention is enough to alter productivity in many situations. If people find that quality and quantity measures are being made, they are likely to assume that increases are wanted in these measures, and they may behave accordingly. If something is not measured, people often assume that nobody cares and this behavior may be safely neglected. Thus, once we begin to measure productivity, people may feel a new accountability, a new incentive to improve their productivity.

This effect can be strengthened in two ways. The familiar psychological process of giving someone knowledge of results very often has the effect of reinforcing behavior and adding incentive. Thus, if we not only measure productivity, but feed the results back to those who are producing, we can, for a time, expect some advancement in productivity levels.

When productivity measurement is undertaken, there is a tendency to become more explicit about the objectives of a production system or an organization. The Riesman-Dean study is a good example of a situation where the measurement process encouraged people to think with renewed clarity about what they were supposed to be doing, what an agency or program was trying to achieve, and what were the goals of the social service system. Productivity is often related to the operation and the clarity of goals; measurement often moves us in that direction. For example, when teachers become interested in stating their instructional objectives in terms of the behaviors they want to see in their students, they have most likely become to some degree more productive, more accountable, and more inclined to engage in productive behavior.

If we measure only the mistakes, the failures, and the counter-productive behaviors of working people, we will certainly cause discouragement. We should, if we believe B.F. Skinner, concentrate on measuring and approving the good things workers do—their successes and their positive achievements. Productivity measurement is an integral part of the strategy of positive reinforcement of behavior. As we look next at particular strategies for influencing productivity, it will be useful to keep in mind that measuring productivity is more than just collecting data.

WHERE ARE WE AND WHERE ARE WE HEADED? Productivity is basic to our economic objectives, and as a matter of fact, to all of our objectives. It is the central concept on which we must depend not only to manage our economic lives but also to manage the broad spectrum of considerations which make up a life style. Getting more for less is about as fundamental a human motivation as one can find.

At the least, we have short run productivity problems, and perhaps the long run outlook is not very good either. Whether or not we are actually headed for a period of working harder and living poorer is uncertain, but there seems to be enough evidence to take this possibility seriously.

Most likely, the strategies we have used in the past to improve productivity are going to be found wanting. Even if they are as successful as they have been in the past, the results will appear unsatisfactory to many people; if these strategies decline in their effectiveness, we should develop new productivity-enhancing strategies. There is, it must be assumed, a potential for productivity improvement in our economic system of unknown and unlimited extent, but the exact nature of this potential and how to realize it are the questions which we must answer.

Broadly speaking, our approach will begin by examining productivity improvement strategies that are "machine intensive" and strategies that are "people intensive" in the next two chapters. Then we will examine strategies that involve working smarter, not harder, and strategies based on our third "soft" source of productivity gains. From this we will turn to new targets for productivity improvement—the service sector, management itself, and the household. Finally, we will try to project the results of this analysis into some sort of fundamental insights and programs for action. By completing this process, we hope to come forward with at least the beginning of a plan for coping with Scenario Y.

Notes

The typical current evaluation of Taylor and Taylorism appears in *Work in America. Report of the Special Task Force of The Secretary of Health, Education, and Welfare*. Cambridge: The MIT Press, 1973.

For the fascinating story of what Taylor actually did and some insights into his personality see:

Copeley, Frank Barkley. *Frederick W. Taylor, Father of Scientific Management*. New York: Harper, 1923.

Kakhar, Sudhir. *Frederick Taylor, A Study in Personality and Innovation*. Cambridge: The MIT Press, 1970.

The surprising career of James Watt as industrial manager and his remarkable innovations are described in Eric Roll, *An Early Experiment in Industrial Organization*. London: Longmans Green & Company, 1930.

The highly creative but frustrating adventures of Robert Owen appear in G.D.H. Cole, *The Life of Robert Owen* London: Macmillan & Company, Ltd., 1933. Also, Robert Owen, *The Life of Robert Owen*. New York: Alfred A. Knopf, Inc., 1920.

One of the most significant documents in the entrepreneurial approach to productivity is certainly Alvin Sloan's biography, *My Years With General Motors*. New York: McGraw-Hill, 1962.

An extremely interesting analysis of the impact of Sloan's innovations appears in Alfred Chandler, *Strategy and Structure*. Cambridge: The MIT Press, 1962.

One of the most interesting ways to approach the McNamara era in the Department of Defense and the measurement revolution is through the work of one of its prominent participants, Charles M. Hitch. His book, *Decision Making for Defense*. New York: Wiley, 1969, is full of insights into the creation of this revolution.

Our summary of the macroeconomics of productivity is based on Solomon Fabricant, *A Primer on Productivity*. New York: Random House, 1969.

The study of social services agencies by Arnold Riesman and Burton Dean is reported more fully in the *Proceedings of the Annual Conferences and Convention of The American Institute of Industrial Engineers, May 22–26, 1972*. Atlanta: AIIE Inc., 1972.

A recent book of the prominent psychologist B.F. Skinner is finding its way into experiments in productivity, as so often happens with new ideas in the world of psychology. See *Beyond Freedom and Dignity*. New York: Basic Books, 1971.

3
Technology
and Productivity

TOOLS

The oldest tradition in the world of productivity enhancement is the transfer of some of the work of production from people to tools. This tradition has been almost overwhelmingly successful as a strategy for increasing our effectiveness as producers, so successful in fact that many people have a sort of single-minded devotion to investment in plants and equipment as *the* way to increase productivity. Today's most exciting tools — the computer, the nuclear power plant, the rocket engine, and the heart pacer — seem to have far outrun the productivity enhancing possibilities that even fit comfortably with words like "tool" or "machine." Indeed, we have recently passed through a period when we were fond of saying that if we can put men on the moon, surely anything is possible given a big enough budget. Happily, we have come out of this period, realizing that committing big budgets to the accomplishment of what has sometimes seemed impossible may be exciting but perhaps not very satisfying.

But the wonders of technology viewed from afar become a little less wonderful as one moves up, gets involved, and establishes a personal stake in creating and using machines. To invest in technology, to have one's income or even one's job determined by it, is to become involved in the uncertainty which surrounds technology. Technological forecasting, which is one effort to cope with this uncertainty, searches for the vague and unreliable regularities in the comings and goings of technologies. Particular technologies have a way of emerging when the economics of the situation move someone to utilize a previously received idea. Until the economics are right, the idea may have enjoyed the status of a curiosity of a natural wonder. When the technology emerges, it may well be accompanied by glowing predictions of its ultimate potential. But in the face of these predictions, actual realization of this potential seems unhappily slow and expensive. Years and dollars flow before the technology really becomes a widespread factor in production systems. Yet, after the first applications show the way, the rate at which the technology diffuses increases, improvements are made, money is made, and we began to think that the technology has an indefinite life. Almost inevitably some other technology is gaining on it and sometimes slowly, sometimes suddenly, it begins to decline. If such a pattern were dependable, some of the uncertainty which surrounds our tools and machines would be moderated. But the pattern is, at best, a rough approximation whose chief function is often to stimulate the identification of technologies whose histories have been otherwise. The very nature of being involved with technologies is to have to cope with hope and fear, to face decisions in which the sources of uncertainty are many and powerful.

STAGNATION

What sometimes happens with particular technologies sometimes seems to happen with our technological enterprise as a whole. In the late Sixties our previous investments in research and development did not seem to be paying off as we had hoped. Technology did not appear to be producing the productivity increases expected of it, and thus it received a good share of the blame when we passed through a period of disappointing annual productivity increments. Both general and particular uncertainty about technological undertakings became popular. Experts seemed to take the position that the spectacular improvements in our productivity that had been the consequence of many years of devotion to technology had run their course and that we had arrived at some sort of plateau. Dramatic future improvements in productivity would have to come from somewhere else. More recently, this opinion has changed; the general uncertainty about technology has moderated, and hope is growing once again.

THE DECISION TO INNOVATE

It is no longer the case, if it ever was, that a new tool or a new machine is created, its superior productivity is easily demonstrated, and it is quickly put into wide use. The crucial factor in the creation and utilization of our technology is the decision to do it. This decision to invest in research, to go ahead with development, and to install equipment is so much a matter of uncertainty, ambiguity, complexity, and the possibilities of both big gains and big losses, that it severely challenges the habitual style and skills of the decision makers involved. Yet the decision to do it is, after all, the element of our technological process which most needs attention. Everything depends on it.

For many years the textile mills of New England moved South. In a classic demonstration of the fundamental laws of supply and demand, the highly labor intensive plants sought out the ample labor pools and the low wage rates of the old, agricultural South. The idea, unfortunately for textile manufacturers, caught on, and other industries have moved rapidly in, drying up the labor supply and increasing the prevailing wage levels. The textile manufacturers were finding themselves increasingly the victims of rapidly changing fashions, meaning shorter production runs and more changeovers. Seeing greater productivity as their solution, and machines as the obvious strategy for increasing productivity, they began converting to "new" technologies. The manufacturers began achieving significant productivity increases by installing "new" looms that were based on a European design which was 20 years old. The looms being replaced, however, were based on American designs which were more than 70 years old. Most American loom manufacturers are producing the same type of machine which was being built 40 or 50 years ago.

The new looms will turn out 70 percent more fabric with 15 percent less manpower. The European shuttleless loom costs about $35,000 compared to some $8,000 for a conventional shuttle loom.

Despite all our concern with "future shock", despite all

our preoccupation with change, there are sectors of our economic system, industries, and institutions where technological change is very deliberate, perhaps even very slow. The harsher critics of the pace of American technological advance see us as becoming too conservative, losing our ability to swiftly transform scientific advancements into practical application. They see the inroads of foreign automobiles in our domestic market as a strong indication that we are not the fountainhead of all great technological advancement. Critics point to our steel industry as unwilling to introduce new methods, to our great oil companies as dependent on tax advantages rather than technological skill for their success, and to our aerospace firms as totally dependent on the government for their share in technological progress.

Similar concerns are heard concerning the way in which we utilize or fail to utilize our great stock of machines. Our railroad car fleet which is called upon to move huge quantities of grain, is pictured by critics as not so much inadequate as poorly managed, poorly allocated, and poorly scheduled. The question which is of central concern is not so much the quality of our technological abilities, as it is our utilization, management, and control of our potentially great technological enterprise. These are the questions to which we now turn our attention, looking basically for a clue to the way machines, tools, and equipment are created and used for some hints about ways to improve our rate of productivity increase.

The Gestation Process

There are two basic facts about machines and tools. First, their productivity is influenced in great measure by the fact that they operate as elements of production systems. Their behavior is intimately connected with this fact. A machine usually requires an operator, some energy and material inputs, some instructions, some maintenance, and so on. For the machine to be operational and productive, all of these elements have to be operational and productive along with it. Thus, the utilization of the machine is intimately connected with the utilization of the operator, with the coordinated availability of the necessary inputs, and with a need for its output: this is precisely what we mean by the notion of a system. Each element finds its behavior influenced by its membership in the system. Productivity improving strategy may be based on machines and technology, and may emphasize these things, but its outcome is intimately related to the effectiveness of the other elements of the productive system.

Second, the process of getting machines into action is a long and complex one. To obtain productivity improvements with technology one must get the new equipment on line and the old, obsolete gear out of action. The central problem of this long gestation period is a series of decisions—decisions about the conduct of research, development, innovation, imitation, maintenance, and, ultimately, replacement. This is the life cycle of the hardware elements of our producing systems. A curious problem which is beginning to clarify itself is the problem of making decisions about when and how to take the various steps in this life cycle. Questions such as these are asked: what kind of research should be undertaken, what research results should be exploited with development effort, when should one be the first to actually install a new machine, when should one imitate one's competitors, how much effort should one devote to maintenance of the equipment, and when should one conclude that its useful life is ended and the next generation should take its place? These decisions have the unhappy attributes of being interrelated in a complex fashion and being filled with uncertainties. What research one could wisely undertake at any given time is a matter of looking far out at a distant planning horizon, foreseeing the life cycle of the dimly perceived possible results, and calculating the possible needs and benefits. Similarly, the question of whether or not to replace a machine, if taken seriously, depends on what is coming in the way of new successors, what maintenance one has done and might subsequently do, and so on. It is impossible to consider the steps in this life cycle independently without seriously over-simplifying the problem. It is these difficult decisions which determine our technological future and thus seem worth a hard look.

The R and D Take Off

During the 1950's we reached some sort of a climax in our enthusiasm for research and development ("R and D"). Companies appropriated ample budgets for research, built large laboratories, hired highly trained scientists and engineers, and resolved to be patient to give their investment a chance to produce almost certain results. It was axiomatic that R and D would produce technological progress and this, in turn, would be reflected in increasing sales.

Edison, in 1876, started the first organized research laboratory in America. It was the beginning of a very big thing. In the next 25 years Kodak, General Electric, and Du Pont established laboratories to do industrial research and development, and in 1907 the Bell System opened its great in-house research activity. In spite of hard times, we were spending $900 million dollars on R and D by 1941 — the beginning of the quarter century of "take off" which brought us to a level of $25 billion by 1968.

Industrial research and development has produced some successes of truly magnificent impact — such as the man-made fibers, the transistor, and the digital computer. But these triumphs have been accompanied by an avalanche of failures. R and D is a very risky business indeed. Some data indicates that 80 percent of all products aimed at industry fail and 90 percent of consumer products fail. In one study of 120 major companies, it was found that on the average 60 percent of all R and D projects produce no useful results. The firm reporting the greatest success had a failure rate of 50 percent. Other informed estimates suggest that of every ten products which emerge from the R and D phase, only two ever reach commercial success.

Overall, there is no question that R and D does produce some technological progress which translates into productivity improvement, but there is a considerable question as to whether or not more R and D leads to more progress. Careful examinations of the R and D binge since 1940 do not support the notion that this great increase in expenditure has made much, if any, increase in our technological rate of advancement. As we saw in our examination of the annual productivity increment data in the previous chapter, there is no evidence here of an increasing rate of change which could be attributed to our surge in R and D expenditures. The productivity data just does not respond in a way which would support the axiom that more research will lead to a faster increase in our productivity or in its companion, our real income. Some of these findings can be attributed to the fact that gross research data includes Defense and other public sector research which is not intended to produce the sort of result that will be reflected in productivity data; however, this is not the total explanation. The number of unhappy firms, disillusioned managers, and board of directors asking for real justification for research budgets, is too great.

Asking the Hard Questions

While research expenditures have clearly been beneficial for some firms, a greater number have been disillusioned and have begun asking serious questions. The axiom that R and D is inevitably blessed on the average with profitable issue has been seriously challenged. The axiom that scientists and engineers are the best, and perhaps the only, judges of what they should be working on has fallen into disfavor. The notion that research budgets must, because of their very nature, be accepted on faith alone is being rejected in favor of some attempt at foresight and justification. The laissez-faire attitude toward the research department is giving way to an insistence that its work be more responsive to the market place. The track record of research and development activities is now sufficiently extended as to suggest the possibility of useful review.

The Evidence

The data, as is often the case, to some degree confirms our popular beliefs and to some degree runs counter to them. The payoff from any particular R and D project is indeed a matter of great uncertainty. In the long run, however, there is a reliable relationship between the amount a firm spends for R and D and the total number of significant technological advances it produces. Thus in a certain sense, R and D works. In industries such as petroleum, drugs, glass, and steel the largest firms are not the relatively big spenders. In these industries the largest firms spend less on R and D relative to their sales than do the somewhat smaller firms. The exception seems to be the chemical industry where the largest companies spend a greater percentage of their sales dollar than do the medium-sized companies. Unfortunately, this does not turn out to be a highly productive strategy for the largest firms. If one keeps the size of the research budget constant, the output of a research program of a given size seems to be less for the largest firms than for the somewhat smaller ones. Thus the bigger the company the less productive is the research budget, assuming that the size of the budget is the same. In this sense the productivity of the research dollar appears, in most cases, to be smaller in the bigger firms. What is different about the largest firms? Is it the way they organize for research? Are their controls on research expenditures too loose? Do they make poorer decisions about the allocation of research funds? Do they take greater risks? Smaller risks? It seems most unlikely that their research departments are second-rate in the quality of their professional personnel.

If, on the other hand, one holds the size of the company constant, the effect of increasing the research budget does not seem to indicate any changes in output which are either more than proportional or less than proportional to expenditures. Again, the exception is the chemical industry where bigger expenditures produce even bigger results. In most industries there is no marked advantage, based on returns per dollar, to having a big research department over having a medium-sized one. Bigness does not seem to permit special kinds of competence or special kinds of management and decision making skills which lead to greater research productivity.

One sort of picture which emerges from this track record data is that R and D is uncertain, that more money produces more in the way of results, but not on a relative basis. Everybody has trouble with the return for their R and D dollar, but the biggest firms have the most trouble. The plausible hypothesis seems to be that it is not the inferior quality of the personnel or of the equipment, but perhaps the decision making problems of the big firm are amplified or their decision making processes are rendered somehow less effective.

R AND D DECISION MAKING

The best strategy for improving the productivity of the new product development and implementation cycle is probably not through the attempt to improve the education of scientists and engineers. The weak point is far more likely to be the decisions which are made about how to conduct the process. The weakness is in the management, the selection of projects to support, projects to terminate, and projects on which to go "all out." One can hardly demonstrate a priority that this is the most favorable route to improvement, but it is held by many to be a highly probable hypothesis which is more than ripe for testing. The decisions we make about R & D, innovation, and replacement offer the key for improving the productivity increment contribution made by technology. While it is difficult at present to defend the hypothesis that these decisions do represent the greatest potential for improvement, they certainly present an opportunity that needs to be investigated.

Planning R & D expenditures on the basis of the industry standard, or on the basis of a fixed percentage of past sales, or on the basis of what has been spent in the past may not be irrational, but it fairly bursts with the suggestion that improvement is possible. These rules of thumb give one an inexpensive way out of a very difficult set of decision problems and lend a certain stability to one's R & D effort, both of which are generally seen as reasonable, but they also suggest that the benefits of investing more in the decision process itself will very likely be sufficient to warrant the costs. Here indeed is a set of decisions which strongly imply more attention could be beneficially allocated.

Better Decision Making

Unfortunately, there are no simple answers about how one can make better R and D decisions. There are answers, but they are not the ones that lend themselves to editorializing or exhortation. One can urge that R and D be directed toward the new targets, toward energy sources, education, transportation, or information handling. Yet, as research administrators know, there is a surprisingly weak relationship between these broad policy objectives and the justification and conduct of a particular program by a particular set of investigators. We will determine, in the next few years, the degree to which our current interest in energy-related research actually serves this end, when funds are allocated and projects actually undertaken and com-

pleted. Many a slip occurs between the proposal and the final·
report, between the project justification and the final audit of
its conduct.

Some have called for greater risks in research budgeting
and some for less. Taking greater risks will most likely produce
fewer successes, but those programs which do succeed will be
programs whose results are of greater consequence. Taking
lesser risks will most likely produce the opposite sort of result.
We will have more successful research projects, but the success
will be of lesser importance. We will have a larger number of
microinnovations, and whether or not this will mean greater
productivity per dollar is just not clear at all.

Some suggest that more elaborate, more explicit justification be required for R and D expenditures. It is sensible to
plan, to predict, and to foresee the various possible consequences of a program, but there is an underlying danger in
even this strategy. This is the danger that looking ahead in research will appear to be so difficult, so fraught with uncertainty,
so much a matter of "pure judgment," that research will cease
to compete with other demands for a company's funds. Making
a reasonable justification for research involves some very long-
range forecasts, and the establishment of a conviction that to
invest in these forecasts will in fact pay off in a more productive research program. It is almost universally the case that one
cannot historically make this kind of connection between that
firm's decision processes and its research results, simply because there are no records on how decisions were made in the
past.

Those who argue that research must be justified on faith
have exactly the same quality of evidence to support their con-
tention as do those who urge clearer, more careful decision
making. The great danger is that managements, unwilling to
have faith any longer and finding little evidence that elaborate
justifications are anything more than someone's opinion, may
well opt to get out of the research business or at least to retreat.
Indeed, there is some considerable evidence that many managements are looking to acquisitions of other corporations as the
way to grow, rather than developing a strategy of growth
through the internal generation of new products and services.
There is evidence as well, that the federal government is as-

suming and being willingly given the role of the nation's risk taker in research. So much of our interest now surrounds the notion of getting private sector benefits out of federally supported research, rather than from the enhancement of the more direct, more efficient route of company R and D.

THE PROCESS

It seems likely that new technology gets into action partly as the result of reasonable decision making methods and partly as a result of decisions which, while not necessarily unreasonable, are intuitive, inspirational, implicit, and not subject to explanation and rationalization. This is hardly surprising if one considers the complexity that would be involved in taking seriously some of the decision problems which arise in a typical research, development, and marketing system. Imagine, for example, a system in which there are essentially five stages through which a project may progress. In the first stage, a basic concept emerges and an initial evaluation of it is made on the basis of readily available data and experience. The decision may be made to advance the project to the second stage at which technical investigations and experiments are carried out to perfect the feasibility of the concept, to create a prototype, and to subject it to bench tests and laboratory examinations. Again one must make a decision. Should the project be scrapped or committed to the third stage in which a more extensive market survey is made, production plans are worked out, and a careful cost and profit analysis are attempted. The fourth stage involves a pilot production run providing enough units for actual field tests and leading to final modifications. If this stage is in some sense successful, the fifth and final stage leads to full scale production and marketing.

Particular systems for development differ in detail from this, but most seem to have similar basic characteristics. They are essentially learning, or uncertainty reduction processes. In the earliest stages the uncertainty about the cost of development, the ultimate demand, and the profitability are very high. Yet the risk of carrying out the first and second stage is relatively low. The data obtained in the early stages is helpful, but uncertainty is reduced only slowly at first. As one progresses through the stages, uncertainty is reduced at an increasingly rapid rate, but the cost of executing the stages also goes up at an increasing rate. Most such systems share a disappointing record of results. Only a small portion of those projects which make it through the early stages survive the third and fourth stages. Only a similarly small portion of those which go into full scale marketing and production turn out to be successful.

The complexity and uncertainty of the staging decisions is extensive. At the end of each stage, what lies ahead must be seen partly in terms of the data which has been so far obtained, partly in terms of explicit experience with similar situations, and partly in terms of the implicit judgments of those who are involved in the actual work and those who manage the development cycle and carry forward the marketing program. One never has "all the facts," uncertainties always remain, risks must always be faced.

Someone must decide how to allocate funds among the various stages — how many people, how much space, what facilities will be committed to each stage. Is it better to pass a high volume of projects through the early stages, weeding them out later when better information is obtained, or is it better to have a "high hurdle" at the first stage in order to save money by running a lower volume of projects through the more costly later stages? Each transition from one stage to the next, or into the reject pile, requires a decision in which one knows that some bad projects are sent forward, and some potentially good projects are rejected. How should one adjust one's policies to behave reasonably in such a situation?

Decision Making Patterns

In some systems, the same people tend to follow a project all the way through the system, taking with them the embodied knowledge and judgment so far accumulated. In other systems, there are specialists at each stage who handle a project only through a particular phase. The specialists are better informed and more competent in the work of that phase, but must rely on what they can learn from those who executed the previous stages in making their judgments. Some systems, of course, involve a blend of both of these strategies. Sometimes the decision to advance or cancel a project is made largely by those who do the work at each stage, sometimes it is made by a central management, and sometimes by committees representing each of the phases in the cycle. Each system involves differing requirements for the reduction of information and judgments to explicit language, for the explicit justification of what is proposed, and brings to bear judgments based on different backgrounds and different experiences.

Those who are responsible for a particular stage must decide how to allocate their resources among the various projects at that stage. How much data to collect in a particular instance, what experiments to try, what literature to search, what experts to consult, and what surveys to commission – all of these decisions are interestingly expensive. These decisions may be made more or less continuously as projects come along, thus reducing delays, or projects may be "batched" and decisions made about groups or projects. The latter tends to produce somewhat "better" decisions in terms of good allocations of resources, but at the price of delays in the progress of the projects. Sometimes the decision to "stage" or to scrap a project is based on a fixed criterion applied directly to that project. The project must have an expected rate of return of 25 percent; it must have a potential of at least 5 percent of the market, or it must show a high probability of recovering its development costs within two years. In other cases, decisions are made about the portfolio of projects at a given stage, and an effort is made to achieve a balance of projects with near term pay off potential, with long term pay off potential, some with high risk and high pay off, some with low risk and lower pay off, and some that will complement and supplement each other in development, production, or marketing. Taken seriously, the portfolio concept – the concept that projects cannot be considered independently – can be extended not only across the projects at a given stage, but across projects at all stages. Furthermore, the portfolio notion could be extended to projects which have not even appeared in the system as yet, the appearance of which can be anticipated on the basis of experience and judgment. No system can as yet afford to give serious and explicit consideration to all of these complex questions. In terms of the state of the art of R and D management, the tools are simply not yet available. Some systems, however, appear to rely almost exclusively on the implicit judgments of a small number of experienced people, with little or no attempt to analyze the decisions involved, examine the track record of the decision makers, or improve the productivity of the entire process. In these systems, there is a tacit assumption that such judgments are the only way to do it, and these judgments are hardly susceptible to either analysis or improvement.

Estimating Errors

It is interesting that we seem to have little or no evidence about the difficulties, the errors, and the uncertainties which characterize the systems which do company supported R and D. We do, however, have the results of a major Rand Corporation study which show these systems at work on the development of major weapons systems. Knowledgeable people suggest that these insights are not unrelated to the case of civilian R and D systems. Prior estimates of the costs of producing various types of military hardware were underestimated by an average of 400 percent. In part, of course, this may reflect a military procurement system which contains an incentive for the contractor to make a low initial investment, since once he is "in" he has an immense opportunity to make up any losses in the resultant production contracts. This cost estimating error was consistently related to the magnitude of the technological step or advance which was involved. The bigger the technological jump, the bigger the error in the prior cost estimate. There were substantial errors as well in estimates of the time to complete a project. On the average, the actual times to completion of ten major projects examined in the study were 1.5 times the estimated times. Here again there was some incentive to give low estimates, but those who work in the civilian context are hardly free from the incentive to present their managements with similarly optimistic views. For big technical advances, big time errors were involved, and the errors grew smaller for less dramatic technological leaps. As the projects progressed, the errors grew smaller as one would surely hope. For moderately difficult projects the average ratio of actual cost to estimated cost was 2.15 at the early stages. The ratio fell to 1.32 at the middle stages, and finally to 1.06 at the final stages. These numbers are by themselves of little decision making value, but they do serve to point up the question of whether the accuracy involved is good enough, whether more money should be spent improving the cost estimates, or whether this process is a level of uncertainty that can reasonably be tolerated for management purposes.

If these figures are any sort of guide to what is happening in the civilian context, it is clear that there is little data on which to base R and D management decisions in the typical case. Judgments implicitly formed and simply rendered play the major role. If one rejects judgment and opinion, and some managers reject all except their own, little remains except faith and inspiration.

The errors of estimation in the time cost and the profitability of research and development are both large and increase as the size or difficulty of the technological advance increases. Furthermore, a significant proportion of projects fail entirely. In this sort of environment, uncertainty is the dominant consideration in the decision process; unless uncertainty can be dealt with reasonably, all sorts of non-reasonable features creep into the process of research and development planning.

Faith and Judgment

There have always been those who argued that research and development decisions had to be made with a very large ingredient of blind faith, and a smaller but essential ingredient called the judgment of experienced people. These people have resisted in principle any attempt to make the decisions more reasonable because reasonableness implies, to a great degree, explicitness, and it was not at all clear how the very great uncertainties involved could be made explicit. They also resisted any attempt at post hoc evaluation of R & D decisions. It did not seem plausible that these decisions could be related in any meaningful way to their outcomes in an attempt to learn about the decision processes themselves. The prevailing philosophy was "You win some, you lose some, and it shall ever be so."

It is difficult to prove that unexamined decisions are capable of improvement on the basis of any sort of logical analysis. The unexamined decision process is the playground of luck, chance, circumstance, and serendipity. It is also the haven of personal biases, premonitions, inspirations, favoritism, self-justifications, anxieties, frustrations, and the variety of human failings which constitute our shortcomings as decision makers.

Gradually, the disappointing results of past R & D efforts have led progressive organizations away from a willingness to make the crucial decisions on the basis of unexamined judgment or intuition. More and more the requirement and the norm have been that uncertainty should be expressed explicitly, that R and D policies should take explicit account of both potential benefits and the associated uncertainties.

The degree to which this supposition will improve the productivity of R and D is difficult to document, but more and more organizations including major investors in R and D such as the Department of Defense are moved to test the hypothesis.

Action

How should effort be allocated among uncertainty reducing activities? Some ways are by modeling, simulation, bench testing, literature searches, hiring consultants, replicating experiments, market tests, prototype testing, pilot production plants, and so on.

The best opportunities for improving the productivity of R and D lie not in some grand pervasive policy, but rather in the intimate details of the decisions which govern its progress. To say that these are decisions involving high uncertainty is not necessarily to say that more effort and resources should be devoted to uncertainty reduction. The trick, the very subtle difficulty, is to identify reasonable levels of uncertainty. The question is not of how to get "all the facts" which will virtually eliminate uncertainty, but rather to determine what levels of uncertainty can reasonably be tolerated and where efforts to reduce uncertainty will have pay offs likely to warrant their costs. The problem is more nearly one of uncertainty management rather than simply uncertainty suppression or uncertainty elimination.

DECISION ANALYSIS

While some technological development cycles may have a simple, low uncertainty quality about them, most it would appear, do not. Complex decisions based on highly uncertain appraisals of the future of a technology are involved. These are difficult decisions in the sense that they cannot be reasonably, clearly, and effectively dealt with by the unaided human decision maker. They severely challenge his experience, his cognitive abilities, and provoke him into a retreat toward manageable simplifications.

Decision analysis takes the view that these decisions should be the subject of a calculated division of labor. Experienced, intuitively capable humans should undertake the parts of the decisions which they can most capably execute, and other parts should be delegated to, and shared by computers, committees, mathematical models, simulations, and so on. Decision aids should be designed to help the decision maker.

Decision analysis takes the point of view that one of the limitations of the human decision maker is simply the finite cognitive capacity which all humans experience when we try to remember large amounts of information and deal with complex problems. Memory is easily aided with lists, files, and computer systems. The basic strategy for dealing with complex problems is one of divide and delegate. A complex decision problem is broken down into basic elements, each of which requires only a relatively simple judgment or relatively simple analysis. The human decision maker performs these simple tasks; a decision model takes these tasks as inputs and reassembles them logically into a final decision. To judge the probability of success of a research project, the project program is broken down into a series of elemental steps. Judgment and data are utilized to evaluate the probability of success for each step, and then a mathematical model uses these results to compute the probability of success for the program as a whole. This is perhaps the most fundamental and reliable strategy which is involved in all attempts to improve decision making in complex situations.

Wishful Thinking

The second basic assumption made by decision analysis is that we are all subject to biases, wishful thinking, and selective perception; we are all in fact to some degree subjective in our thinking and deciding. The worst part of subjectivity, the most troublesome aspect of the way in which our needs and desires control our thinking, is that we are largely unaware of it. This is the basic reason why most approaches to the improvement of decision making suggest that much of the decision process be made explicit. Judgments, opinions, evaluations, assumptions, calculations, and reasoning are all to some degree spelled out with the aid of rating scales, opinion and attitude analyses, and goal formulating tools. This process permits one to examine his own opinions for bias, to check them with others, and to police his decision making for the effects of his inner needs and desires. The defense against subjectivity is explicitness and awareness of its presence.

Delphi Panels

The Delphi method is one of several approaches which takes advantage of the fact that in certain situations, many heads, properly put together, make better decisions than one. As we saw in the previous chapter, the judgments of a Delphi panel, refined by a process of iterative feedback, have been shown to be effective in predicting and deciding in cases where there is little explicit information available and uncertainty is high. This method has been usefully applied in many phases of the R and D process with a very reasonable expectation of improving the decisions involved.

Stress

It is well documented that human decision makers find their abilities degraded in the face of physiological pressures, psychological pressures, frustration, anxiety, and conflict. Decision aiding methods are often designed to make decision making situations explicit, impersonal, and unemotional, in order to remove decisions from the influence of these kinds of human shortcomings. We are not often as clear about our goals as we might wish, nor are we as capable of dealing with uncertainty as R and D situations would often require. Among the most popular and useful decision analysis tools is the use of probabilities as a language with which to express uncertainty. Once this expression is achieved, one is in a position to take advantage of other tools which help in the difficult problems of how much uncertainty may reasonably be tolerated, how much information it is worthwhile to collect in order to reduce uncertainty, and how one may consistently choose between high payoff—low probability of success projects on one hand—and low payoff—high probability of success projects on the other.

The strategies of decision analysis are based on the ideas that decisions will be made more reasonably if they are broken down into manageable elements, made open and explicit, and tested for consistency against logical analysis. While this does not guarantee making the "right decision" every time—for there are always some uncertainties which cannot be eliminated—it does rather reliably increase the probability of making the right decision. The problem that remains is to develop the tools of decision analysis so that they are less costly and more widely adopted as parts of the management styles of R and D managers.

Thus, the challenge of improving productivity in the R and D process, and as a result improving the possibilities for technological innovation and imitation is not a simple one. To say that more or less should be spent on R and D, to say that greater or lesser risks should be taken, to say we should be more conservative or more adventurous, are only ways of oversimplifying the problem. Better decisions will not emerge from such approaches with any sort of assurance. The problem is unfortunately more subtle, more complex, and more a matter of making reasonable improvements in the decisions involved by attacking the complexity, the subjectivity, and the human weaknesses that are involved. This sort of suggestion is immensely frustrating to those who expect a simple remedy, but if there were simple remedies the chances are we would already be using them.

INNOVATION

When a new product, process, or technological advance is first introduced into an industry, the decision to do so is technically called an innovation. When an industry already has some firms using the advance, the introduction of it into another company is a decision to imitate. Being first is often a significant advantage if it gives a firm a lead over its competitors which it can hold for a period of time. Being first also has the potential for disaster, for if the new technique does not work out as hoped, the first firm simply does some very expensive testing to demonstrate to the others what they do not want to undertake. Many new products and new processes emerge from the research and development stage with a high degree of uncertainty in the view of potential innovators. Laboratory tests and pilot runs are less than perfectly predictive of what will happen under actual conditions of applications. Full scale field demonstrations are often prohibitively expensive. Someone has to be the first to finance and actually try what has been proven in principle and in prototypes. Good market research, or at least expensive market research, may only produce an Edsel or a Corfam. Here again, however, the data that is available is enough to give one pause.

Diffusion Rates

The evidence which is available suggests that for major innovations the average time between invention and first application is from ten to fifteen years. However, there are considerable variations in the actual times. This, remember, is the average time from invention to the *first* application or innovation. This lag is somewhat shorter for consumer products than for industrial products. The lag between invention and innovation is also somewhat shorter for advances developed with government funds than for the results of privately financed research. It is just not possible, because of the almost total absence of data, to say whether this apparently very sedate process of innovation is reasonable or not. The decisions involved may have been quite sensible, given the uncertainties perceived, the costs of reducing those uncertainties, and the potential for large gains and large losses. The lag between innovation and invention, however, does appear to be a factor one could decrease. Decision analysis is again the answer. Should potential innovators be insisting on more information, or should they be willing to tolerate greater uncertainties? Are their attitudes toward risk consistent with the company goals? Is the decision to innovate strongly related to the interests and backgrounds of particular managers who do not necessarily reflect in their decision making the objectives of their organizations? As before, to urge more rapid innovation is to take only a most simplistic view of the problem actually faced by managers.

Imitation

Much the same thing may be said of decisions to imitate, which are only innovation decisions with dramatic reductions in the uncertainty involved. Once others have tried a technological advance and pretty well proven it in practice, those who follow have strong assurances of the outcome of their decisions to install the new technology. The data available on innovation decisions has an extremely reasonable quality about it. The evidence about imitation among large firms suggests that the probability that a firm will introduce a new advance increases with the proportion of firms in the industry already using it. The more exploitation and demonstration that a technique has received, the more likely it is to find its way into still other companies. As the uncertainty is progressively reduced, the technique, reasonably enough, becomes more attractive.

The greater the profitable effect of a firm's use of a new technique, the more likely the firm will make the decision to imitate. The smaller the investment required to undertake the imitation, the greater the chances that a firm will decide to do so. This is all very reasonable. When we depart from considering only the larger firms, however, other effects show. The length of time a firm waits before making a decision to imitate depends on the size of the firm. The bigger firms are quicker to imitate than are the smaller ones. The time a firm waits before imitating, if one factors out firm size and profitable effects of the imitation, does not appear to be related to how profitable the firm is, or to how fast it has been growing. Firms which are not very profitable are neither faster nor slower in their decision to imitate than are their more profitable competitors. Whether or not a firm is growing rapidly has little effect. Nor does its profit trend, whether increasing or decreasing. Even its liquidity, the funds potentially available to finance innovation, does not seem to be an important factor. The age of the firm's president, some kind of a rough indicator of the progressiveness of its attitudes and the aggressiveness of its policies, does not seem to be related to the time the firm waits to imitate. These inferences leave room for the full play of other variables in explaining the rate of imitation in a given firm. The personalities, interests, and styles of influential managers are probably significant. Likewise, the presence or absence of "champions," men who believe strongly in an innovation and press for its introduction with great vigor, is often an important aspect. Here once again, we have room to suppose that the process of imitation is partly reasonable and partly less than reasonable— explained by particular personalities and particular organizational arrangements. Also, the approach which avoids oversimplifying the problem is through decision analysis—by putting ourselves in the shoes of those who must make the decision to imitate and by attempting to develop aids which will increase the degree to which these decisions meet our standards of reasonableness. Imitation decisions, involving markedly lower levels of uncertainty, appear to be more reasonable than R and D decisions or innovation decisions; however, the rates at which new technologies diffuse are sufficiently low to strongly suggest the hypothesis that this is a process which might also be examined with an eye to speeding it.

WHEN ARE MACHINES WORN OUT?

Sometimes machines are replaced when they break down, sometimes when they are very, very old, and sometimes when it appears to be economical to do so. The Japanese have found it economical to replace an operating steel mill every seven or eight years in order to use a more productive one. This sort of drive for high productivity and economic facilities stands in marked contrast to some of our own replacement policies and leaves us wondering what they know that we don't.

Deciding to replace machines on the basis of productivity and economics usually involves looking at the annual cost of a given amount of output for various service lives or replacement intervals. If equipment is replaced very, very frequently, then one always uses new, highly productive equipment which tends to be the most modern available. The cost per year, however, is likely to be very high because of the high initial cost of the new equipment and the very rapid decline in its resale value during the early years of its life. Like the family automobile, the market value of which may drop by $500 the first time the owner drives it, much equipment used in production systems has only modest trade-in value even if it is only a few years old. On the other hand, if we keep equipment for a long time, its productivity seems worse when compared to the best available each year. Its maintenance and operating costs begin to climb as it grows older, and once again we find that keeping equipment for a long time results in a high average cost per year. An interesting factor about the average cost per year is that it is often high if equipment is replaced frequently and high if equipment is held for a long time, but in the middle range, the cost may not vary much for service lives within a four or five year interval. The cost function has a flat bottom and there is a range of replacement intervals for which the cost per year is about the same. It may turn out for example, as one analyzes the problem, that replacing a major item of equipment every ten years results in an average cost per year of, say, $100,000. If we replace the equipment every eleven years, the average cost per year goes up to, perhaps, $105,000. This flat bottom hypothesis, which appears frequently in replacement decision analyses, has a number of interesting consequences. The hypothesis means, for example, that it ought not to be too hard to get fairly close to the minimum cost per year, even with a "rough and ready" study of the problem. It also means, as is often the case with the family car, that since there are a number of trade-in lives at which the cost is about the same, in the absence of a detailed analysis people are likely to argue about the best time to trade, and everyone involved in the argument will be nearly right.

The Temptation

The hypothesis suggests something far more tempting and dangerous from a productivity point of view. Suppose the machine we were discussing has a purchase price of half a million dollars. Suppose the minimum average cost per year, when all relevant costs are considered, occurs at a ten year life and amounts, as we said, to $100,000. Suppose a management finds itself with a ten-year-old machine which it knows should now be replaced if they are to minimize the average cost per year. The machine is still running well and the management, looking at the flow of funds from its depreciation charges and retained earnings, finds itself a little short of cash. If the management postpones replacement of the machine for a year, it will be freed of the necessity of coming up with the half million, and the "cost" of such a postponement will be an increase in the average annual cost of, say, $5,000. This is an extremely tempting way to raise cash or cut one's cash requirements, and managements frequently succumb to the temptation. Having done it once, it is tempting to postpone replacement for a second year, and then a third. Each time, the average annual cost rises, each time the equipment in use grows more obsolete, and each time competitors who are making economical replacements become more productive. If one persists, the difference between costs must eventually be reflected in price differences and profit differences. Postponing replacement will eventually be reflected in declining earnings. Somewhere along the line management will realize that its equipment is growing old, its earnings are falling, and its ability to borrow capital funds is waning. They are stuck with old machines, low and declining earnings, and find nobody interested in lending money to such a company. At this point only radical surgery can help. Bankruptcy, a government guaranteed loan, or being acquired by someone who wants a "turnaround" situation are the likely fates at this juncture. Replacement policy, when the very seductive flat bottom hypothesis is operating, is a decision of major consequence from a productivity point of view.

Depreciation

Replacement decisions are matters of some complexity and of some uncertainty, as are the other decisions we have examined. Depreciation is important, not because it tells one when to replace a machine, but because it is a tax deduction and helps to determine the cash left after taxes. This cash is what most firms use to replace old equipment. By far the largest portion of all replacements are financed out of retained earnings. Depreciation, the amount of the investment in a machine charged off against current earnings in each year, is an historical recording fiction which helps one make more reasonable statements about past earnings to stockholders and to the Internal Revenue Service. What is relevant for replacement policy purposes, however, is not what has happened in the past, but our options for the future—the action alternatives. If we keep the machine, this decision by itself produces no cash flow one way or the other. If we sell the machine, we realize a cash flow equal to the resale price or the trade-in value. The resale price has nothing whatever to do with depreciation charged in the past nor with "undepreciated value" or "book value." This minor point of confusion strikes with interesting frequency and with devastating effect in replacement policy discussions. Taken seriously, the replacement policy decision is a hornet's nest of uncertainties. Not only is one typically uncertain about future operating costs, maintenance costs, and future resale values, but one is also faced with the problem of what new possibilities will become available as a result of research and development efforts. How much better and more productive will next year's model be, and the models that will follow in the years after? How far in the future should one extend one's analysis? When we replace today's equipment depends partly on what equipment we would replace it with, how long that equipment would be used, what sort of successor would follow, etc. Somewhere we must say "enough" and adopt a planning horizon. What will happen to the future demand for the output of the equipment in question? Will it even be needed, or will its capacity be insufficient to meet the growing needs in the future? These sources of uncertainty are both difficult and expensive to consider seriously, and it is natural that actual replacement policies should be characterized by some simplification. Yet how much simplification is reasonable?

Studies of actual replacement policies indicate that some of them are simple indeed. Whenever the money seems to be available, whenever we find a new machine which will pay for itself in two or three years, whenever we find a new machine which will give us a twenty percent return on our investment, then we replace the machine. It is not difficult to show that in many situations these policies delay replacement beyond the economical point, beyond the point at which the cost per year begins to rise sharply. Simplicity in these cases is bought at the price of lower levels of productivity than are economically sensible. Replacement policy, as it is sometimes practiced, is a good example of what we mean by oversimplification.

Maintenance Decisions

When a machine is replaced depends partly on the maintenance it requires to keep it functioning and the productivity lost while it is being repaired. This, in turn, depends on the choice one makes between preventive maintenance—fixing the machine on a preplanned basis in order to minimize expense and lost production—and emergency maintenance—fixing the machine when it has malfunctioned. Preventive maintenance has a sort of public health, preventive medicine quality about it. It sounds so good and seems so rational, and in fact, some degree of preventive maintenance is often very good from a productivity point of view. But here again simple answers are not the useful guides to maximum productivity. By doing enough preventive maintenance one can virtually eliminate unplanned outages and emergency repairs. This much preventive maintenance is likely, however, to be very expensive, both in terms of manpower and in terms of the time devoted to the planned outages. At the other extreme, doing no preventive maintenance at all will typically result in an expensive amount of unplanned downtime and disruptions resulting from breakdowns. The problem, unhappily, is to find some point of moderation between these two extremes, some point where the costs and productivity losses resulting from a combination of preventive and emergency maintenance combine at some low level. Uncertainties abound—chiefly those associated with trying to predict when failures, breakdowns, and malfunctions will occur. Since such predictions are usually extremely difficult, designing a sensible preventive maintenance policy is likely to be subtle, complex, and a task which once again can benefit from liberal applications of decision analysis. Maintenance policy may well be one of the great neglected areas from which future productivity increases may be drawn. The problem just does not yield to the simple sort of recommendation that one should do more maintenance or less, since what one should really do is almost never self-evident.

SIMPLIFICATION The complex web of decisions which determine the availability of technology to our productive systems turns back on itself. How much maintenance a machine requires—its reliability—and how easy or difficult it is to maintain—its maintainability—are largely determined in the stages of research and development where our story began. Such complexity, such interrelationships, and such a multitude of uncertainties must always generate responses from human decision makers which simplify. It is necessary to overlook some relationships, suppress some uncertainties, and substitute rules of thumb, conventions, and simple reasoning for the formulation and analysis of complicated decision problems. The keys to greater productivity through the development and application of new technologies are in understanding the decisions involved, finding ways to aid the overburdened decision makers who must cope with them, and singling out management information gathering and technology planning systems as the currently most vulnerable point for productivity enhancing efforts. It may even be, as some recent evidence might suggest, that the decisions we make about our technologies are pretty good on the average. It is, however, the decisions which stray from the average which are so costly in terms of productivity. When one looks at all of the sciences involved in our technological enterprise, the science of planning, forecasting and deciding is the least well developed.

MACHINE PRODUCTIVITY

How well, how fully are we using the technology which we already have in place? The greater the need for the output of a machine, the more costly it is to have it down; the more productive it is, the more likely we are to know the answer to that question. Great care is devoted to keeping track of the utilization of steel mills, commercial aircraft, and major power plants. On the other end of the spectrum are the great numbers of machines and tools which are kept on hand for occasional use, which individually represent a modest investment, and which are not especially productive by themselves. For these, there is only the mildest concern about levels of utilization. In between are the machines which represent the greatest portion of our investment, the machines for which the question of how well they are being utilized and how well they ought to be utilized are matters of some subtlety.

The typical machine requires an operator, some maintenance service, some material to work with, a client to serve, some operating instructions, and a schedule by which to bring all of these system elements together. All this clearly depends on complex and uncertain decisions about capacity, future demand, and on an examination of whether it is better to make or to buy the machine's output. It is often possible to overuse equipment—running it too fast, too long, too hard. Neglected maintenance and demands which exceed the design capability are likely to produce lower utilization, poor quality output, and the need for early replacement. Pushing hard is seldom the way to maximize productivity. Since machines assembled into production systems have intimate relations with each other, it is often the case that one machine's idleness is another's productivity. When a large generating plant is taken out of service for preventive maintenance, the outage is managed with great care and great precision. Everything needed to service the generating equipment must be at hand, together with a detailed plan of just what is to be done on a minute by minute basis. The outage is planned perhaps even more carefully than open-heart surgery, such is the importance of returning the generating plant to service as rapidly as possible. One implication of this is that a very large investment in cranes and other equipment must be made, and that this equipment is almost always idle and unproductive. When the equipment is needed, it must be there, but it is needed on the rarest of occasions. Looking at utilization data on the crane says little, for its idleness is a necessary ingredient of an attempt to achieve high utilization for the power system as a whole.

Thus the problem of utilization is another one of those complex decisions where, unfortunately, single-minded devotion to increasing something is not the answer. The doctor increases his utilization at the expense of the waiting patients. The generating plant increases its utilization at the expense of the crane. In Russia, high in-process inventories are used to keep work ahead of machines so they will have virtually no chance of running out. We can increase the utilization of equipment by making things which are produced more effectively by others—by keeping men, managers, and materials ready but underutilized. Because machines operate as elements of production systems, the best level of utilization is never 100 percent. The best level of machine utilization is related to the best level of utilization of the people, materials, maintenance resources, and management skills which are also part of the system. The thought that productivity could be increased by seeking to more fully utilize the equipment we have on line is an excellent thought, but, unhappily, not a simple one.

Planning Idleness

The people who tend machines in the typical textile plant are idle a large portion of the time. They walk among their assigned machines, occasionally mending a thread or making a small adjustment. It is important, however, to the productivity of these machines that the tenders be quick to discover the need for their services, however infrequently this may occur. The temptation to use fewer tenders and to give each person more machines to oversee is strong. This change will be done, however, at the price of reduced productivity of the machines. We could trade machine idle time for human idle time; that is the very essence of the utilization decision. It is generally clear that we don't want so many people that we force the machine down time almost to zero, nor do we want so few people that their idleness time approaches zero. Machine idleness is people utilization and contrariwise. The most productive plan is to have people and machines idle some of the time. Just how much of the time is a matter of some complexity, a matter which can be the subject of some fairly sophisticated analysis.

The notion that the greatest system productivity will result if both the people and the equipment are not fully utilized is not only a complex notion, but it also presents management with a basic cultural challenge. It implies that management, having discovered the best idle time for the people and machines in the textile mill, or the various elements of any production system, will have to undertake the achievement of this degree of idleness. Managers have a long tradition of trying to keep everybody and everything as busy as possible. To deliberately sanction idleness—to make it a matter of explicit policy that somebody or something should be unutilized for some percentage of time—is not in any way a part of this tradition. It is a difficult step for a management to take. Visions of what will happen to operations when it becomes known that some people are supposed to be idle—that it is a management objective that they be idle—suggest disaster. The simplistic program of insisting that everybody and everything should be busy all the time seems the only way to prevent everybody and everything from degenerating into a state of intolerable laxity.

Utilization data does tell us some things about machine productivity, but seldom anything very obvious. The question of how to manage production systems in order to increase their productivity is seldom answered in the same way as the question of how to maximize the productivity of the machine elements of these systems alone. The unutilized potential of our production equipment is probably a good source of productivity improvement, but beyond a few cases, horror stories of machines grossly and obviously underutilized, the problem is one which requires some subtle analysis. When, for example, we become concerned about the low level of utilization of our railroad car fleet, class rooms, or port facilities, how to increase utilization and how much to increase it are less than obvious. We will return to these delicate problems in Chapter 5.

MACHINES, PEOPLE, LOVE, AND HATE

Machines, seen as components of production systems, interact with people, materials, maintenance support, and operating policies; their productivity must be understood in terms of these interactions. Of particular interest is the complex of relationships between people and their machines, between people and the tools of production. Some considerable attention has been given to the physical aspects of these relationships. Human engineers have devoted many years of skill and experimentation to designing machines which are easier to operate, easier to communicate with, easier to control, safer and less tiresome as work companions. The current problems are heavily involved with the relationships between people and computers—relationships which involve attempts to communicate at a very high level indeed. Considerable effort, as well, has been expended on questions of just how best to divide work between people and machines. We have considered very carefully how much of the physical effort, skill, precision, reliability, and decision making involved in a great variety of tasks can be effectively transferred to machines.

Those who have been involved with production systems have often noticed that there is a whole dimension of relationships between people and machines which has been little documented and barely considered in the development of productivity improvement strategies. These are the emotional, the affective, the loving, hating, trusting, and doubting relations.

Emotional relationships are first seen in the artist, the craftsman, the artisan, whose tools are his own, and who, according to some psychologists, is in love with his tools. They are intimate parts of his art, deeply familiar, and in many senses, are extensions of his own person. As we transfer more and more skill and effort to machines, they come to dominate production systems and to no longer belong to their operators.

Pride of ownership is replaced by a special relationship

which arises out of the continued and exclusive assignment of one machine to one operator. The machine, the truck, or the computer terminal, that is assigned to one operator is his in a very special sense. The fact that it is owned by someone else ceases to be a consideration. As long as nobody else uses it, adjusts it, or abuses it, the operator can come to know the personality of the machine, to enjoy the relationship, and to take productive advantage of it if he wishes.

Machines, as every car owner appreciates, have special sounds, smells and vibrations which become well-known indeed. Any variation in these will be quickly sensed by one who is intimately familiar with the machine, and malfunctions can be detected far earlier than by routine diagnostic methods. The operator can eventually sense very slight changes in the way "his" machine is running and may be able to make minor adjustments of far greater subtlety than anything conceived even by the machine's designer. The operator is deeply interested in the care and maintenance of his machine, an interest which is notable by its absence among those who check vehicles in a motor pool, or who are assigned frequently to different machines. Operators are quick to detect the use of their machine by someone else and equally quick to complain that it has been "fouled up." Multi-shift operations have the effect of weakening the relationship between people and their machines in just this way. And with the weakening of this relationship—responsibility, interest, and productivity are very likely to decline. Just how important this decline is likely to be is something about which little is known. It is more than reasonable to suppose, however, that this is an important aspect of the productivity of the man-machine system.

Sensitivity and Productivity

As people learn the special, not generally known, things about their machines, they come to not only be able to make useful adjustments and to detect impending difficulties, but also they develop emotional patterns which influence their own productive behavior. Machines which are accurate, reliable, responsive, easy to operate, and which "do a good job" come to be liked and to give their operators pleasure in their use. One's personal well-being becomes identified with the well-being of the machine, and when both are "working well" the combination is very productive indeed. Machines which are erratic, inaccurate, unpredictable, and difficult to operate are less liked, and this inevitably influences the behavior of the operator. The person who has trust, confidence, and some pride in the output of his equipment is far more likely to exercise that kind of discretion, creativity, and persistence which can make such an important difference in productivity of the system.

Machines which are forgiving of operator mistakes, which do not extract too severe a toll in injury or defective output are, of course, appreciated and used well. Those that are not are often sources of frustration and anxiety.

As machines grow larger and more complex, they seem to dominate the people in some production systems. The role of the machine is such that the significance of the operators seems reduced to nothing more than mere servants. Some big machines such as the digital computer appear as an extension of one's powers, making it possible for the operator to do things which greatly enhance his particularly human abilities. Other big machines such as the automated assembly line seem to depreciate the contribution of the human operators. In part, there is an element of boredom and fatigue which is involved, but more important is the question of who's in charge. The fundamental difference between the machine which sets the pace and requires a rigidly regular behavior from its operator and the machine which is not directive but responsive is one of the most widely noticed emotional hypotheses about our production systems. Although the computer requires communication in a very special language, the operator is very much in charge, very much in command of what the machine does and when. While there are no simple generalities about whether man-paced operations are likely to be more productive than machine-paced operations, it is very clear that the distinction between the two is an important key to emotional interactions.

These sorts of hypotheses have been widely noticed by those involved with combinations of people and equipment. Little has been done, however, to systematize our knowledge of the effects of these relationships or to use them in enhancing productivity. People-machine combinations are more productive when people like their machines, take responsibility for them, and find satisfaction in using them, but how much more productive we really cannot say at this point. It is interesting to speculate about the possibilities that might emerge if these relationships were acknowledged and used in the management of production systems. Even better, what would be the result of understanding these feelings to the degree that they might have an influence on the design and selection of machines, the assignment of people to them, and the training of people to relate effectively to equipment? We have begun to feel sensitive about the emotional relationship between the executive and his management information system. Might it not be useful to become sensitive about similar relationships in other sorts of production systems? To do so would require a new tendency to see people and machines as individuals, as unique elements in the production system. This tendency we have resisted for a variety of reasons, not the least of which is the suspicion that it is just too costly. We may be on the verge of revising our opinions about this in ways which we will be exploring subsequently. It may well be that there are important opportunities to control productivity which involves an intimate and detailed knowledge of production systems—a level of knowledge which is far beyond anything that could be expected from management. Only those within the production system may be in a position to bring the system to the level of productivity which approaches its potential.

TECHNOLOGICAL UNEMPLOYMENT

In the spring of 1974, members of Local 6 of the International Typographical Union voted overwhelmingly to strike the major New York newspapers. Among the issues which had been brewing for years and had been the subject of thirteen months of intensive negotiations, was the automation of the printing process, in particular, computerized typesetting. The publishers made a wage increase offer and agreed to guarantee jobs for all of the regularly employed printers. The union demanded more, asserting that it should have jurisdiction over all new technological developments and over any facilities where new technology was introduced into publishing operations. The publishers became more and more insistent on maintaining effective control of the new technologies and of finally escaping from the "make work" practices long associated with unionized printers. Here was a technology that was well developed and in wide use and that was ideally suited to the large newspaper—yet, the union leaders were able to effectively block its installment.

The view that machines take away jobs is older than industry itself. The fear of technological unemployment has persisted, become institutionalized, and has colored our very thinking about the productivity of machines. It has had its emotional impact on those who make decisions about the development and introduction of technology, as well as its effect on those who must accept and operate the machines when they are installed.

Job Security

There has seldom been a more persistent and troublesome question than the question of whether technology is good or bad. Technology means productivity; thus, it is a part of the more general question of whether productivity is good or bad. One whose job is about to be eliminated as the result of a new machine finds it especially hard to see this question in a relaxed fashion. This is not very difficult to understand, but what is more difficult to accept is the pervasive, general and conventional notion about what is going on.

Unions have organized around militants to whom it is clear that new technology is but one of several productivity increasing strategies—the major effect of which will be to reduce the need for labor, to displace union members, and to create unemployment. Job security has become, for many unions, the top priority objective in all of their negotiations. But unions are not alone. The general human belief and the conventional wisdom about the introduction of technology is consistent with the unions. While calm and dispassionate thinking surely cannot be expected from a person about to make a major investment in a machine or one about to lose his job to a machine, the popular view of this problem seems to be consistently disfunctional.

We seem to share a persistent belief that technology is basically a labor displacing strategy. We are reluctant to see the problem in terms of our failure to find really satisfactory ways of dealing with displaced people. Transfer, unemployment assistance, and re-education all leave something to be desired. Nor can we recognize our failure to accept labor displacement as a fact of organizational life and a fundamental correlate of the productivity changes which accompany our rising real wealth. All of these serve to color

* our attitudes toward technology,
* our decisions about it,
* our motivations to accept and improve it,
* our need to become apologetic for it, and
* our tendency to place on technology the blame for other social problems such as pollution, overcrowding, energy shortages and so on.

Nothing is more important than changing some of the facts about machines and jobs held by conventional wisdom, both so we can more readily work toward productivity development, and so that we may grow interested in dealing more effectively with some of the problems which this approach to productivity does involve.

THE EFFECTS OF TECHNOLOGY

In thinking about the effects of technology we have not been very careful to distinguish several different cases. There are those cases in which technology was essential to the life of the enterprise, without it there would have been no enterprise and no jobs; those in which technology increased productivity and ultimately wages, with little if any immediate changes in employment level; those in which technology was delayed or introduced in a way which permitted the changes in employment levels to occur naturally, by normal attrition; those in which technology has given people opportunities to learn higher skills and earn more; and those in which technology has furthered the safety, fatigue, and boredom of the job.

There is a strong possibility that the effects of technology will be to move the skills and talents required toward the more sophisticated, higher responsibility, greater versatility end of the spectrum. When tools are utilized which increase productivity by factors of ten or one hundred, this means people are displaced; the jobs which remain require a good deal of judgment, responsibility, and intelligence, because these systems, too, are not without their operating problems. We tend to greatly overdramatize the effects of technology in displacing people. We ignore those who find employment almost immediately in the same plant, firm, or area. We ignore the changes in jobs which would take place anyway. Firms which are using new technology at a high rate are likely to be expanding firms which can soon absorb any displaced workers, and which are in the process of reshuffling and rearranging people and jobs at a high rate in any case. The labor displacement process (which incidentally involves people at all levels of management as well) is a fact of industrial, governmental, and institutional life. While technology is a cause, things will not be much improved if we eliminate it.

An even more serious cause of the labor displacement process lies in the fluctuations of demand, the shifts in tastes, and in the effects of foreign and domestic competition. It is far more important to understand and deal with recessions than to respond only to the cry that appeared after the Civil War, "machines have taken over the jobs."

Early in the eighteenth century, a bill was introduced in the French Assembly specifying that all wood cutting was to be done with a dull axe. Although we have surely made some progress since this attempt, society's failure to do a good job of assisting those who are displaced has increased the antagonism of many people concerning technological innovation. Changes in aggregate unemployment are the result of at least four factors:

1. changes in aggregate demand for goods and services,
2. changes in the size of the labor force,
3. changes in the output per man-hour, that is, changes in productivity, and
4. changes in the average hours of work.

Thus the introduction of technology need not result in increased aggregate unemployment. What is important is that government and the market increase aggregate demand, not so fast as to cause inflation, but fast enough to avoid increases in aggregate unemployment.

Overall, these changes are fine; however, there is still the question of the specific worker—his skills, and his opportunity and capacity for retraining. There is little support for the "structuralist" view that workers and jobs are becoming more and more mismatched. There are surprisingly few occupations, few industries, and few localities which show a significant tendency for unemployment to increase with time. Although a substantial portion of unemployment may have been structural, there is little evidence that this has been increasing in recent years.

Although aggregate demand may prevent an increase in aggregate unemployment, unfortunately it cannot prevent displacement of particular individuals. These adjustments are an unhappy essential to productivity growth, accommodation to consumer change, and rising real wealth. The problem is to make these displacements as efficient and painless as possible. They are not painless for anyone, but are especially difficult for farm workers who must move to the city (the greatest displacement of all) and for older workers.

Emerging Concepts

We cannot possibly say the last word on this ancient problem of technological displacement, but some indications of where to go are beginning to emerge. Some are revolted by technology and see the solution as a return to the simple life, a withdrawal from patterns of high consumption, and thus a liberation from the host of social evils behind which they see the forces of technology. Others see the forces of technology as inevitable, not to be stopped, controlled only at our peril, and a prominent force in our progress toward some utopia. On balance, of course, there are both good and bad effects of technology. The question is a difficult one, characterized by subtle trade offs which many of us are poorly prepared to make confidently. Several things, however, seem likely to move us away from emotion and perhaps somewhat more toward reason.

What we need are not more of the economist's aggregated data about unemployment—data which largely masks the detailed causes and ultimate human consequences of technological displacement. What would be more useful is individual histories—detailed studies tracing the results of introducing particular technological innovations. What are the alternative strategies for innovation and imitation, and what are their effects on individuals? Which working people are displaced, how are they prepared, where do they go? What strategies for placement, retraining, and retirement have what sort of consequences? To understand the problem, we must look at individual situations and become sensitive to individual differences.

Technology, unlike some other sources of layoffs, has a planned, predictable quality about it. Companies plan far ahead for major equipment introductions, and this planning usually includes detailed considerations of how job changes will be managed. Demand fluctuations, on the other hand, are far more difficult to predict and, as a source of layoffs, have a far greater degree of uncertainty and surprise about them. Surely a more reasonable target for the union's efforts would be to demand of their management some improvement in demand forecasting. Some greater level of effort in foreseeing these fluctuations would be a far more effective, far more basic approach to greater job security than simply the resistance of technological change. We have always been interested in perfecting the labor market and in making job information more widely available, but the weakest aspect of this effort has been the forecasting of short run employment requirements. It takes little imagination to envision a nationwide data bank which contains not only job openings and job seekers, but short run forecasts of needs. The real villain in the problem of job security is the company (and there are a considerable number of them) which hires several hundred people one week and lays off several hundred a few weeks later. Such a forecasting system is technically feasible if incentives could be developed to entice private sector employers to participate:

The irrationality of the struggle between labor and technology must someday surely give way before the mass of data relating increases in productivity to increases in real wealth. The problem is one of balance. If one sector of the economy suddenly becomes dramatically more productive than the other sectors, displacements will of course occur. It is difficult to see why we should be so consistent in our determination that the few who are displaced must pay so heavily for the benefits which accrue to the many.

MACHINES AND PRODUCTIVITY —
A SUMMARY

Looking at productivity improvement strategies which emphasize technology has suggested some hypotheses which, we have argued, hold some promise as the next steps. The kinds of opportunities we have to make decisions about improving productivity through new technologies are a direct result of the decisions we make about research and development. The key point is that we are moving somewhat painfully from the era when R and D expenditures were based on faith, inspiration, guts, and rule of thumb to the era where somewhat more reasonable decisions are made about uncertainty reduction programs. R and D will always, by its very nature, be a matter of high uncertainty, but there is an important opportunity for improvement in the productivity of R and D through more reasonable decision making procedures—more reasonable management of that uncertainty.

For all of our biases in favor of technology as the classical key to more productivity, we have been somewhat less than sensitive to the powerful impact that the emotional relations between people and their machines may have. The love, the hate, the trust, and the feeling of responsibility seem often to be key variables in explaining why some man-machine combinations are more productive than others. As we will emphasize again and again, the behavior of people in production systems is, like all human behavior, complex. People behave to some degree like other individuals whose individual feelings toward the technology may be well worth exploring. He who operates "his" machine is, more often than not, more productive than he who operates a machine.

Nothing is more fundamental in determining the productivity of our technology than the view of those whose decision it is to utilize it or not, and the view of those who operate it, live with it, and make their living in daily association with it. If technology is fundamentally bad, a basic threat to job security, it may be sought by some, as were computers in the early days, as a primary means of reducing the work force. Technology will be resisted by others who see their own jobs, quite reasonably, as too great a sacrifice for what may be an infinitesimal increase in the real income of the rest of us. The more rapid and more reasonable diffusion of technology is linked to this curiously persistent problem—a problem that seems no more challenging than others we have faced, yet a problem with which we have made remarkably small progress. The view that technology is to some degree a labor displacing strategy is not wrong. What is somewhat difficult to understand is that this displacement can be foreseen, can be managed, and will result in long run increases in our real wealth if we will only foresee it and manage it so that a few do not suffer disproportionately.

Notes

For a quantitative understanding of technological change, innovation, and imitation, we have relied heavily on the pioneering work of Edwin Mansfield.

Mansfield, Edwin. *The Economics of Technological Change*. New York: W.W. Norton, 1968.

Ibid. Industrial Research and Technological Innovation: An Econometric Analysis. New York: W.W. Norton, 1968.

Victor Ferkiss provides a brilliant and stimulating study of the broader social impacts of technology in *Technological Man, the Myth and the Reality*. New York: George Braziller, Inc., and New American Library, 1969.

On the question of looking ahead to the future development of technology as a basis for further perfecting the labor market, see the excellent papers in Bright, James R., ed. *Technological Forecasting for Industry and Government*. Englewood Cliffs, N.J.: Prentice-Hall, Inc., 1968.

4

Working People

PEOPLE LOOKING AT
PEOPLE WORKING

Without losing sight of the essential fact that the machines, people, materials, and concepts which go into a production system must, if we are to make any sense of it, be seen as a system, we have been looking at productivity improving strategies which place their major emphasis on machines. We move now to those strategies which are strongly oriented toward people, working people who might just be moved to work harder or work smarter. There is a long and fascinating history of some people's attempts to figure out ways to make other people more productive, only a little of which we will try to assimilate here. The tone of much of this history is set by the terms used for the central characters. They are always referred to as "workers" or "employees." Those who are presumed to be fully productive already and who assume the task of motivating the "workers" are not called workers themselves but rather "managers" or "supervisors." How different the literature might have been if it was recognized that everybody involved is working, almost everybody is an employee, and almost nobody involved is working at their fullest level of productivity. The business of enhancing productivity through strategies which direct their emphasis at working people has certain game-like, manipulative qualities which are not lost on any of the participants and which always stand ready to erupt into sources of open antagonism.

TAYLOR'S ONE BEST WAY

We may best begin the story with Taylor whose unusually creative efforts we have examined previously. Taylor's view of people was surely not a foolish one, but his work seemed completely directed toward the goal of productivity from a management point of view. The concept which absorbed Taylor was that productivity would be maximized if human working behavior could be completely regularized. If all variation in work methods could be eliminated, if working people could be programmed to relentlessly adopt the one best method for each job, then productivity would be sustained at the highest possible level; fatigue would be reduced, and any waste of energy would be eliminated. The concept of individual differences in work methods, of individual preferences or capabilities, were not part of his model of working people. The way toward "efficiency" was to make people as regular and reliable as the machine components of production systems. All this might have worked far longer than it did if people had not developed some now predictable resentments. They did not function identically, either from a physical, or from an emotional point of view. Though some people doing simple, repetitive tasks could turn in the machine-like performance of the one best way, for others the attempt ran counter to their most basic aspirations. They were not willing to adopt the required behavior, even if it did mean more money. There was a limit to what they would do for money.

Worse yet, Taylor began a practice which has persisted with modern day managers, and which working people receive with the deepest distrust and antagonism. The productivity gains which result from what working people often see as speed-ups are not always shared with them. Still worse, some managers will share the gain for a while, and then when productivity gets too high, when earnings grow beyond what they find reasonable, the rate on the job is cut and the operator has to accept lower earnings or increase his efforts again to recover a part of what has been taken from him. This problem of rates which get "out of hand" exists in many plants today, and managers are still busy trying to find ways to cut them. The extreme shortsightedness of this policy is a part of the conflict, the distrust, and the bitterness which is deeply embedded in the attitudes of working people toward management today. It is a natural consequence of Taylor's approach perhaps, but its cost in terms of productivity and its conditioning of authoritarian management styles marks it as one of the basic problems of our production systems.

There was, as is very well known, a good deal of resentment at the experts' attempt to change work methods and to dictate in detail the most minute step in every job. If complete regularization of behavior could be achieved, people would become simply interchangeable elements of a production system — uniform reliable, efficient, and would, of course, be treated much like machines. We are a very long way from freeing ourselves from this systematic ignoring of individual differences. It is a model of working behavior which has a powerful appeal — so powerful in fact that we tend to ignore the unhappy result. It simply doesn't work very well, probably leading to more harm than good. Nevertheless, Taylor made a critically important start at understanding the behavior of people at work.

THE OPTIMUM ENVIRONMENT

The next step led us toward the model work environment. Perhaps illumination, music, wall colors, temperature, ventilation, and coffee breaks would do it. The results tended to be conflicting and, at best, not very dramatic in terms of productivity improvements. However, in the process of one of these investigations into the design of the model work environment a curious discovery was made. By the early 1930's it was becoming clear that the attitudes, emotions, and personality characteristics of working people were at least as important as the model work environment. We began to look into what we were pleased to call the "human" aspects of work, and thus began the human relations movement.

The Hawthorne Effect

More than once, fundamental discoveries have emerged from the tactical blunders of researchers. At the Hawthorne

Works of Western Electric in 1924, an elaborate and expensive series of experiments began which was designed to find the best working conditions for a group of working people who were engaged in assembling telephone components. What would happen to productivity on these relatively simple, repetitive assembly tasks if a paternalistic management was to vary the length of the working day, the coffee breaks, the illumination, the pay scale, the availability of hot meals, and so on? What, in short, would be the ideal work environment? For the time, it was not an unusual type of experiment—an experiment of the sort which had been done in many other plants. What happened, however, was very curious indeed. When the illumination was increased, productivity went up. When the illumination was decreased, productivity went up again. So it went with the other variables in the experiment. When conditions were "improved," productivity improved. When conditions were worsened, productivity improved. This was the famous "Hawthorne Effect."

The Hawthorne investigators developed, after some time, an understanding of what seems to have happened. Participation in the experiment was voluntary, and the working conditions which were used had dimensions which had not been anticipated. The subjects were freed from close supervision which typified the plant; they were set up in a special work area; they were able to converse more readily, to form a cohesive group, and to develop the concept that they were special people, singled out by management for individual attention. They were in fact being viewed as individuals, as people, as the interesting subjects of an investigation which was important to management. The Hawthorne researchers came to the conclusion that considerations of morale and attitude were of an importance which completely swamped the effects of the physical work environment. Thus began a long period of investigation and theorizing about "human relations" as determinants of productive behavior. Teachers have regularly cited the Hawthorne studies to their students as the classical example of an overwhelming effect of mere participation in an experiment on human subjects. Making the fundamental error of creating an experiment in which participation was so attractive and complimentary had the result of confounding the effects of the variables which the research team had set out to study. What has to a great extent been lost on managers and researchers as well is the marvelous potential for practical applications which lies within the Hawthorne effect. We will return shortly to this potential because it contains the germ of a special productivity enhancing strategy.

Human Relations

Once the dam had been broken by the Hawthorne "mistakes," there came a series of experiments, theories, and attempts at applications which steadily increased in tempo. This series of experiments is best seen as the repeated discovery of the efficacy of some special approach to working people in a particular situation, followed by rapid attempts to institutionalize and label the approach so that it might be marketed for immediate application. First came a long series of experiments designed to find out what working people valued, what influenced their morale, and their attitudes toward their work. How could they be made happier, better adjusted, and more satisfied with their working situations? Some of these studies seem hopelessly simplistic as we look back on them. Working people were endlessly asked what they wanted, what they thought was important. These investigators first pounced on the fact that money seldom ranked first on anybody's list and interpreted this as further fuel for the study of attitudes. Next they assumed that, unlike the rest of the human race, working people were fairly clear in knowing what they wanted, would be willing to make an effort to get what they said they wanted, and would be happier if they succeeded. People, when asked what their desires are, seldom produce very good predictions of their own behavior. Yet some interesting things were learned about the attitudes of people who worked in production systems. They wanted job security, good supervision, recognition for their contributions, fair treatment, some measure of independence, and in one place or another on the list, more money.

MORALE AND PRODUCTIVITY The difficulty really came when it was time to take the next step. If one could improve morale and increase job satisfaction, would this mean an increase in productivity? Things, unfortunately, did not work out this way. In fact, the findings were conflicting, confusing, controversial, and essentially useless if one was intent on raising productivity. A lot of effort went into attempts to measure job satisfaction and to relate these measures to output, absenteeism, and turnover. Unfortunately, it has turned out that no reliable relationship seems to exist. When relationships have been found, they were weak at best, and not of great significance if one wished to justify a human relations program.

Democratic Management

Among the next series of experiments which came along were those which emphasized the behavior of supervisors. If a supervisor was democratic, it was hypothesized, his people would be more productive than if he was authoritarian. Theory X and Theory Y became the favorite subjects of management seminars. Theory X — people are children and need to be controlled, directed, and disciplined like children — was bad. Theory Y — people are adults, want to be productive, take responsibility, participate in the planning of their work — was good. Participation became the subject of extensive experiments and as before, some results were good and some not very good. There were indeed cases in which it could be demonstrated that different supervisory styles did produce differing levels of productivity. Unfortunately, there are studies which show that authoritarian supervision characterized by a high degree of power wielded by the supervisor sometimes produces greater productivity than does democratic supervision with its sharing of power and participation in decision making. Even more unfortunately, there are a number of studies which detect no really useful differences between the two styles. Once again the rush to apply these concepts and to install participative methods is interesting, but not based on any clear evidence that productivity is likely to be improved.

Self-Actualization

The experiments have continued, often blending theories, often asserting the efficacy of the teachings of some prominent psychologist. A small, privately held electronics firm in California, named Non-Linear Systems, Incorporated, was run by a man who became interested in the ideas of the distinguished advocate of self-actualizing work, A.H. Maslow. Maslow spent an extended period in the plant on a sort of fellowship; his ideas about the arrangements of work which would be not only productive but psychologically healthy for the working people were gradually translated into a sort of revolutionary experiment in the early 1960's. The assembly line was abandoned in favor of small teams of six or seven workers. Each team was free to organize itself, plan its work, and operate however it wished in order to produce whatever product had been assigned to it. People were freed from the pressures of any monetary incentive and freed from having to punch a time clock. Everybody was put on salary at a level substantially above the prevailing wages in the area. Both working people and managers were given far broader responsibility and far greater decision making powers than they had ordinarily experienced. Record keeping and controls were decentralized, and the top managers of the firm turned their attention to long range planning.

Like so many such experiments two things seemed to happen. Productivity went up in the first five years by 30 percent. Customer complaints about product quality dropped dramatically. The company was growing. Then things went to pieces and the company began losing money. Top and middle managers were busy with their experiments in participative management and sensitivity training sessions. Inventories got out of hand; new products were introduced which did not do well; salaries seemed to get out of line. People began to have the feeling that they didn't know what was expected of them, and some of the production teams seemed to be slipping in their performance.

The second thing that happened at Non-Linear Systems, which is frequently seen in these experiments, was that along with the general degradation in results came a serious setback in product demand. The decline in the aerospace industry that occurred in the early 1970's was coincident with these disappointments in participative management. All the experiment really left us was an argument over whether participative management and work restructuring could have continued to work if the firm had not faced a deteriorating market position, and whether the experiments were in some way implicated in the hard times which followed them. The firm was not about to find out and moved back to more traditional methods of production and management in an attempt to rescue itself.

As so often happens when things go badly, experiments must be abandoned because the business of the company is not, after all, a laboratory for the testing of new productivity strategies. There is little evidence that working people, beyond the special few, find fulfillment in their work. Indeed, it has been suggested that they are able to remain mentally healthy only because they refuse to get overly involved in work which simply cannot be rewarding intrinsically, or self-actualizing. They are willing to work for other reasons, but letting work become a central aspect of their mental well-being just doesn't make sense to them.

Restructuring Work

Experiments in the restructuring of work took on a new urgency when the productivity slowdown of the late 1960's became evident. Job enlargement, job enrichment, the building of entire products by individuals or teams, the revolt against the division of labor and the assembly line were tried by literally dozens of firms in the U.S. and Europe. High absenteeism, the Lordstown syndrome, the decline of the work ethic, the younger work force—all motivated more and more experiments in modifying the arrangements of work in production systems. The attitudes of working people began to be classified in terms of job alienation, the blue collar revolt, and just plain boredom. The team building of automobiles came from Sweden to America. At General Motors, team building of motor homes seemed to work for a while and then was abandoned. The same sort of result occurred wherever these experiments were made. Sometimes they didn't work and were quickly set aside. Sometimes they seemed to work for a while, but their effects were not clearly measured, were confounded by other events, and eventually seemed to die out.

Mitchell Fein's penetrating analysis of work restructuring concludes that even the most expensive, successful, and well supported program, that of Texas Instruments, achieved after fifteen years the participation of only between ten and fifteen percent of its workers. Only the fifteen percent which Fein calls the "achievers," responded as management had hoped to job enrichment and participation. Fein goes on to analyze other data from all over the world in an attempt to show that there are rather consistently only fifteen percent of the workers who respond to these strategies. Beyond these individuals, Fein convincingly demonstrates, the widely heralded expectation that job enrichment and participation would lead to productivity growth simply has not materialized.

B. F. SKINNER New hypotheses continue to appear on the scene. Another noted psychologist, B. F. Skinner, produced theories which picked up labels like "behavior modification" and "positive reinforcement." Skinner's ideas, which he has eloquently elaborated and fully demonstrated in his laboratory, were naturals for application in industry. Essentially, managers were to use praise, positive feedback, and recognition to emphasize and reinforce the good things working people were doing. Behavior that was reinforced would be repeated. Most important, working people need continuous feedback about their results, what they are actually achieving. Skinner is firm in his insistence that theorizing about what people are thinking or feeling and attempting to psychoanalyze them is not only useless, but meaningless. Experiments in which working people have been invited to keep track of their own results, and supervisors have been careful to praise improvements, have produced dramatic increases in productivity. At the moment it remains to be seen whether other experiments in "behavior modification" will simply turn out to be adventures in trying "this year's current solution to productivity problems" or whether something more permanent will emerge.

What Does It Mean?

It is important to step back and see what is to be learned from these experiments in people-oriented productivity strategies. First, and clearly most important, what we are seeing is a series of experiments, and a continuing series. The problem of what sort of arrangements will bring working people toward their productive potential is an unsolved problem. The question of whether the series of experiments is making progress in this direction is highly problematical. To a great degree, the experiment as carried out in actual production systems are experiments without memory. If it doesn't work, abandon it, forget about it, go back to the old days. They are often, as we have seen, quite poorly designed experiments, and experiments in which confounding of the results occurs in spite of the best efforts at design. We must particularly note the ever-possible explanation, the pervasive suspicion, that the Hawthorne Effect is with us again and again. In how many of these experiments, which suggest that lots of things work a little bit, are we indeed seeing mere participation in the study as the best explanation one could offer? Experimentation may be the really influential aspect of what managers are doing. Experimentation may be the practice to which working people are responding.

Second, each of the experiments tends to involve one concept, one rather narrow strategy, or one approach to productivity improvement. They are not based on broadly conceived, comprehensive models of what may influence the behavior of working people. Even work restructuring is essentially a simple strategy. The results of such investigations have two special qualities. There are a lot of things which seem to improve productivity a little bit for a little while. There isn't much of anything which seems to have a marked and lasting impact on productivity. From this kind of observation two very important conclusions are possible.

The Complexity of Behavior

The behavior of working people, these experiments are showing us, is an extremely complex phenomenon. It depends on a great many things which vary from the physical design of the task to the ideals and aspirations of the individual. The enormous number of variables which have been shown to have some effect on working behavior warns us that oversimplification is the greatest danger, both in explaining and in attempting to influence this behavior. The weakness of simple explanations and the general failure of simplistic strategies for increasing productivity present an overwhelming array of data to which it is time we attended. The search for the simple, powerful explanations of behavior in production systems, on the model of the theories of classical physics, is not likely to be met with early success. This is, in a way, the entire message of the accumulated research in the behavioral sciences at large.

Approaches to increased productivity are destined to be only fads if they are restricted to simple formulations such as job enrichment, participative management, or organizational development. The simple, effective, easily formulated approach is not a very likely prospect, and the related data says this quite strongly. Human behavior in work situations is an extremely involved affair, and the best strategy is to be highly suspicious of the simple strategy.

Next Steps

If, however, we are serious in our search for new ways to increase productivity, it will not do to stop with this sort of analysis. What should be done next, where should we go from here? Three things seem clear from our review of people working. First, more experiments are necessary. We face an unsolved problem, and experimentation is the only route we have to follow. Second, we need to stop looking for great generalities about human behavior and begin at the other end. We need to look at particular people in particular work situations. We need to concentrate on the way in which individuals differ, not search vainly for useful ways in which they are the same. Finally, throughout all of the research we have examined there is indeed one variable which seems to be a candidate for prime importance and singular relevance. This is the concept of job security, of having and holding a job and doing nothing to cause a colleague to lose a job. Our next steps will be to pursue these concepts in some detail.

THE UNREALIZED POTENTIAL

As is the case of productivity strategies which emphasize technology, various attempts have been made to estimate the unrealized potential which characterizes the productivity of the working people in production systems. One may look at the variability of productivity levels among people and make estimates based on the assumption that the less productive might be raised to some higher level, say the average level of productivity. Other approaches involve identifying specific non-productive acts, or specific instances of counter-productive behavior such as tardiness, absence, grievances, strikes, turnover, and the production of unacceptable work. One may then speculate about the levels of productivity that might be achieved if these acts were reduced to various lower levels of occurrence. While these may be useful beginnings, the present conclusion must be that we don't know very much about the unrealized productive potential of people.

It is sometimes asserted that the majority of people in industry, at all levels, are working at considerably less than their maximum potential. While this may be so, it must remain as merely an hypothesis for the present. What ultimate potential is conceived is itself a complex problem, depending on sustained performance, individual differences which are accentuated at high performance levels, and so on. Even more important, we don't have much of an idea how to approach the achievement of anything near the ultimate in productivity. As we have seen, it is a fundamentally unsolved problem. We may need to remind ourselves once again that people are only elements of most production systems, and their productivity is intimately related to the behavior of the machines, the materials, and the management skills which go into the system. Finally, efforts to increase the productivity of people are costly, and we know little or nothing about the even more complex question of what the cost-benefit relationships are for various possible strategies. In this situation, lacking empirical knowledge and a theory to guide us, we must rely on uncertain decisions and experiments. In fact, the key to productivity improvement strategies lies in the skillful design of experiments. Experiments based on whatever experience may be available, but experiments designed to reduce our uncertainty about what might be the costs and benefits of various approaches to productivity growth. This fundamental point will require further analysis in order to see some of its practical implications for practicing managers.

THE LUMP OF LABOR

Increased productivity is one of those rare variables which turns out to be a central driving force in a complex system. If we can get our hands on productivity, we can do something about most of the things we want our economic system to accomplish. We could, for example, not only eliminate poverty, but in time give every family the material wealth now reserved for the few well-to-do. If we could influence productivity we could sustain a high rate of economic growth, control inflation, have full employment, and a favorable export-import balance. It seems very plausible to those who work in production systems that if there were some way of separating one person's influence on productivity from another's, a generally unexpected conclusion might emerge. Those who are managed have a greater influence on the productivity of a system than do those who manage. The most basic problem in our path is that those who are managed—the working people—generally believe that productivity increases are not in their interests. Many a young person entering the "work force" eagerly and energetically finds himself almost immediately called aside by one of his older colleagues who remembers the 1930's era of high unemployment. The message is simple. Go easy. If we get the work done too fast, we'll be out of a job. This is the famous "lump of labor theory." The need for labor is something which comes in fixed amounts. If it is satisfied too rapidly, someone will be out of work. However marvelous productivity increases may be in the long run for somebody else, they are not good for working people.

The National Commission on Productivity in 1972 conducted a survey of 1,578 people by Louis Harris which quantified anew the currency of the "lump of labor" theory. In fact it suggested the remarkable possibility that the theory was held by substantial numbers of executives and professionals, as well as by skilled and unskilled working people, by clerical people, sales people and by union members. When asked whether employees benefit a lot from increased productivity, only 20 percent of all those surveyed would agree. Indeed, 23 percent said employees did not benefit at all. One of the surprises of the survey was that these percentages did not vary dramatically with income or with age. As one might expect, 15 percent of executives thought employees did not benefit at all, as compared with 35 percent of union members who held this view.

On the question of who did benefit a lot from productivity increases, 70 percent of those asked said that it was the stockholders who did, and 68 percent thought that management did. Some 30 percent felt that the country as a whole benefited a lot from productivity increases; 30 percent thought customers did, yet only 20 percent thought employees did.

The data indicated some curious conflicts in the public mind about the effects of productivity growth. The statement, "The nation as a whole benefits from increased productivity through general economic growth," brought agreement from 73 percent. Yet at the same time, a majority of the respondents felt that one of the implications of productivity growth was the exploitation of the "workers." Two-thirds of those asked agreed with the statement, "Companies benefit from increased productivity at the expense of workers." In rating the productivity of various people, 9 percent thought doctors and nurses had lower than average productivity; 15 percent thought the productivity of factory workers was lower than average; and 19 percent thought this was true of company management. Some 26 percent felt that their own productivity could be improved while 15 percent felt they were being pushed too hard.

This kind of data tends to support the notion that there is a clear link in many people's minds between increases in productivity and short run decreases in employment. However worthwhile in our long run interests, productivity is a basic threat to job security. While the ultimate benefits of greater productivity may not be well understood, the immediate dangers are clearly perceived. A lot of people do seem to believe the "lump of labor" theory.

In-Process Inventories

Another sort of behavior shows the workings of this theory inside production systems. If work piles up ahead of a work station—if the "upstream" in-process inventory grows above its normal levels—the operator's pace is very likely to increase. If the work waiting falls below some normal level, his pace is very likely to decrease. The effects of in-process inventory levels on work pace are beloved by managers from at least one point of view. If one has a series of work stations, the output of one becoming the input to the following station, this effect keeps things in balance. If the work between two stations piles up, the upstream operator slows down a little, and the downstream operator goes a little faster. The result is to give the impression that the line of work stations is beautifully matched and balanced. The industrial engineers have done a beautiful job of planning the system. It is often extremely difficult to alter this behavior with financial incentives. Not only does a person not work himself out of a job, but he doesn't want to make his buddy downstream look like a slacker.

THE ECONOMIC FACTS

If all other things were to remain equal, increases in productivity would directly reduce employment. All other things being equal, productivity is more than just a threat to job security. Job security is reliably very high on the list of what working people say they want. In a 1973 survey of 2,535 sewing machine operators, it was overwhelmingly number one, rated above "pay equal to other plants," "more fringe benefits," and far above "meetings to talk about how work is done and how it could be done differently." If indeed, all other things remained equal, it would not be difficult to see why working people would be clearly opposed to anything that tended to boost productivity. We have already seen that in the long run other things do not remain equal, and increasing productivity results in increasing real income for most everyone. What is so important and so little appreciated is that even in the short run all other things do not remain equal. Things have a way of changing, and these changes are crucial in their impact.

Let us look at some of these factors in the short run at the industry level. As an industry's productivity rises, there is good data which suggests that the selling prices of its products tend to fall. In fact, the faster the rise in productivity, the faster the decline in selling prices. Now in most markets, declines in selling prices will stimulate demand, and the industry's output will go up. If demand responds strongly to reductions in selling price, the industry's output could even go up more than could be accommodated by its increasing productivity. The result could be more jobs, not fewer. What is so little appreciated is that a look at the data suggests that this event is not particularly rare; in fact, it occurs rather frequently.

Industries which have had productivity increases greater than the average for the economy as a whole have very often experienced an increase in the number of jobs they provided. More than this, these industries have often experienced greater employment increases than the employment increases in the economy generally. And the converse is also well supported by the data. Industries which have achieved smaller productivity increases than the economy as a whole have also experienced smaller employment increases or even reductions in the number of jobs they offered. The data, moreover, indicates that these things do not just happen sometimes, but usually, more often than not.

The electric utility industry is a good example of one in which productivity has risen rapidly, and prices, until rather recently, have been falling rapidly. The result has been a classic example of increasing output and increasing employment. The trend in employment has been not only increasing but rapidly increasing. The lumber mill products industry is the classic counter example. Productivity has been lagging behind that of the economy, prices have risen, output has lagged and employment has dropped. In the service sector it is not surprising to find that the productivity of barber shops has not increased much since 1939, nor has there been an increase in the employment of barbers. In broiler chickens, output per man-hour has shot up dramatically, accompanied by an increase in employment as well as an increase in the number of farmers raising these birds.

This sort of data is simply not known, or if known, is perhaps just not very believable. It gives very strong indications that the greater the productivity increases in an industry, the greater the job security.

There is some general feeling that all this has been changed in recent years by something called automation—which is regarded as a threat to job security of a whole new order of magnitude. Here again, the data does not support this view as we have seen before temporary job dislocations do occur. However, there is nothing to indicate that these are any more rapid nor any different in their nature or long run effects than we have previously experienced.

What is more, the nature of productivity increases is such that he who helps himself in this way also helps his brother. An increase in productivity in industry A contributes to rising real income generally. The rising real income may result in an increase in the demand for the products of industry B. Even if productivity was not rising in industry B, even if its prices were going up, people would have more money to spend as a result of what was happening in A and might want the products of B at even higher prices. Thus industries that are in trouble with their own productivity may actually experience an increase in employment which ultimately derives from increases in the productivity of other industries. The health care industry is a familiar, if painful, example of lagging productivity and rising prices, but at the same time it has experienced increasing demand and increasing employment. A worker rarely appreciates the fact that if he increases his productivity, he may very well increase not only his job security but that of his neighbor as well.

Dislocations

Even in the face of this evidence, it cannot be denied that jobs do sometimes disappear when productivity increases. The problem is to understand what happens to the people involved rather than to simply count, as we have almost always done, the number of jobs that were eliminated. New jobs are often created and people are transferred. Jobs are preserved until attrition and retirement provide people with voluntary alternatives. Productivity increases tend to create new jobs which are higher paying and often more interesting, safer, cleaner, and generally more desirable. People are eager to transfer. When we begin to see in detail what happens to people, it is very likely that the loss of jobs is not at all the same as the loss of job security. It would be foolish to argue, however, that job security is assured. Displacements do occur; people find it difficult to learn new skills, to move to new jobs, and to accommodate to the changes which seem to overwhelm them. It seems very likely, however, that this is a far less frequent occurrence than is supposed by conventional wisdom and the outlooks of working people in particular. The interesting question is whether or not the attitudes of working people seem to be at all consistent with this evidence.

UNIONS

There have long been examples of unions who supported the notion of productivity increases such as the International Ladies' Garment Workers and The United Mine Workers. There have been far more unions, however, who based their programs on the "lump of labor theory," fighting, as they saw it, for job security by fighting anything that tended to increase productivity; winning when they could, work rules and time off which tended to reduce productivity; and holding on fiercely to contractual arrangements which made it extremely difficult to increase productivity. Lately, an increasing number of union leaders, perhaps seeing themselves as labor statesmen, have begun to talk about the virtues of increasing productivity. The president of the United Steel Workers has been featured prominently in advertisements speaking out on the importance of increasing productivity. Labor, he says, has always sought "more," but if they are going to continue to get more, people must become more efficient, absenteeism must go down, and we must get the most out of technology. The construction trades, at least as personified by their union leadership, are beginning to relax their insistence on their notoriously restrictive work rules. Slowly and suspiciously, some segments of organized labor leadership are beginning to talk about the stake which their membership may have in increased productivity. They are beginning to bargain in productivity terms, exchanging restrictive practices for pay and explicit job security. How-

Such anecdotal evidence as we have so far indicates continuing great suspicion on the part of local union leaders and little if any change at all in the attitudes of the membership. Although some union leaders may talk of increased productivity, working people are extremely reluctant to become involved unless it is perfectly clear that either their jobs are at stake because the company is about to fail, or everyone is likely to benefit in terms of a substantial wage increase, or unless they can see clear guarantees which remove any threats to the job security of anyone involved. They still find it impossible to abandon the "lump of labor theory" and to dispel the fear that they will be penalized as a result of anything they may do to raise productivity.

In one of the most publicized examples of unions leading their membership into cooperation with management in the improvement of productivity, the United Steel Workers in 1971 agreed to enter into a joint labor-management program to help the productivity of the steel industry. At least, the top union leadership entered into this hitherto unprecedented agreement. In each steel plant, a high level union and management committee was established to work together in an effort to find ways of raising productivity. I. W. Abel, the union president, told his membership that they wouldn't get anything by dropping a bucket into an empty well. The steel industry was suffering both from imports and from the competition of other materials. The results of this undertaking were virtually zero. In some plants the committees simply did nothing; in some plants misunderstandings and uncertainties actually made things worse. At the base of the difficulties seemed to be the old "lump of labor theory." Productivity was widely taken by the working members of the union to mean more work with no more pay, to mean a serious threat to job security, and to mean nothing more than old fashioned attempts to get more work from them at their expense. Although Mr. Abel made the success of the productivity program one of his top priorities, he ever interesting and "trend setting" these developments may seem, the place to watch is not at the top. The place to look is among the local unions, the shop stewards, and the working people who are the membership.

was unable to make any progress at all in convincing his membership that productivity improvements were, in any sense, in their interests.

WORKING PEOPLE LOOK
AT PRODUCTIVITY

The attitudes of working people toward productivity increasing strategies are, of course, far from uniform, but there are some strong generalities which seem to explain a good deal of what is seen in production systems. Productivity is restricted by the powerful forces of peer pressure to protect other people's jobs, and the individual's strong desire for job security— the protection of his own job. No working person will freely and willingly do anything to improve productivity because he knows that to do so is, in one way or another, to injure himself or his fellows. He feels that increasing productivity will make it necessary to work harder and make less work available; also, it will increase the supply of labor and thus inevitably lower the price, his wages. Even such schemes as suggestion systems which offer monetary rewards for ideas that result in productivity increases have limited effectiveness, probably as a result of these notions.

The belief that we can get people interested in improving their own productivity is a very dubious one indeed, at least below the supervisory level. The long development of the adversary relationship and the ample grounds for the mistrust of management, leave working people without any reason to be interested in becoming more productive. They do not, in general, see their interests as in any way coincident with those of management, at least until the very life of the company is clearly hanging in the balance. From the working person's point of view, increasing productivity is not so much a matter of the extra effort it might require. It is simply inconsistent with the adversary relationship which is the product of long years of mismanaged incentive systems and union militancy. Anything that one might try to willingly increase productivity would set a very dangerous precedent indeed. Who could tell how many jobs such an attempt might ultimately cost. Even the arguments from the economical viewpoint are unlikely to persuade many. They see themselves as being asked to trade an almost certain short term sacrifice for a highly uncertain long term gain. Besides, as the data indicates, we rather regularly achieve some sort of annual productivity increment for the economy as a whole. Why should any individual be called upon to take unusual risks while productivity goes right on increasing anyway? The real wage increases are going to be available anyway—immediately if we leave things alone, far in the future for a particular individual who puts his job in jeopardy.

The notion that resisting productivity growth is consistent with job security is about the most fundamental, reliable, and significant effect with which any productivity enhancing strategy must contend.

The Unspeakable Hypothesis

Every transaction between managers and working people says something about the attitudes of one group toward the other. One of the most difficult aspects of this relationship concerns the reaction of some working people to management strategies designed to increase productivity. We know for example, that the history of wage incentives and rate cutting has caused many working people to mistrust managers and to resort to playing games with the incentive system. But we have never explored the question of whether or not there are large numbers of people who see all attempts to motivate them to make them more productive as attempts at manipulation. Just when one person is manipulating another is very difficult to define, since much of our behavior is designed, whether consciously or not, to influence the behavior of others. Yet when what management does is seen to some degree as dishonest, as forcing people to make difficult choices in favor of company goals, and as the creation of games which must be played to get one's reward, what is going on probably captures many of the meanings of manipulation. It seems likely that there exists a significant group of people who resent being "motivated," resent being put "on incentive," and resent what they see as treatment for laboratory rats in a maze. They view this policy as manifesting an attitude of elitism, subtle contempt, cynicism, and superiority on the part of managers. They see management, for example, as offering them chances to make decisions about their own work situation, but carefully arranging things so that the decisions have only the most trivial of consequences. They see participation as an impression that management wants to create, without permitting any effective participation to occur. They see much of what management does as having purposes other than those openly declared. Job enrichment, for example, is sold as a way of making work more interesting, less dull, but clearly it is just another scheme for getting more work for the wage dollar. If job enrichment were so great, working people would be asking for it, and their unions would be negotiating for it. No major union has ever asked for job enrichment. All of this must surely suggest to some people that managers regard them as stupid.

These kinds of hypotheses are unlikely to be investigated in any situation over which managers have control. If it became clear that the reason some working people respond in the wrong way to management strategies because they do not want to be motivated, manipulated, or forced to behave in response to whatever system of rewards and reinforcements managers decide to invent, then things would be at dead center. It would be very difficult to imagine anything that could be done, as management is presently conceived, to move toward greater productivity. We have told ourselves for so long that one of the basic functions of management is to motivate people, that we would be faced with the necessity for some very basic rethinking. Yet, this is surely one of the hypotheses that ought to be openly discussed. What are the characteristics of people who have a low tolerance for being motivated and manipulated? What should be management's relationship with such people?

IN SEARCH OF INDIVIDUAL DIFFERENCES

The current fascination with job enrichment or job enlargement is a good example of our long standing difficulties with productivity enhancing strategies based centrally on the attitudes of working people. Job enrichment, or the movement toward the restructuring of work has been advocated as a great national priority by the report of the HEW Task Force, "Work in America." Numbers of companies are experimenting with it; behavioral scientists are advocating it with enthusiasm which sometimes approaches moral fervor. Many managers seem skeptical and mistrusting, but their current difficulties with absenteeism and other counter productive behaviors, emphasized by more than adequate coverage in the popular press, have given many of them a kind of desperation attitude — "we'd better try it because nothing else we have done seems to be helping."

Work restructuring means permitting working people greater latitude in determining their own work pace, giving them the responsibility for inspecting and controlling the quality of their own work, making them responsible for the setup and repair of their own machines, and giving them a wide choice in the work methods they adopt. The result of work restructuring is supposed to be greater autonomy for operators, greater skill requirements, and less monotony.

Now the benefits of such restructuring of work are predicted on the basis of a three step theory, which sounds very plausible indeed. Simple, repetitive, short time cycle jobs are, it is predicted, perceived by working people as being dull, monotonous, and unstimulating. Step two: dull, monotonous jobs produce feelings of boredom and job dissatisfaction, so the theory goes. Finally, boredom and job dissatisfaction lead to an increasing incidence of nonproductive behaviors, such as absenteeism, turnover, and restriction of output. By this chain, it is reasoned that the process of division of labor, of creating simple, routinized jobs, has become disfunctional and is now leading to lower productivity levels than would result if we moved in directions opposite to the division of labor, namely job enrichment or work restructuring.

We have already dwelt at some length on the evidence which surrounds the final step in this linkage — the relationship between job satisfaction and productivity. We concluded, as others have, that the relationship is vague, ambiguous, and too weak to be useful. This led us to the conclusion that the factors which influence work behavior are complex, and that to understand them we will have to search for explanations at a more microscopic level. Work behavior will have to be viewed in terms of individual workers rather than searched for broad powerful generalizations which simply do not seem to be forthcoming. By looking at the first two steps in this theory of the efficacy of work restructuring, we serve to confirm these conclusions.

Monotony

Let us look first at the presumed relationship between monotony and the performance of simple, repetitive jobs. The evidence continues to accumulate that there are numbers of working people who simply do not find these jobs monotonous. In some work groups, the simplest most repetitive jobs—the jobs that seem to require the least thought—are taken by those having the highest seniority, those who have their choice among all the jobs within the group. In some studies, significant numbers of working people have been identified who find these simple jobs not monotonous at all, but in fact pleasant and positively motivating. No matter what conclusions may be advocated by the popular sociologists, the carefully controlled, well planned experiments consistently indicate that this relationship is very much a matter of individual differences. Broad generalizations are simply not useful here.

The second link in the theory of work restructuring is that boredom leads to job dissatisfaction. Again it has been repeatedly shown that it is simply not true that the vast majority of workers enjoy making decisions about their jobs. Some clearly prefer the simplicity, the security, and the safety of not having to make these decisions. Again, it is very much a matter that must be understood in terms of individual differences.

In view of this kind of evidence, it is not surprising that both the carefully planned experiments on work restructuring and the attempts by managers to implement programs of work restructuring have produced very mixed results indeed. Once again, it would appear that the relationship on which this strategy is based is far too simple to be consistent, and far too inconsistent to be useful. Comprehensive and detailed reviews of the available data simply do not support any useful relationship, even between job specialization and job satisfaction. Yet would-be reformers continue to argue in favor of work restructuring as the greatest available strategy for enhancing productivity. In other aspects of the behavioral sciences, individual differences are often vitally important and fully acknowledged. Yet there is a pervasive tendency for the zeal of reform to lead otherwise reasonable behaviorists to expect that everybody should react in the same way to a given job design. It may well be that the scientist's own reaction of total inability to tolerate what he sees as being some of the incredibly dull jobs which people do in industry, hopelessly colors his outlook. The fact that these jobs might be intolerable to the sympathetic behavioral scientist leads him to conclude that something must be done to relieve those who seem to be stuck with them.

THE EXPERIMENTAL DEMONSTRATION

In 1965 two investigators, Turner and Lawrence, set out on yet another study of the effects of work restructuring. They examined the hypothesis that working people would respond with high satisfaction and low rates of absenteeism to jobs which were characterized by more complexity, variety, authority, and more decision making responsibility. They did an extensive study involving 470 people from 11 industries working on 47 different jobs. A curious thing happened. The part of the hypothesis which concerned absenteeism was confirmed. Jobs which were "enlarged" or "enriched" did produce lower absentee rates. Yet the other part of their basic hypothesis, that job "enrichment" would be accompanied by higher job satisfaction, was not confirmed. In reviewing this troublesome result, it occurred to them that it was possible that the subjects of their experiment might be usefully viewed as being composed of two separate and distinct groups. After some reanalysis of the data, they came to an extremely important conclusion. People from plants located in small towns seemed to respond in a completely different way than did those who worked in large city plants. The investigators were on the trail of the first real understanding of the individual differences that might explain the conflicting results obtained from work restructuring. Their data suggested that people in small town plants behaved just the way they had supposed. They responded to more complexity, more freedom, and more responsibility with lower absentee rates and higher job satisfaction. People from the big city plants showed no response at all to work restructuring so far as their absence rates were concerned. Job enrichment just had no effect. On the other hand, they responded negatively as far as job satisfaction was concerned. Indeed the big city working people exhibited significantly high job satisfaction on the supposed dull, simple, repetitive jobs.

As social scientists, Turner and Lawrence immediately began explaining their findings in terms of worker alienation, cultural background, and the development of strong or weak subcultural norms. All of this is interesting, but the real point is that here we began to see the expansion of highly simplistic theories into slightly more complex but experimentally confirmable explanations. Work restructuring worked for small town people but didn't work for big city people. Just by adding this third variable to the theory, by attending only in this limited degree to individual differences, a significantly better understanding of this particular productivity improvement strategy was produced. This insight has since been tested thoroughly, and it has been used to make some sense out of much of the previously conflicting evidence. The cultural background of working people, the type of environment in which they live, the size of the work group of which they are a part—all are clearly useful in predicting their response to work restructuring. Where attempts to discover a general relationship have failed, this modest attention to individual differences has been most helpful.

Having said that the best hope for the understanding of work behavior lies in the pursuit of the ways in which people differ rather than the ways in which they are similar, we are left with a series of very difficult problems. Once one sets aside the hope that a sudden technical solution, a new, simple, powerful theory of working behavior is going to appear, what should be done?

The basic question is, of course, how to look at people. If we are not going to assume that all working people will respond in the same way to work situations, how should we characterize people, what aspects of their working styles and personalities should we begin to investigate? If there is some evidence that cultural background and location are important, what next? Obviously we will never be able to afford to study each individual person in detail. From a practical point of view, the question will be one of finding categories, classifications, and constellations of attributes which are neither too broad to be useful in explaining working behavior, nor too narrow and specific to be prohibitively costly to establish and apply. If anything is to come of the proposition that successful productivity growth is not likely to come from simplistic approaches, we must find some cost-effective midpoint between the concentration on human characteristics and the focus on the ultimate individuality of the person. This belief is consistent with the basic proposition that people behave in some ways like all other people, in some ways like some other people, and in some ways that are uniquely their own.

The Graves Study

In an interesting and little noticed study, Professor Clare W. Graves of Union College has shown one sort of direction the exploration of individual differences might take. In a study which extended over fourteen years, a pattern of seven categories was established which represented reasonably distinct personality types or personality levels. Roughly speaking these levels were:

1. Childlike, psychologically run down, discouraged;
2. Primitive in outlook, superstitious, preoccupied with taboos;
3. Wide awake, objective, but frightened of the complexity of the world;
4. Aggressive, power seeking, angry, troublesome;
5. Sociocentric, secure economically and psychologically, concerned with making society run smoothly, joiner of groups;
6. Individualistic, self-confident, works well toward a goal, reacts negatively to supervision;
7. Individualistic, pacifistic, goes his own way, does not react negatively to supervision, but simply ignores it.

Now it turned out there were two very interesting things

about this set of personality categories. In the first place, they were practical in the sense that they could be readily recognized by a competent industrial psychologist. While it might not be inexpensive to classify individuals according to this scheme, it was not hopelessly complex and prohibitively elaborate in application.

The second remarkable thing about these categories turned out to be that when employees in a large manufacturing organization were grouped in this way, and with a small amount of interdepartmental transferring it was arranged that each employee was under a supervisor appropriate to his personality type, some behavior changes resulted. The plant, which had been characterized by some discontent, experienced a 17 percent increase in productivity, an 87 percent reduction in grievances, and a reduction in turnover rate from 21 percent per year to 7 percent.

Again we do not know how long these effects continued nor how well the experimental conditions controlled against the effects of other variables, but it is still a challenging experiment.

PRODUCTIVITY STRATEGIES

In Chapter 11 we will have a close look at the question of whether or not a practical, cost-effective, non-manipulative approach to productivity could emerge from this necessity to attend to individual differences. Nothing is more useless than to talk endlessly about the importance of individual differences if not, at least, some prospect that the consequences of such a view could eventually result in an approach that tough-minded managers might find worth a try. So much of the experimentation and advocacy of the behaviorists of the past twenty-five years has lacked any real consideration of the management viewpoint. The result has been that a great many managers have regarded the experiment as not quite believable, as highly risky, and not to be tried until someone else has spent their money testing it very thoroughly. It is useful, however, to take a preliminary look at the possibilities which lie ahead by examining one of the current fads of motivational strategy—the flexible work schedule.

Suppose that absenteeism is a problem which is hampering productivity. Suppose it is not simply asserted that everybody has bad attendance records, but rather the data is examined and reveals that most of the problem seems to be with ten to fifteen percent of the working people. Suppose we look at other attempts to control absenteeism by means of prizes, point systems leading to possible dismissal, job enrichment, and so on. We might easily conclude that these experiments, which have more often failed than succeeded, suggest that for some people, the problem is less related to the job than it is to outside demands—the haircut, the doctor, the child's dentist appointment, the conference with the teacher, the need to try out a new boat, the desire to go fishing on the first day of the trout season, and so on. Suppose that we resist the temptation to make value judgments about which of these do and do not warrant staying away from the job. Suppose we just view the people as individuals with their own needs and values, and decide to avoid getting involved with rules that say certain kinds of absences are acceptable and certain kinds are not. Suppose we avoid the very expensive process of trying to sit down with each individual in an attempt to understand and accommodate his unique constellation of outside demands.

Freedom and Flexibility

Whether with these sort of considerations in mind or not, in 1973 Lufthansa Airlines introduced a policy so simple, yet so radical, that it commanded immediate widespread attention. Employees who did not have to deal with the public during set business hours were permitted to come in any time they wished between 8:00 a.m. and 10:00 a.m., as long as they worked eight hours each day. Notice that this is not simply staggered starting times dictated by the management, but a real degree of choice open to the people employed by the airline. Notice, too, that this can't be done with all jobs—some necessarily have fixed time constraints. Where it is practical, however, this choice represents a substantial measure of accommodation to individual needs, individual styles of working and living, and individual demands which arise outside of the work situation. Flexible work scheduling has been well received by working people at Lufthansa; their morale is up, and problems of getting people to work overtime have been reduced. Whether or not productivity is up is difficult to establish because it is difficult to measure, but everyone seems quite optimistic about it. Whether this policy will last or fade in a few months or years remains to be seen. What is significant about the Lufthansa initiative is that it demonstrates some very important possibilities and points us in some extremely interesting directions.

New Directions

First, from the management point of view, it was seen that it was not essential to treat all working people in all jobs the same way. People could understand that flexible scheduling was possible in some cases and not in others. It turned out that the problems of work scheduling, of coordination among jobs, and of being to a degree uncertain about when people would come and go, did not present severe technical problems. How far flexible scheduling can be carried will depend on the degree of interdependence among jobs, the need for simultaneous presence of groups of people, and so on. These, however, are technical problems which can now be examined because the tradition of common starting times has been successfully challenged.

The most important factor of flexible scheduling is that the essence of the strategy is not to get involved with studying the individual differences among people, but rather to maximize the freedom and the flexibility in the work situation so that the people themselves may adjust their behavior according to their own needs, styles, and preferences. Management takes the position of providing the freedom within which scheduling may happen—not of trying to understand, to direct, and to manipulate the situation. The cost of a productivity strategy which aims at responding to individual differences is the cost of increasing the freedom available within the job situation. All of Taylor's efforts, as frequently pointed out, were directed in the opposite way—toward the complete elimination of freedom.

What is perhaps of equal importance is the strong possibility that flexible work scheduling, or gliding work hours, will be seen by many as neither manipulative nor as reflecting attitudes of superiority on the part of management. In the first place, everyone is quite open about what is going on. Management hopes that by giving this measure of freedom at reasonable cost, those who enjoy it will be more productive, more regular in their attendance, and less distracted from their work by outside obligations which they find difficult or expensive to discharge. There is nothing more, nothing subtle, nothing in the way of hidden motives. Each party is willing to give something and hopes to get something.

As we have remarked, it is difficult to predict which management behaviors are likely to be perceived as manipulative and which are not, by those individuals sensitive to such things. It seems reasonable, however, that the granting of greater freedom in the behavior required of working people—the granting of this freedom for reasons which are well understood to be the legitimate interests of the company—is about as unmanipulative as any management action could be. In a sense, the increase in freedom of choice is the very opposite of manipulation, if it is in fact a real increase. The reality was, in this case, clearly demonstrable to the people involved.

Finally it should be noticed that gliding work hours represent a move toward one of the work relationship models which is held in highest regard by many people. This is the work relationship of the professional person. The professional tradition is that people will assume responsibility for getting work done before a deadline, not during a specified working period. Professionals work toward meeting an objective, not toward meeting a time obligation. It has been repeatedly shown that professionals are highly admired, and that they are regarded as being very productive. For instance, this was noted by the Louis Harris survey for the National Productivity Commission. Furthermore, numerous studies have shown that professionals with highly flexible work hours devote more time and effort to their jobs than do those who have a defined working period. Management is, in this situation, essentially testing the hypothesis that if they want people to behave like professionals, they should treat them like professionals. It seems very likely indeed that the compliment being paid to working people—the expression of trust, of regard, and of respect—is not at all lost on these people. Giving someone a modest choice about when he or she starts work may not be the ultimate in professionalism, but neither should it be overlooked.

Thus, in this small experiment one may see some fascinating possibilities. There just may be ways to make work situations responsive to individual differences—to do it without seeming cynical or manipulative, and to do it in a way which argues strongly for a favorable balance between the costs and the benefits. However, we need to develop the possibilities of this approach to productivity growth somewhat further. Flexible work scheduling is unlikely, by itself, to solve our productivity problems, and it very much remains to be seen whether the principles it suggests can be extended in ways which will be found credible to managers and to working people.

Leaving People Alone

Many experts and managers think that whatever gains may follow from new work scheduling will be short-lived. While a given company may have an advantage for a while, this advantage will quickly disappear as competitors make the same experiments, and as the effects of the initial experiments decay. Again, not everybody will like flexible working hours; not everybody will have the poise and the self-perception to come in late and willingly work late. Absenteeism, tardiness, short hours, and eventual turnover may result from this strategy. There are, however, reasons to expect otherwise. This is a strategy which represents both an increase in freedom and a recognition that work may not be, and need not be, the central factor in one's life.

The concept is really one of leaving working people alone as much as possible. Rather than attempting to force everyone to conform to rigid job specifications, the objective of those who design production systems would be to create systems which would accommodate as much diversity on the part of the working people as possible. This is the basic statement of a productivity strategy based on the concept of the primacy of individual differences. The question at issue is whether this, too, like so many other strategies, will have a moderate short-term effect but almost no long-term effect.

Assumptions

The behavior of people at work is a very complex phenomenon which has been viewed from many vantage points: technological, economic, psychological, social, historical, and moral. We have experimented for many years with ways of arranging the work situation to motivate or permit people to be more productive. The problem remains essentially unsolved, and we are presented rather regularly with new schemes, new fads, and new approaches to making people more productive. It seems at least possible that our difficulties may be one day understood in terms of three assumptions on which many of our efforts are based. We have assumed that working people would respond rather uniformly to productivity approaches. We sought "the approach" which would work for nearly everybody, and we have yet to find it. For everything that has been tried, the results have been mixed.

We have assumed that people could in fact be manipulated, and be motivated by wage incentive systems, by participation in decision making, and by restructuring the design of their jobs to provide more of the intrinsic rewards of work. It may very well be that there are significant numbers of people who resent this sort of control of their behavior. These people will respond to a degree when the control strategies are new and strong, but their responses will tend to disappear quite rapidly with time.

Finally, we have assumed that if people were given what they wanted in the way of working arrangements, if they were brought to a condition called "high job satisfaction" they would respond by being more productive. That data seems to be saying that this assumption is sometimes weakly correct, but not generally useful.

TOWARD EXPERIMENTATION

Where to go from here? The answer must be more experimentation with real work situations and real working people. This experimentation should try to avoid the memoryless trials of the past and more nearly approach the scientific ideal of a program of cumulative knowledge; each new experiment should be well related to those which have gone before. The kind of experimentation which is consistent with our present state of knowledge, which would seem to coincide most reasonably with what has been done, is investigation into the significance of individual differences. Working behavior, it would now appear, is likely to be strongly explained not in terms of great, simple generalities, but rather by a closer examination of the working styles and personalities of individuals.

To argue for more experimentation is to undertake an exercise in futility, unless we can make some progress toward showing that experimentation is a strategy which might be seen by managers as a realistic productivity development strategy. Unless we can give some indication that the cost of such experimentation will be more than covered by its benefits, little will come of such suggestions. We must further examine the concept of productivity development through experimentation in an attempt to see how it could be construed as a strategy with reasonable risks and reasonable payoffs. For the moment, however, we will suggest some of the implications of experimentation from the point of view of the working styles of people in production systems.

The Meaning of Hawthorne

The implications of the great Hawthorne studies have been explored in detail for many years, but little has been done to either acknowledge or document what may be the most important implication of all. If experimentation produced productivity increases among the women at the Hawthorne works, no matter what the direction of changes made in their working situations, perhaps experimentation itself is the key to an effective productivity enhancement strategy. If people become more productive when they participate in experiments concerning their working arrangements, why not undertake experiments to serve this purpose? If and when the effects of an experiment decay, why not undertake another experiment? In fact, why not implement a policy of more or less continuous experimentation as the essence of a productivity development strategy? Such a suggestion presents us with several problems, the outlines of which we will only suggest for the present.

Was the result obtained in the Hawthorne studies a peculiarity of the people and work situation in that plant, or was the effect something to be expected in a variety of situations? One of the results we have seen rather consistently in reviewing the fads and experiments that have been made over the years is that many of them seem to work sometimes and for some period of time. Clearly one strong possibility for interpreting this kind of data is the hypothesis that almost any reasonable kind of an experiment will result in a productivity increase, at least for a while. It matters less what the exact nature of the policy or strategy may be. What is important is that an experiment is being made; people find themselves the object of management attention; management is seen to be interested in productivity and concerned about the arrangements which surround the people in the production system. These are the conditions which attend experimentation and lead to the productivity increase, rather than the particular hypotheses that are being tested in the experiment. Now such an interpretation must surely be kept within reasonable limits. Not just any policy made the subject of an experiment will produce productivity increases among all sorts of working people. Rather, there seem to be a lot of policies, perhaps some which seem somewhat plausible to working people, which can be strongly relied upon to produce higher productivity when tested with many groups. Just what the practical limits of this interpretation may be, must be the subject of subsequent investigation. Still, interpreting the history of productivity experiments as being often effective simply because they were experiments is strongly plausible.

There is a related effect which, like so many observations that do not fit with any well developed theoretical structure, has been largely ignored and completely undocumented. Familiar to many who have worked in production systems is what we may call the "just paying attention" effect. In one plant which had been having considerable difficulties with product quality, a quality control engineer was brought in to see what could be done. After a certain amount of preliminary observation, the engineer hung some very technical looking pieces of graph paper at strategic points around the plant. From time to time he would inspect a few items of the product and plot points on what were prominently labeled "Quality Control Charts." Without any other action on his part, the engineer soon noticed that quality problems began to disappear, and things once more returned to an acceptable level of good output. No technical solution was involved. The people working in the system simply became aware that management was interested in quality, was paying attention to quality, and they made the necessary corrections themselves. The working people were fully aware of what to do to correct the quality problems, but until the arrival of the engineer and the appearance of his charts, they simply didn't bother because they had no indication that management was concerned. "Just paying attention" was enough to produce some correction of the problem. In the same sense, many productivity enhancing strategies have signaled people that management is concerned about productivity and is paying attention to it; therefore, they will for a time respond. The posting of the "control charts" eventually lost its effectiveness, and quality problems gradually reappeared again. It was time to make a new experiment of some sort, to indicate once again that management was paying attention.

Time Decay

There is a great deal of anecdotal evidence that productivity enhancing strategies, work restructuring, new wage incentive plans and participation often work for a while and then lose their effectiveness. The same thing occurs in other ways and at other organizational levels. In one large engineering department employing some 1800 people, morale was poor, and there was considerable lack of communication and lack of coordination; also, productivity was low and projects were falling behind. A new director of engineering planned a total reorganization of the group. He took considerable pains to explain to everyone over several weeks just what their positions would be in the new organization. Then over one long weekend, he implemented the changes. People came in on Monday, took up their new jobs, and went to work. Morale was obviously higher; people worked together more effectively, and deadlines began to be met once again. The director, a very experienced man, later admitted privately that the nature of the new organization structure was important, but there were a considerable number of structures which would probably have been equally effective. What was important, in his opinion, was that reorganization itself was intrinsically functional. He fully expected that the good effects of his reorganization would eventually wear off, and he had already begun to think about the next reorganization which would have to be undertaken in a matter of months or years to once again involve the people in the excitement of an experiment—to show them once again that management was paying attention. The functional character of reorganization is not a new hypothesis, but it is one that we have been reluctant to admit and to discuss, and one which we dare not document. If people decide that experiments are being made just for the sake of making experiments, and not for real and carefully considered substantive reasons, the functional character of the experiments will be lost.

The Functional Aspect

The manager of one of the largest and most progressive industrial engineering departments in the country, one which serves one of our most prominent manufacturing firms, acknowledged this recently. His firm, he said, was involved in experiments on the restructuring of work, as were many companies. His data had begun to suggest that these experiments were very likely to increase productivity, and this increase was likely to last for a while and then decay. He was, he said, perfectly willing to plan for the next experiment and to make this sort of use of the Hawthorne effect, as long as his staff could keep devising reasonable experiments. It was, however, absolutely essential, in his view, that his efforts not be interpreted in this way, nor even be open to any such suspicion. It was, he felt, almost disastrous for him to even admit to himself that this was what seemed to be under way.

Thus a policy of productivity enhancement through continuous experimentation has the strong advantage that it appears to be consistent with much of our experience. At the same time, there are serious practical difficulties which surround the deliberate espousal of such a policy, and no company has done so explicitly. We must return later to the exploration of whether or not a plan of continuous experimentation can be reasonably undertaken in the expectation that it will have a favorable cost-benefit relationship.

Experimentation has another functional dimension which

is now being explored by social scientists in research studies involving community problems and community decision making. One of the payoffs these investigators are discovering is that involving members of a community in research studies is not simply that one may get useful, problem oriented data, but that participation in the experiments has a powerful educational effect on the members of the community. Participating in these experiments makes people think about community issues, makes them reflect on possible futures for their community, define for themselves the problems facing their community, become explicit about their values and uncertainties, and think about the alternative problem solving processes that might be available. The same thing, it seems very probable, was occurring among the workers in the Hawthorne studies. They began to think about the problems and constraints of their working environments; they began to understand that productivity was a central issue and that little was known about what influenced it; and they began to be more self-perceptive about their own likes, attitudes, and motivations in their working situations. We don't, of course, have any evidence that these things happened, and here once again, we can only suggest that the anecdotal evidence from those with long experience in production systems seems strong enough to warrant more careful tests of the educational effectiveness of participation in productivity experiments.

Personal Experiments

We have strong indications that much of the turnover among new employees represents their own experimentation. When unemployment is low, significant numbers of people try out jobs, sometimes for a few days and sometimes for a few weeks. If they don't particularly like the jobs, they move on. Sometimes they leave without even picking up their last pay check, without even answering the personnel department's request to come in for an exit interview. When jobs are hard to find, of course, the rate of experimentation goes down drastically, but when jobs are easy to get, when everybody is hiring, the labor market may have significant numbers of what one plant manager called "rollers." They are probably better called "experimenters." They collect data on both their own likes and dislikes, on job characteristics; they are generally more self-perceptive and knowledgeable about their own work styles. These are clearly very expensive experiments in terms of individual efforts and of the productivity losses due to this turnover. A heavy equipment manufacturer hired 276 welders one year; one year later only 21 of these were still on the payroll. Much of this turnover must be accounted to working people trying out this job to see how they liked it. Experimentation as a productivity enhancing strategy needs to pay some attention to this process of having each individual study his own working personality and style by a series of job changes. This seriously inefficient process, if it could be refined and made less costly to all concerned, would represent a substantial productivity pay-off potential both to working people and to their employers.

A SITUATION SUMMARY

Thus, our situation is the following. It appears that productivity growth strategies which emphasize people and their behavior will have to be understood less in terms of generalities and more in terms of the particular personalities and styles which set us apart from one another. We simply do not presently know what dimensions of individual work style are useful, nor what dimensions of the working situation are useful. We must therefore move toward more experimentation. This experimentation presents a set of serious practical difficulties which we will shortly examine. On the other hand, there are grounds for optimism. The Hawthorne effect, the "just paying attention" effect, suggests the strong possibility that experimentation is intrinsically functional, that doing experiments increases productivity for a while. Whether or not this theory could become the basis for a productivity development strategy is an intriguing question which will require some further exploration.

Experimentation is an effective strategy because productivity and the response to productivity increasing strategies are strong functions of individual personalities, particular working groups, particular managements, particular historical developments, and special local conditions. Experimentation, our only resort in the absence of strong, reliable theories, is the way to begin to learn and to adapt. It is not the alternation of conditions, attitudes, and the structure of work which will improve productivity. It is far more likely that experimentation with these factors will lead us to discover the route toward productivity growth.

Notes

The Hawthorne studies are described in Roethlisberger, F.J., and W. J. Dickson. *Management and the Worker.* Cambridge, Mass.: Harvard University Press, 1939.

There is a vast literature on the human relations movement; a good picture can be obtained from:

Dubin, R. *The World of Work: Industrial Society and Human Relations.* Englewood Cliffs, N.J.: Prentice-Hall, Inc., 1958.

Herzberg, F., and others. *The Motivation to Work.* 2nd ed. New York: Wiley, 1959.

Sutermeister, Robert A., editor. *People and Productivity.* New York: McGraw-Hill, 1969.

The work of A. H. Maslow is reflected in his very extensive writings. A good beginning is his *Eupyschian Management.* Homewood, Ill.: Irwin-Dorsey, 1965.

The famous Theory X and Theory Y are presented in McGregor, D. *The Human Side of Enterprise.* New York: McGraw-Hill, 1960.

Mitchell Fein's analysis of work restructuring is described in his *Motivation for Work.* American Institute of Industrial Engineers. Atlanta, 1974.

The classic study of the restriction of output was first published in 1931. It has since been reissued. Mathewson, Stanley B. *Restriction of Output Among Unorganized Workers.* Carbondale, Ill.: Southern Illinois University Press, 1969.

The results of the Harris poll on attitudes toward productivity are given in *The Second Annual Report of the National Commission on Productivity.* Washington: U.S. Government Printing Office, 1973.

The study of attitudes of sewing machine operators was published in the *New York Times,* March 23, 1974.

The economic data on the consequences of productivity is summarized in Solomon Fabricant. *A Primer on Productivity.* New York: Random House, 1969.

The key studies on the effects of individual differences are:

Hulin, Charles L. and Milton R. Blood. "Job Enlargement, Individual Differences, and Worker Responses," *Psychological Bulletin.* 1968, Vol. 69, No. 1, 41–53.

Turner, A.N. and P.R. Lawrence. *Industrial Jobs and the Worker: An Investigation of Response to Task Attributes.* Boston: Harvard University, Graduate School of Business Administration, 1965.

Turner, A.N. and A.L. Miclette. "Sources of Satisfaction in Repetitive Work," *Occupational Psychology.* 1962, 36, 215–231.

Vroom, V.H. *Some Personality Determinants of the Effects of Participation.* Englewood Cliffs, N.J.: Prentice-Hall, Inc., 1960.

5
Working Smarter:
Productivity as a Soft Science

SMARTER NOT HARDER

There is hardly a more self-evident proposition than that of the virtues of applying intelligence and reflection to the design of work of all sorts. If the job of anyone in an organization can be made simpler, more productive, less tiresome, safer, and more satisfying by giving some thought to how it is performed and how it is coordinated with other jobs, then surely it should be done. It is sufficiently difficult, as we have seen, to interest people in working harder, but it has often been done. It is much more difficult to interest people in working smarter, and this has seldom been done.

Work simplification, the exciting notion that everybody is the outstanding expert on his own job and ought to be interested in redesigning and improving it, was a strongly advocated concept in the 1930's and 1940's. Hundreds of companies sent representatives to work simplification seminars, and they came home with the intriguing notion that if people could be stimulated to examine their own jobs, then some basic, common-sense notions to direct their thinking would bring about significant productivity improvement. Work simplification approached the fervor of a crusade, and the logic of every man improving his own job seemed immensely appealing. Unhappily, the results were far less exciting than the concepts. Apparently the ideas never really received much acceptance below the supervisory levels—in spite of the seminars on company time, the posters, and the contests.

Efforts have been made to get people interested in their

own productivity by making them profit sharers and participants in the success of the organization as a whole. There have been some outstanding examples of the success of this approach, but it has failed at least as often. The effects of profit sharing are weakened by the separation of the action and the reward. The connection between an increase in a person's productivity today and an increase in his profit share when profits are distributed, seems tenuous and uncertain.

Thus the notion that everybody ought to be interested in working smarter has not been of great practical consequence, and the result has been to "expertize" the improvement of work design and production system design. The first great move of the experts was, as we have noted, in exactly the opposite direction from asking those who did the jobs to redesign them. The experts developed elaborate wage incentive systems which were based on their designs. Each job was examined in minute detail; the best method for doing it was specified as well as the expert could determine it. Detailed operations sheets were produced which gave the working people virtually no room for experimentation and variation. Standard performance times and, in turn, wages for better than standard performance were based on the assumption and the expert insistence that the job be performed exactly as specified. Today, some 26 percent of working people are operating on this sort of expert designed job specification.

THE SPECIALISTS

The notion that work is so important that it ought to be designed by specialists has flourished. The specialists have grown from time study men to operations research analysts, systems analysts, and management scientists. Although these people have somewhat different historical and cultural backgrounds, they are more similar than different. They share a devotion to the basic "working smarter" hypothesis. Neither more machines, nor more people, nor people working harder, nor more energy will yield substantial productivity improvements. All of these factors must be combined in better ways. The specialists are interestingly different from the "machine" people who see machines as the only way and the "people" people who see motivation as the only way. These work designers are fully sensitive to what can be done with machines and with people, but their focus is on the "soft" aspects of production systems — the operating methods by which all the inputs come together. They are interested in big, one time jobs and in small, frequently repeated operations. They are looking at operations which extend from the production floor all the way to the chief executive officer. Their basic hypothesis is that planning, experimentation, design, and measurement of the ways in which work is performed, the ways in which operations are conducted, and the ways in which coordination is achieved, will produce significant productivity growth. Some analyses suggest they are right, indicating that as much, if not significantly more, of our past productivity increments have come from this source than from more capital equipment. Yet, of all the ways to improve productivity, the design of work and operations is probably the least understood, the least appreciated, and the most poorly recognized for its potential.

VISIBILITY

In part, the above finding is the result of our tendency to ascribe advances in productivity exclusively to machines like the digital computer and the nuclear power plant. Soft improvements have a very low profile. It is easy to talk about the capacity of the computer to process information, but difficult to illuminate the fact that much of the benefits that are ascribed to it may have been the result of improvements in the way the information was used in making decisions. The computer may be, in fact, quite incidental to the accompanying review of an organization's whole approach to generating information and using it for planning. Similarly, the nuclear power plant is the beneficiary of many soft improvements in the way power is distributed.

The improvement in the productivity of thousands of basic assembly jobs as the result of work design gets little notice. Placing the parts to be assembled in convenient trays, designing and positioning special tools, and providing jigs and fixtures to hold the work is not really exciting, but it results in immense productivity changes in the aggregate.

In one major metropolitan area there were 31 police jurisdictions and a serious crime problem. Machine proposals, people proposals, more cars, more computers, more patrolmen were the obvious answers, but unfortunately the money to do these things was not immediately available. Operations designers noticed that much of the crime occurred on Friday and Saturday nights and that apprehension and deterrence depended heavily on how fast a patrol unit could communicate with its headquarters. They noticed, too, that each jurisdiction had one radio channel and that there was a 90 percent chance that the channel would be tied up at any given moment on a Friday night. By simply having two jurisdictions share two channels, the probability of not being able to reach headquarters was reduced to something like 90 squared, or about 81 percent. If seven channels, the probability of a patrol unit not being able to reach headquarters at all would fall below 50 percent. Yet this kind of operations improvement, involving no more people and no more equipment, is little recognized either as an accomplishment or as a possibility.

There are many similar examples involving inventories, schedules, budgeting and allocating resources, predicting capacity requirements and so on, which are resulting in significant productivity growth, almost in spite of their low visibility.

Neglect

There are other reasons for the neglect of the "working smarter" approach, which, taken together, constitute a kind of cultural bias against "efficiency." The early image of the "efficiency expert" which surrounded the first disciples of Taylor was similar to the image which attached to many "technocrats" who were interested in the idea of efficiency as a principle for designing not just production systems but entire social systems. The efficiency expert image provokes several responses. The efficiency expert can't possibly tell managers how to improve their operations (some of them think) because all that he is an expert in is efficiency, and they understand their operations better than anyone else. In this business, things are so uncertain, so variable, and so confusing, that the ideas of efficiency which apply to simple, repetitive industrial operations are simply irrelevant. Some managers feel they've been carrying out these operations for years, and they are not about to listen to anyone who walks in and tries to suggest that the operations could be done differently or done better. Efficiency strikes at the heart of the problem of changing people's behavior, of their resentment at being told they could improve, and of their personal conviction that they are pretty much alone in understanding what they do.

The cultural bias against efficiency thrives on the notion that it means a general neglect of all human values in favor of some narrowly defined criterion of maximizing output per man-hour. It is supported also by the tendency to see that productivity improvements become ridiculous if pushed to extremes. Efficiency in the bathroom, the bedroom, or in the symphony orchestra can easily be made laughingly ludicrous. This ridicule, however, has been recently reinforced by a general disillusionment with the expert who has received the blame, not without some justification, for many prominent military and diplomatic failures, as well as some not-so-minor disasters in the fields of economics, welfare, health, and education. The cultural bias has taken as its recent target these attempts to bring those who have special knowledge into working contact with those who have the responsibility and power to act. When things have not worked out so well, the "experts" have taken much of the rap.

The bias against efficiency is also close to Veblen's famous notion of conspicuous consumption. As we prosper, one of the first things we want to buy with our wealth, usually without even thinking about it, is the privilege and pleasure of waste and inefficiency. Perhaps one of the basic luxuries in which we somewhat unconsciously indulge ourselves, is the luxury of not having to be careful, efficient, and considerate in the way we do things. Working smarter, consuming more satisfyingly, making the most of what we have—all of these require effort, attention, and time. One of the things we seem to want and seem willing to pay for is the freedom from having to exert this effort and invest this time.

It is our basic hypothesis, then, that operations design has been overall one of the most important sources of our past productivity increments. The question now is if it were a source more widely recognized, more widely understood, more frequently considered for substantial future productivity growth—what would be its potential, what could we reasonably expect?

UNDERLYING EFFECTS

Suppose we look beyond the varying titles and backgrounds of those who make a profession of operations design. Suppose we take industrial engineers, management scientists, operations analysts, and systems designers together under the more or less neutral banner of operations designers. Suppose, further, we consider operations to be a very general term including all occasions on which we bring together people, materials, equipment, computers, money, and intelligence into some sort of goal-oriented activity. Suppose we consider operations as including not only what goes on in industry but also what is happening in the service sector, in households, in government agencies, in airlines, and in hospitals. What are the common threads, the essential underlying concepts? What is the basis for the working smarter hypothesis—the idea that significant productivity growth can result from paying attention to operations design?

First, the basic belief in the futility of planning is not warranted; attention devoted to conscious design of operations will be adequately rewarded in productivity terms. The feeling that planning is futile stems from the complexity of operations, the great uncertainties about the future conditions under which they will be carried out, and the belief that those involved in operations are to a great degree powerless to anticipate and prepare for future contingencies. The futility of planning also stems from the experience that things tend to get worked out, tend to get taken care of one way or another as operations evolve. Looking ahead is not only futile, it is to a certain extent unnecessary. It seems more reasonable to accept inefficiency, lack of coordination, and the waste of resources as an irritant but part of the nature of things. It seems more sensible to put one's faith in expediters who unscramble troubled operations rather than in planners and designers who attempt to foresee these difficulties and prepare for them.

This sense of the futility of planning is neatly reinforced by the pressures of immediate affairs, the daily preoccupation with firefighting. The pressure of immediate operating problems tends to drive out planning for future operations. The structured nature of immediate problems tends to distract one's attention quite easily from the unstructured problems of the future. The necessity for working harder drives out the opportunity for working smarter.

Planning

Operations designers believe that planning is not quite futile. They believe that many, if not most, operations are undermanaged in the sense that there are pay offs to be realized from analyzing them and redesigning them. They suggest that common sense, long experience, and direct involvement may lead those who create and manage operations to do a pretty fair job, but there is a point beyond which common sense and the unaided human mind cannot go. When operations become complex, are plagued with uncertainties, depend upon subtle interactions, and are launched in pursuit of not very clear goals, then people who have the time, the mission, and are in possession of some helpful techniques can make a useful contribution to planning and design.

Perhaps the most basic precept of operations designers is that they can improve operations, not so much because they are more intelligent or have more sophisticated techniques, but because they have the mission and the time. Much of what they do is obvious once it has been done, but the point is to have the freedom from other distractions in order to do it. Many are free to admit that although some of their work involves great mathematical and experimental subtlety, some could be readily done by anyone who took the time to examine and question the way operations are being planned and conducted.

Uncertainty

In close second place is the belief that uncertainty, those aspects of the future which seem beyond our control, can be dealt with reasonably—not eliminated, not banished by clairvoyance, but dealt with reasonably in ways which yield productivity increments above and beyond their cost. How much inventory to hold, how much plant capacity, what to charge, how much material will be avilable, what future opportunities will present themselves, and a host of other questions at the very center of operations planning are matters of greater or lesser uncertainty. Operations designers believe that using historical data and expert judgment, one can be explicit about these uncertainties, and they can be stated in quantitative terms. This, then, represents the first step in moving from hunches, "seat-of-the-pants" decisions, and pure inspiration toward decisions in which we actually calculate the risks and weigh explicitly the chances of various possible futures.

Goal Clarity

In similar fashion, operations designers hold that most organizations are not particularly clear about their objectives. To say that a government is trying to achieve the greatest good for the greatest number, that a company is trying to maximize its profit, that a hospital is trying to furnish the best possible health care, and so on, is to say something which is of little use when it comes to making hard decisions about uncertain futures. Decisions which require one to trade something which is good for other things which are also good demand greater clarity. Knowing one's objectives with a clarity that is useful for decision making purposes requires some effort, some attention, and sometimes some special techniques, all of which operations designers believe are worthwhile in some situations. Explicitness—in terms of objectives, of uncertainties, and of alternative courses of action—is the price of planning.

Part of the difficulty is, of course, that it is not sensible to try for perfection in these things. It is sensible to tolerate some uncertainty, some vagueness about objectives, and to live with some confusion, some inefficiency, some idleness. The subtle aspects of the problem begin to appear when we wonder what these levels of tolerance should be. How much uncertainty or ambiguity is reasonable to tolerate? It is here that the operations designer begins to put to work some of his mathematical and experimental tools. It is here that he begins to function in the role of the traditional expert who brings some very special knowledge to the design of operations.

Operations designers also share some basic beliefs about the nature of operations themselves. It is a very tough job to find the underlying regularities which govern operations, the basic laws which will reliably predict their behavior. This means that most cases will have to be studied de novo, in the absence of very much prior theory or prior data. The study of operations thus becomes very much a research activity in which theories are newly developed, tested, and applied for each specific situation. This, of course, has strong implications for the costs associated with carrying on operations design and the uncertainties which must, in the beginning, be associated with how it will turn out.

Operations designers operate from the premise that operations, however well planned and coordinated at one moment, will with time tend to disorganize, to degenerate, and to fall apart. This means that part of the design of any operating system is the design of methods of monitoring its behavior of feedback, of the properties of self-correction, of learning from experience, and of self-innovation and self-modification. The basic dynamic law of operations may well be that organization tends to disorganization. Natural systems may be self-organizing and homeostatic; however, it is tough to create systems which will reliably recreate themselves, just as it is a tough problem to create life.

Complementarity and Coordination

Operations designers operate on a basic trade-off. Productivity can often be enhanced by bringing together activities. Two men can often be brought together in an operation in such a way that they are more than twice as productive as one man working alone. Two small computer centers can often be brought together in such a way that they are more than twice as productive as each operating separately. Indeed, two great railroads can perhaps be brought together in ways which take advantage of efficiencies, synergies, or just plain operating economies. Thus, there are advantages, technically known as complementarities, which often attend the bringing together in a system of previously distinct operations. There is, however, a price and that is the price of coordination. If two men are going to be more than twice as productive as one, somehow this will happen only if their common efforts are coordinated. In the same way, the merging of two major railroads will only succeed at the price of very considerable effort devoted to coordinating their operations. Thus, for every possibility of productivity gain through complementarity, there is the price in terms of the necessary coordination. Coordination involves managers, planners, management information systems, control systems, reporting systems, and so on. The basic trade-off with which operations designers struggle is the attempt to discern when the benefits of complementarity will exceed the associated coordination costs.

Implementation

Finally, operations designers acknowledge some special difficulties associated with the implementation of their work, with its actual translation into operations and operational practice. Their work is "soft." It is hard to demonstrate its payoff, its effectiveness in advance. Unlike the builder of the better mousetrap, they cannot give the client a demonstration. The client must have faith, be willing to accept a degree of uncertainty, and be able to see that investments in operations design may contend reasonably with his opportunities to invest in machines or in motivating people. It is hard to give prior assurance of the effectiveness of operations design; even after the design is finished, it is often difficult to attribute the various good and bad results to the work of the operations designers. They must often be content with sharing the credit with others who participated in the creation and execution of the operations. Their work tends to fade unless constantly attended to, because organization, they believe, tends toward disorganization. Innovations in operations design, techniques for achieving productivity growth from this source are slow to diffuse, compete unfavorably with hardware innovations, are not capitalized, and have no market value in most cases. Operations design is often seen as being nice but not essential to the conduct of producing activities and may be among the first to go when the decision is made that something must be cut back in order to "save money." Thus, operations designers realize and struggle to cope with some very special problems associated with the implementation of their efforts—problems which are central to our estimate of the future potential of productivity growth from this source.

METHODS FOR DESIGNING OPERATIONS

How do operations designers go about their business? What are the essential characteristics of their methods? The answer is that their business is much the same as what is done by engineers and scientists generally. The science of trying to understand the productivity of operations and their engineering design are not fundamentally distinct from other logical and experimental attempts to plan and to create. Like all engineers and scientists, operations designers have their individual and personal styles of professional activity. Some like to read the literature first, and some do not. Some begin by formulating models and theories; others begin by getting some casual data about the phenomenon in question. Some are loners, and some need the stimulation of groups; some have their best ideas in the middle of the night, and some are inspired by two-martini lunches. Behind their personal styles, however, can be detected some basic methodological regularities.

The essence of their methods is not in the exotic mathematical structures they create, the elaborate data collection programs they arrange, or the quantities of computer time they find necessary. Rather the essence lies in three basic activities, which are alternated, iterated, varied, extended, or attenuated as the particular design situation seems to require. The basic step is an explicit examination of the operational system in question—trying to be specific and explicit about what it is supposed to accomplish, what outputs it may yield, what inputs it may require, what methods it will employ, and what uncertainties surround its behavior. This examination is carried on with an ever-present set of questions in mind. How can the operations be improved, made more productive, more reliable, safer, less demanding of resources? Sometimes this examination leads directly to ideas which are obviously useful, obviously valid, and can be implemented directly. These are the improvements which are widely attributed to something called "common sense," the ideas which, after they have been created, seem obvious.

Models

Sometimes this examination discloses that the system is complex and subtle, and that possibilities for enhancing its productivity are likewise going to be complex and subtle. In these cases, the work of the operations designer is to create a laboratory animal whose behavior he can study experimentally without the prohibitive cost of studying the behavior of the real production system itself. The laboratory animal turns out to be a mathematical model—a mathematical representation of the production system itself. The model tries to capture the essential decisions involved in operating the system, the behaviors of the machines, the people, and the resources which enter the system. The model tries to capture the uncertainties which surround these behaviors and the objectives toward which the operation of the producing system is directed. If the model is large and complex, it will be mechanized by programming it on the digital computer. If the model is simple, its behavior may be studied by the designer using only paper and pencil.

The creation of the model is not simply an exercise in mathematical logic. It requires a good deal of qualitative observation about the composition of the producing system and the way it generally works. In addition, a lot of quantitative data will be required to give reality, life, and precision to the statements contained in the model. All sorts of data on capacities, responses, interactions, rates, and levels will be sought. More often than not, this data will not be readily available in the organization. Much of the cost of operations design arises from the need to get data on costs, benefits, operating relationships, and so on, which are not already a part of the system's existing information gathering arrangements.

With the model brought to life by the data, its behavior can be studied. This is essentially a process of asking the model questions, asking it to predict the behavior of the real production system if various sorts of productivity enhancing strategies were carried out in actuality. What would happen if some things were increased, some were decreased, and some left alone? What would happen if resources were allocated in a different way, if decisions were based on more information and alternative logics, if the work was distributed differently among people and machines? What would happen if alternative sets of assumptions about the future are made? What will be the possible behaviors of our customers, our suppliers, our working people, our stockholders, and so on, in the future? All sorts of questions are asked of the model, and it responds by making predictions about the productivity of the real producing system.

Predictions

The quality and the reliability of the model's predictions are obviously the central issue here. Models may be roundly criticized for being incomplete, inaccurate, or even simplistic; but the basic issue is whether or not they are better than their competition. The competition is the unaided human manager, who may have lots of experience but still has the severe cognitive limitations which we all share to a degree. Models generally seem to be simplifications of reality; they seem lacking in the infinitude of subtleties which experienced humans claim to consider, and lacking in the flexibility of the active mind. Yet, there is a general and growing experience that decisions made with the aid of models have a very good chance of being better than decisions made without them. Models supply a consistency which humans often lack; they supply a capacity for detail, and a capacity for complex and extended reasoning which humans cannot hope to approach. The data which seems to favor models is interesting and to some extent surprising.

One sort of study is producing evidence which shows that managers may be pretty good operations designers on the average, but they are not very reliable. That is, their variations from being "good on the average" are frequent and costly; their selective attention to variables, all of which they cannot simultaneously consider, produces an inconsistent pattern of results. Models do better than unaided humans, this data is indicating, primarily because of their consistency and their capacity for detail.

Still another type of study is challenging our basic conceit about the effectiveness and subtlety of human judgment. In a classic study of clinical psychologists, the presumption of these professionals that they could make all sorts of subtle judgments through personal contact with their clients, and that these subtleties were essential to making good predictions of client behavior, received a stunning shock. A mathematical model, and not a very complex one at that, taking as its input some readily observable data and some test scores, was able to make consistently better predictions of client behavior than were the psychologists themselves. This immediately produced an excited flurry of attempts to repudiate the superiority of the model; but similar findings have been produced in the case of professional financial managers, physicians, and managers themselves. The conceit which we all share about the effectiveness of our judgmental processes, when applied to the design of production systems, may not indeed be really warranted.

Into Action

The third element of the methodology of operations designers is implementation—the test of the hypothesis which the model has advanced in its predictions about how best to design the system. Will the model turn out to be even partially correct in its predictions about the productivity of particular policies and arrangements? Designers persist in regarding the predictions of their models as hypotheses, although they see these as the hypotheses most likely to succeed, most likely to turn out to be effective in enhancing system productivity.

This third and final step involves the decision on the part of management to innovate, to actually make the experiment with the real system. As with other sorts of innovation decisions, this one is characterized by high uncertainty about the results and the payoffs. The implementation decision creates a special set of difficulties for the operations designer which may well be either a limiting constraint on this source of productivity improvements or the key to far greater results if it can be better understood.

This method, which roughly characterizes most production system design efforts, is not inexpensive. It often takes more time, more money, and more manpower than the client anticipates. It often requires the client and his people to participate actively with the designer in the process of creating the model and collecting the data to bring it to life. It requires sufficient lead time to carry out the design process, sufficient skill to turn vague problems into well defined models, and sufficient patience to gather the necessary data. It is not unreasonable to wonder whether the cost of such an approach to productivity growth is likely to be matched by the benefits. It is not unreasonable to hesitate when one comes to appreciate the uncertainty which necessarily surrounds all answers to this question. It is perhaps very reasonable to wonder about the potential of productivity as a soft science.

THE POTENTIAL

The potential for productivity enhancement through working smarter is not especially clear. In part, this is a result of past overselling of the approach—creating false expectations which tended to be optimistic, followed inevitably by disappointments which lead to the extremes of pessimism. In part, it is due to the work of operations designers themselves who have sometimes been quite justly accused of being more interested in the development of their methods and the creation of mathematical models than in the achievement of actual results to improve productivity in real production systems. In part, it is also the result of the flat-top hypothesis, the hypothesis that there are a rather broad range of systems designs which are nearly as good as the very best design. An alert and experienced management is likely to be able to get the system in the neighborhood of the best design without too much difficulty. The refined methods of the operations designer then serve to produce only small percentage increases in the system productivity. Although these may be small percentages of very large numbers when big systems are involved, they are, nevertheless, small percentages. The greatest uncertainty about the potential of operations design stems, however, from the twin sources of the apparent uniqueness of each individual production system and the special difficulties associated with bringing a management to make the decision to innovate, to try out the design.

We have the macroeconomic data which attributes a significant part of our past productivity increments to the work of operations designers. We have, from time to time, the public record of what has been achieved in particular systems, in particular situations. The curious thing, however, is that in spite of this growing record of past results, most managers see this as only the most limited help in estimating the payoffs from future benefits. It is a property of both the current state of the art in operations design and the current state of our understanding of the similarities and differences among production systems, that this record permits only the weakest of inferences about future payoffs. There appear to be such important differences among production systems, that only the weakest kind of generalizations seem warranted on the basis of our experience so far.

The potential also depends heavily on the seemingly unique approaches of different management groups to the decision to innovate in the field of proposals for working smarter. This innovation decision is, as we have emphasized, typically a high uncertainty choice, with heavy losses a possibility as well as heavy gains. It is a decision which is seen as being irreversible to a great degree. Once in, it is hard to get out. It compares unfavorably in the view of many managements with other productivity enhancing strategies. Operations designers are beginning to make some progress in understanding implementation, however. It is beginning to appear that the probability of actually seeing their work translated into action depends on their past record of success within the organization. If they can demonstrate competence through a series of rather quick, high payoff projects which produce a kind of validating basis for their work, they have a markedly greater chance of achieving further implementation. It appears that the probability of implementation is proportional to the degree of client involvement in the design process. The method of simply producing an expert, master-minded solution is inferior to having client personnel participate in the creation of the model, the development of design concepts, the interpretation of the data, and the judgments that must be made about the output of the model. Continuous and active client participation in the process seems to be significantly more effective than having experts reveal a solution at a final briefing. Designers are beginning to understand, as well, that the probability of implementation depends on how well the design matches the personal management and decision making styles of those involved, how well it matches the style of working and innovating which characterizes the organization as a whole, and how well the history of the organization predisposes it toward the sort of design being suggested. Still the understanding which is available regarding the implementation decision and the effectiveness of various implementation strategies is weak and confronts us with very considerable difficulties when it comes to estimating the potential payoff from operations design.

This incomplete knowledge, these uncertainties, the uniqueness and the individuality of particular situations leave us with only one alternative for the rational development of working smarter strategies. We must adopt a plan of continuous experimentation as the only route possible in the absence of well developed general theories and reliable experience.

DEVELOPING A STRATEGY

The basic formula of the operations designer is prediction, planning, and productivity. The reasonable management of uncertainty will, he hopes, result in predictions of the future demands on his system and the behavior of the people and equipment which are its elements. These predictions, while not representing complete elimination of uncertainty, provide the basis for planning the production systems. His plans are aimed always at arranging, combining, eliminating, and modifying the operations and the decisions in order to produce highly productive systems.

In spite of all the data on the effectiveness of operations design in the large, individual situations, particular working people, and particular management decision makers resist generalizations about what the payoff will be in any specific instance. Lacking a general theory, the basic strategy for this sort of productivity improvement must be one of continuous experimentation to accumulate knowledge about the rewards that may be expected for each production system.

The operations designer has before him two fundamentally opposed organizational strategies; which will be the more effective is not very clear at this state of our knowledge. He may, on the one hand, take the view that everyone in an organization should become involved in the improvement of their own productivity and should have a strong incentive to do so. In such a situation, profit centers are created to stimulate and attribute productivity growth to the individual managers of these centers. Working people are given a considerable measure of freedom to plan their work and to experiment with ways of increasing their productivity, combined with a responsibility and an incentive for productivity growth. In this sort of atmosphere, the operations designer functions as an internal consultant, providing specialized tools and offering suggestions drawn from his background of experience. In this atmosphere, everyone is supposed to have a strong interest in productivity improvement and some basic competence which will permit the achievement of such improvements. Whether or not these conditions can be found or created in a given system is difficult to foresee, and experimentation again appears to be the only route to understanding.

On the other hand, the operations designer may operate as an expert by studying the system and involving the participants in his work—and taking the intellectual leadership in productivity improvement. The designer cooperates with managers in the selection of projects and consults widely with those whose behavior is likely to be influenced by the results of his work. He retains, however, the central role of the professional who defines opportunities to improve the productivity results of the system and takes the leadership in seeking the implementation of his solutions. In some organizations this may very well be the only way anything will get done; yet in others, it may succeed only in suppressing the great contribution which the managers and the working people might otherwise make to productivity improvement. If there is an expert around to worry about it, perhaps everyone else will simply forget about it. If everyone else forgets, those simple basic, common sense things which have such a significant productivity payoff will not get done. The basic choice of organizational strategy is one in which there is some history of success and some history of failure associated with each option. Experimentation, because of our imperfect understanding of these experiences, would appear to be the only alternative in dealing with these fundamental uncertainties.

Likewise, the actual conduct of the work of operations design is itself very much a matter of experimentation. Only in these most simple situations is the solution achieved in one system useful to another. Each system must be studied, and experiments made with a mathematical or conceptual model of the system; the resulting indications should be tried out experimentally in the real system. It is a field in which innovation is the rule and imitation a rarity. Experimentation is consistent with our state of knowledge, but it is also the route to some grasp of the natural laws of operations which would permit far stronger generalizations than we now find possible.

FROM THE MANAGEMENT POINT OF VIEW

It is by no means clear, however, that such a strategy of experimentation with ways of working smarter can ever be translated into an appealing policy to management. We may argue that experimentation must be continuous because operations change, learning occurs, and organization tends toward confusion. We may argue that clear understanding of an organization's goals is important to productivity growth, and that this difficult task is essentially an experimental undertaking. We may argue that experimentation is functional in itself; that it raises the level of interest in productivity, increases involvement in the goals of the organization, enlists the knowledge and the creative forces of everyone involved, gives people an openness to change and a confidence in meeting it, and that it is a route toward the growing effectiveness of coordinated operations and interested people. Yet, from the viewpoint of many managers, the very notion of experimentation smacks of risk and demands extreme caution.

It is clear that the decision to innovate in operations design involves considerable uncertainty—typically greater uncertainty than capital investments or perhaps even research and development. But it seems equally clear that the payoffs associated with success are very high, as unfortunately are the penalties for failure. The question before us then is whether or not a strategy of experimentation could be proposed which would be widely attractive to managers. Could the risks and the rewards be arranged by judicious experimental design so that there would be a more general willingness to act? Clearly the degree of risk involved is a plausible explanation of why the diffusion of innovations in the area of operations design appears to be significantly slower than the diffusion of other sorts of innovations. Can we suggest that the potential for productivity growth is, in a specific situation, of the same order of magnitude as it has been in other similar situations? Can we suggest that experimentation, even when it seems to fail, raises the general level of reasonableness in an organization, increases the knowledge of the participants about their system and each other, and that experimentation, if it just takes place, carries the strong message that the organization is interested in productivity and that this message will have its own effects? It remains to be seen whether or not a broad management conservatism can be overcome, a conservatism which often appears as a bias in favor of investing in machines or schemes for making people work harder rather than smarter. In too many situations, when it is time to cut costs, the "working smarter" people are among the earliest to be considered expendable. We will turn to these questions shortly in an attempt to suggest positive answers.

Notes

A good example of one of the modern classics is Barnes, Ralph M. *Motion and Time Study*. New York: McGraw-Hill, 1949.

Two outstanding reflections of the trend since 1950 toward

quantitative and experimental approaches to larger scale problems are:

Giffin, Walter C. *Introduction to Operations Engineering*. Homewood, Ill.: Richard D. Irwin, 1971.

Wagner, Harvey M. *Principles of Operations Research*. Englewood Cliffs, N.J.: Prentice-Hall, Inc., 1969.

There is much literature on decision analysis. Two excellent works which illustrate the experimental and the analytical points of view are:

Raiffa, Howard *Introductory Lectures on Decision Theory*. New York: McGraw-Hill, 1971.

Schlaifer, Robert. *Analysis of Decisions Under Uncertainty*. New York: McGraw-Hill, 1969.

6
On the Grand Scale

IS BIGGER BETTER?

What economists call economies of scale constitutes what seems to be an obvious strategy for achieving high productivity. The economic ideas involved are old, clear, and of great generality. The more one produces, the cheaper the production costs. There are some fixed costs involved no matter how many products are made; even if a large number are made, these fixed costs remain pretty well fixed. The larger the number of units over which one "spreads" the fixed costs, the lower the unit cost. It therefore makes sense to get big, to standardize, and to mass produce. But this involves some subtle balancing of capacities and resources. The equally famous law of diminishing marginal returns says that if one tries to make too many products by increasing one of the resources relative to the others, the returns from these increases will fall. Things will start to get expensive again. If a person has a plant of given size and capacity, and he tries to get more and more production out, he will pay overtime premiums and neglect maintenance; workers will get tired and careless, and costs will start to go up again. But even with this caution, productivity ought to increase in an interesting way if operations are enlarged.

Bigness, real bigness, however, may be a mixed blessing. In the 1930's during the Depression, Justice Brandeis suggested that the major corporations ought to be broken up because they had become too big for human beings to manage. We have had ambivalent attitudes toward such big organizations for a long time. Social commentators continue to say that they are too large and have grown overly powerful and unresponsive. They are seen as inefficient, noncompetitive, uneconomic in the user of resources, dedicated to minimizing risk and uncertainty, and more interested in continuity and expansion than in human needs. It seems clear, on the other hand, that as customers we prefer the reputation of the big appliance manufacturer, the service organization of the big auto manufacturer, and the route structure of the big airline; and when we want somebody to really do something about a social problem, we prefer the power of big government. Productivity for the consumer translates into huge markets, high volume production, and low prices—all the work of big corporations.

Bigness, on the other hand, holds the possibility of market dominance and the threat of anti-trust proceedings. Some congressmen continue to talk about the necessity for breaking up General Motors, and one staff proposal suggested making each of that firm's plants an entirely separate company. There is a well established belief in the auto industry, however, that one cannot even cover one's costs unless one makes 250,000 cars a year.

Thus, the basic problem is despite the productivity advantages associated with getting bigger, there is at least the fear that one could get too big, encountering not only legal difficulties but perhaps productivity difficulties as well. Is it possible that the strategy of becoming more productive by producing more can be carried too far? Is it possible that it already has been carried too far by our big corporations, big hospitals, big railroads, and big government agencies?

ORGANIZATIONAL GROWTH

Large organizations can be managed not by a single brain, but through coordinated decisions made by many. Just how decisions are to be delegated and the resulting actions coordinated is the central question in organization design. It seems clear that since the information handling and decision making capacities of the chief executive are finite, the organization must eventually grow beyond the point where the executive becomes a limiting factor bringing about diminishing returns. Things begin to get out of hand, and the organization is regarded as too big.

As a firm grows, one might imagine the transformation of its internal structure taking place along the following general lines. When the chief executive finds his information processing and decision making capacities taxed toward their limit, he delegates some work to his subordinates. Thus begins the emergence of an elaborate hierarchy of line managers who come into existence through delegation of the work of managing. This immediately raises the problem of coordination. How are the actions and decisions of these managers made compatible, with each other and with the objectives of the firm as a whole? As the lines of communication multiply and lengthen, the possibilities for delays in decision making, uncertainty about what is going on in the firm, and incompatible decisions increase.

As these processes are taking place through delegation, another kind of change emerges. The volume of decisions grows to the point where specialized information and advice to support various classes of decisions are not only required but can be easily justified economically. Thus begins the evolution of staff services within the company to fill these two needs. Some staff services, such as accounting, function chiefly to provide information for coordination and control and help to assure the compatibility of decisions made by various managers within the firm. Other staff services give specialized advice — such as the legal, marketing, or personnel staffs.

Some have been concerned lest the progress of delegation lead eventually to such a large and complex hierarchy of line managers that increasing costs of administration per worker and increasing delays in making decisions would result in a firm uneconomical to manage. When the chief executive finds that the number of subordinates who report to him has grown beyond some vaguely defined point of effectiveness, another level in the organizational hierarchy is instituted. This process continues by increasing the number of levels of management as the size of the organization grows. The number of subordinates reporting to a superior is called the span of control. Both experience and evidence tend to indicate that, contrary to such fears, the growth of line management will not itself create an excessive burden on the organization. If the span of control is kept constant, the number of line managers tends to grow exponentially with the number of levels in the hierarchy, but so also does the number of workers. Thus, the ratio of managers to workers tends to remain nearly constant. In the companies studied by Mason Haire, it also appeared that as they grew the span of control tended to increase. (See Notes at the end of this chapter.) In firms having between 20 and 50 employees, the average span of control was 11.5 subordinates per superior. When, however, these firms grew to a size of more than 200 employees, the span of control had increased to 21. Haire also discovered that the precentage of employees in top and middle management dropped over the same growth span from 13.6 percent to 4.1 percent. It may well be that in the long run the capacities of top management are not the limiting factor in the growth of the firm.

As the line functions grow, they must, however, be supported by the addition of staff services. How does the staff emerge and grow? Again, the four companies whose histories Haire examined in detail give us the first clues. He defined the term staff as all those who provide specialized support, advice, and help for line personnel. Line personnel, in turn, include all those directly concerned with the making and selling of the product. The companies he examined began with nearly everyone falling into the category of line positions. During the first six to ten years in the lives of these companies, the proportion of staff increased very rapidly indeed. At the end of this period, however, the percentage of staff people tended to stabilize — in two of the firms at about 50 percent, and in the other two at about 20 percent. If one were to generalize from this, it might be suggested that in the early years the staff will grow geometrically while the line grows linearly; but later, this relation relaxes into one of parallel growth. It is interesting to note that staff employment appears more stable than line employment, which remains quite insensitive to reductions in the work force.

Another study, somewhat differently conceived from that of Haire has been done by Baker and Davis. They also were interested in the emergence and growth of the staff, but chose to study some 211 companies of various sizes at a single point in time rather than examine the life histories of individual firms. Out of such data came a number of interesting insights.

They suggest that every time a firm adds 100 direct workers, the number of indirect workers increases by 75, regardless of the size of the firm before the addition. This finding agrees in general with the pattern of parallel growth that emerged in the later years of the companies Haire examined.

These studies suggest some useful hypotheses. Apparently, the emergence and early growth of the staff is rather dramatic when the firm is small and young. The staff groups quickly achieve an institutional existence and may come to constitute an important portion of the organization. As time passes and the firm grows, the expansion of the staff settles down to a pattern paralleling that of the line or direct employees. At the same time, the number of middle and top managers increases at a decreasing rate, so that this group eventually comes to constitute a smaller portion of the organization.

The types of changes in form and structure that take place as an organization grows are those that are necessary to meet and overcome the forces tending to destroy the organization. This principle, drawn from studies of the growth of organisms, suggests that the emergence and growth of the organization's staff functions, in association with and in response to delegation, support the organization where the need arises. The functions of the staff groups include the gathering and processing of information for decision making, coordination, and control, and furnishing specialized advice in particular fields. Thus the staff is the chief bulwark against lack of communication, conflicting and incompatible decisions, and general disorganization —the potential destructive forces that threaten a large firm.

From the negatively accelerated growth of top and middle management one might also draw the conclusion that the staff is an effective means of increasing the abilities and capacities of management. It appears that the staff groups make possible the management of larger firms with relatively fewer managers, but without a runaway increase in the size of the staff itself. Clearly, it does not appear that the staff-management hierarchy is going to become a limiting factor in the growth of the firm.

As the firm expands and accommodates itself to the capacities of management through delegation, the need for coordination increases. Studies of how executives use their time reveal large portions of it spent in giving and receiving information.

Some have supposed the difficulties and costs associated with coordinating widely delegated decisions would eventually operate to limit the growth of the firm.

When decision making responsibilities are delegated, responsibilities for coordination of decisions at lower levels are delegated as well. Thus the demands of coordination placed upon different members of management may be varied by altering the structure of the organization itself. A critical variable in understanding the problems of coordination in any organization is the degree of self-containment of the organization's various subunits. When two or more units compete for a share of some common resources, such as the capital budget of the firm, or when the output of one subunit forms the input of another, they cannot be considered highly self-contained. The less the degree of self-containment, the greater the need for detailed coordination and control.

An important aspect of the problem of organization design involves making these divisions self-contained to a large extent and thus reducing the burden of coordination. The ultimate extension of this line of development, which is often discussed but seldom truly approached in practice, is to permit the divisions to operate as virtually independent business units so that coordination will be reduced to a minimum. The trick, of course, is to do this and yet assure that the division operates in order to advance the objectives of the firm as a whole.

The evolutionary changes in the design of the subunits of the organization are often thought to proceed along the following lines. When the organization is small, the subunits tend to be formed by grouping similar processes together, as for example in the typical departmentalized manufacturing plant. As the organization grows, however, the advantages obtained from process-organized subunits tend to be outweighed by the increasing costs of coordination. The advantage shifts eventually to the organization of subunits according to purpose or end product, thus substantially reducing the need for coordination.

There are a variety of assertions about the virtues and vices of bigness, none of which seem to be decidable on the basis of the data which is now available. It is argued that big organizations are not innovative, and that relatively few inventions or major innovations have come from them. It is argued, on the contrary, that only large organizations can afford the expenditures necessary to undertake major research programs and can accept the risks associated with the decision to innovate. Some have asserted that big organizations are sluggish, unwieldy, and unresponsive to the changing demands of the market. Others have responded that only large organizations can afford the market research and the great market contact which makes it possible to anticipate changes in customer desires. Large organizations are praised for providing a great variety of opportunities for people, and at the same time they are condemned as being the chief perpetrators of the highly specialized, routine, repetitive jobs which are supposed to dehumanize working people.

Growth, even in the terms of this simplified description, is thus a complex process. As an organization grows, some things get better and some things get worse. In an attempt to accommodate to these effects, the company changes its organizational structure as it grows. The question of whether the balance is in favor of those things which are getting better or in favor of those which are getting worse, is something that is really not well understood by those who control organizations or those who study them. If this is true—if in fact organizations are growing without really understanding whether or not they are becoming more productive or relatively more profitable—then we would seem to have at least two serious problems. First, if organizations are continuing to grow without knowing whether or not this is increasing productivity or return on investment, why are they growing, what drives the process? Second, do we have any idea whether what is driving growth has driven it beyond the point of economies of scale, beyond the point where greater size means greater productivity?

THE VIRTUE OF GROWTH AND
THE PROBLEM OF SIZE

It is some help to separate the process of growth, which is generally seen as good, from the result of growth, which is not as clearly appraised. The process of growth is most likely strongly driven by considerations other than productivity. To grow is to build security, to reduce the threat of competition, to have the strength to survive adversity. To grow is inherently good because it demonstrates accomplishment and achievement; growing is synonymous with succeeding. It is not surprising that there is a managerial bias in favor of growth. Growing permits new things to be done without taking resources away from old things. Growing means excitement, stimulation, and high morale. Growth means big deals and big results, and the opportunity to neglect, at least for a while, the petty, uninteresting details of careful management.

There is the somewhat mystical view that an organization must either grow or perish. For reasons that may not be entirely clear, a stable organization is not viable. Growth is a sort of American good—a good which is seldom really challenged by those who are in a position to influence the progress of major organizations. Thus there seems to be a plausible case for the notion that many of our organizations are growing and will continue to grow, not only for reasons other than increased productivity, but also in the absence of knowledge of the consequences of further growth for greater or lesser productivity.

The problem of size is that size alone is not a very powerful factor in explaining productivity. It is not just size, it's synergies. If several totally unrelated and independent companies are combined in a conglomerate, then all of the companies can, it is supposed, benefit from a higher level of management skill, a greater strength of capitalization, and an ability to withstand adversity that none of the companies alone could achieve. If a stamping plant and an assembly plant are put together, cars can be produced more economically than if the two plants are independently managed. If one division makes cameras and another makes films, the productivity of each is enhanced by its relationship with the other. If two truck lines are merged, the productivity of the two is greater than twice the productivity of either separately. Large organizations can get along with proportionately less working capital, less inventory, less computer capacity, and less of many shared resources than can small organizations. Synergism means simply that when activities are put together under the same management, they achieve results which are proportionately greater than when they are managed separately. Synergism is simply the enrichment of the notion that when two men work together in a coordinated fashion, they can very often achieve more than twice the output of either working alone. How synergistic a large organization is depends in part on the nature of the activities it encompasses and in part on the skill of management in bringing about the necessary coordination of actions.

Size alone does not tell the story of productivity. Size is not, in spite of the simple appeal of the notion of economies of scale, a strong explanation of how productive an organization may or may not be. From the point of view of productivity, size has some "goods" as well as some "bads."

Beyond Economies Scale

Given that growth is driven by considerations which are likely to be other than those of productivity; given that the relationship between size and productivity is unreliable, little understood, and difficult to understand, it would appear that there may well be a number of large organizations which have grown beyond the point of productivity enhancement. They may very well have gone from the region of economies of scale to diseconomies. Further growth, while it may have its own special virtues, is not likely to increase productivity. Thus, it may be a good time for our very large organizations in all sectors of the economy to at least ask themselves the question of whether further growth will enhance or detract from their productivity. It is clearly a complex question, and it is unlikely to yield to any simple hypotheses about the optimum size for any kind of an organization. But there seems at least to be the real possibility that for some organizations, further growth will not produce productivity increments.

EXPERIMENTING

Just how this question is to be asked and answered is far from a trivial matter. It is easy enough to call for the breakup of organizations which are supposed to have grown too big, but it is virtually impossible to produce much in the way of evidence to support the case. Nobody has ever demonstrated that an organization, simply because of its size, has entered the region of diseconomies of scale. It is all very well to suggest that when management detects that diseconomies are about to begin, they should plan to give birth to new, highly independent organizations that can have a capacity for growth and can benefit once again from economies of scale. How is this really to be done?

We have little or no useful general theory about what happens to productivity as growth occurs. What happens seems to depend very much on the specific, individual situation one is considering. We have not only little theory, but really very little data for any particular organization concerning what happens to productivity as it grows. Growth is typically being motivated by other considerations, almost nobody takes a look at what would happen to productivity if the organization got smaller rather than bigger. In such a situation there is little one can do except experiment.

The way in which we will discover the onset of diseconomies of scale is through the careful consideration by large and growing organizations of what happens to productivity as they are growing. Each increment of growth needs to be preceded by careful estimates of productivity changes and followed by auditing and analysis of what actually happened to productivity. Continuous experimentation of this sort appears to be the only rational basis for viewing the productivity effects of size. Clearly, size may have other advantages, but it would seem reasonable that these other advantages be weighed a little more explicitly against the productivity considerations which go along with them. A number of very knowledgeable observers have questioned the productivity advantages of further growth for our big organizations, and it is perhaps time to enrich the discussion with some data; data which does not seek vast generalities, but indicates the results of specific experiments in specific situations.

Notes

Senator Phillip A. Hart's bill to break up some of our biggest corporations, and the staff proposal for the dismemberment of General Motors are discussed in *Business Week*, March 2, 1974.

A current example of social commentary on the evils of bigness is Goodwin, Richard C. *The American Condition*. New York: Doubleday, 1974.

The studies by Mason Haire and by Baker and Davis are described in Haire, M., editor. *Modern Organizational Theory*. New York: Wiley, 1959.

An outstanding explanation of what happens as organizations grow is presented in Leavitt, Harold J., and others. *The Organizational World*. New York: Harcourt Brace Jovanovich, 1973.

Among the latest and most prominent calls for an examination of the possibility that further growth may be unproductive is that of Peter Drucker in *Management: Tasks, Responsibilities, Practices*. New York: Harper and Row, 1974.

7
New Targets:
The Managers

THE GENTLE HERESY

Managers are almost universally comfortable with the notion that a prominent part of their opportunity and their responsibility is the development of productivity growth in the organizations which they manage. It is an opportunity they generally accept rather readily and an accomplishment they strive for. Heresy of heresies: the productivity of managers themselves, as distinct from the systems they are managing, might be usefully examined. It is important to be clear—we are talking about the productivity of those who manage, not the productivity of the production systems which they manage. This is an idea which might be entertained in the context of a few smiling and ridiculous classics like Parkinson's Law or the more recent Peter Principle, but surely if there is any bite behind their humor, it has no serious local application. Managers, after all, are judged practically, pragmatically, and in the hardest of hard-nosed traditions. They are judged not by what they decide, nor by how busy they are, nor by anything that could be called their output. They are evaluated on the basis of results, of what happens, of the "bottom line." If the bottom line looks good, then managers are, by definition, being effective, and the question of their productivity is not only meaningless but irrelevant.

Nonetheless, it might be interesting to fearlessly raise the question of how productive managers are, and whether or not one of the keys to the resolution of the productivity crunch might possibly be discovered here. Nobody knows how productive managers generally are, largely because nobody (or hardly anybody) has looked. Ultimately, we will have to consider the potential for management productivity improvement in terms of individual differences, not in terms of broad generalities; but let us begin, at least, with a few of the generalities which have some currency.

The marvelous notion that work expands to fill the time available in which to do it, in spite of its persistently plausible interpretation of much that we see going on around us, is not fact, nor data, nor the sort of evidence on which to base a serious examination of management productivity. On top of which, super-scientism comes quickly to the rescue once again. Nobody could possibly define or measure "objectively" the productivity of those who manage, and what we cannot measure does not exist. What does not exist is difficult to improve. Productivity is, after all, a concept that is useful in looking at the behavior or working people, not managers.

Yet we must, to some degree, honor our experience and recognize that our predispositions are not entirely prejudices. The suspicions, the stereotypes, and the folklore of management do say some things which might just be the smoke which signals the presence of at least a little fire. If we consider that the nonproduction working people constitute 62 percent of our work force, and that management, broadly defined, includes a lot of these people, it ought to be worth a look. If we recall that in 1970, companies were "laying off" managers to the point where it was reliably estimated that the unemployment rate among executives was 10 to 14 percent, then obviously somebody thought they could get along without all the managers they once needed. Managers have been singularly secure in their jobs in the face of business recessions (one of the prerogatives of being a manager), but in October 1970, executive employment firms were estimating that more top management people were out of work than at any time since the Depression of the 1930's. There is thus some reason to suspect the presence of what is technically called "organizational slack."

MODELS OF MANAGERS

The folklore runs the gamut from the rational model of the manager, fully engaged in his appointed tasks (planning, organizing, integrating, and controlling), to the "dealer" whose major activities are office politics and empire building. If there is any substance at all to these ideas, then management productivity is probably highly variable and strongly a matter of individual differences. If this is so, then one can invoke the fundamental law: the greater the variability in productivity, the greater the potential for improvement.

At the top of our great organizations, so the folklore goes, are those who have arrived, whose work and lives seem incredibly productive. These are the people who operate in a highly self-directed fashion in a world of very long hours, private planes, and executive secretaries. They are the super-achievers, stimulated by success, who are well along the road toward realization of their full potentials. No need to worry about their productivity. They create new functions and new activities almost at will. They have no motivational problem, seeing freedom, power, rewards, and self-realization as fully within their grasp if they only do what they are fully confident they know how to do.

At the bottom of the management ladder, at the base of the pyramid, at the lowest levels of the hierarchy, are the "firing line" types, those who are directly in charge of the production operations. They hope they have the appropriate caliber which will tend to float them toward the top, partially because of the big payoffs in power and money, and partially because as a front line manager one works very hard indeed. "Float" they think is a good word for it because how far one rises depends partly on their performance, partly on circumstances totally beyond their control, and partly on politics and diplomacy. One needs luck, skill, and contacts. As the operating managers, they must cope with all the immediate crises of the ongoing production system. The breakdowns, the absenteeism, the grievances, and the union stewards hit these people first. There is rarely anyone to delegate things to, nor anyone to put in charge while the operating manager takes care of something else. How things go depends a lot on the kind of backup support the manager gets from above, but he has very little control over that. There is no need to worry very much about the productivity of the "firing line" people—at least if there is any truth at all to this sort of stereotype.

The Middle Men

Between the chief executive officers and the front line people are the mass of the chosen, the elect, the emergent of the managerial group, known simply as middle management. They would like to see themselves and to be seen as bright, hard working, "upwardly mobile," and very much on top of things in their own areas of responsibility. It is here, however, that the evidence which isn't really evidence keeps leaking out. Here is the area where stories keep coming forth about managers creating new activities, new jobs, and new empires. The more people he supervises, the bigger his organization, the better off he is. Here is the area in which it is virtually impossible to get a manager to admit that he has too much of anything. Nor can he readily admit uncertainty or indecision. From the middle management area comes a steady trickle of studies indicating the amount of time spent in meetings, the vigorous reading and writing of interoffice communications, and the amount of effort devoted to office politicking. From here come the studies of "daylighting," that wonderful possibility of spending lots of time in each others' offices, in conferences, and in very pleasant seminars which handle all types of interesting topics and give every appearance of the energetic pursuit of one's duties. This is the area of a very high degree of self-definition of jobs, of "buck passing" and blame casting, and of proving one's real executive potential by delegating. It is also the province of those whose frustrations have finally reached an equilibrium with their achievement drives. They no longer see the top spot as a real target. They have, with great skill indeed, discovered that level of activity which assures them the stability and the security of a salaried semi-retirement.

Middle management is also the province of that contemporary rediscovery of pragmatism, "Management by Objectives," The policy is: let's get together and set some goals, some objectives for the coming year, then your job is simply to achieve.

If you make it, wonderful, but often vague things are promised. Your chances for advancement will be markedly improved. The important thing is to achieve the goals which "we" set for you. Nobody will worry much about how you do it, the details of how you spend your time, the methods you use, or the decisions you make. These are pretty much up to you; all that really counts is whether or not you reach the objectives. Never mind that the tendency to see everything in terms of results distracts us from the development of management methods and decision-making techniques which may improve the reliability of the results. After all, it takes both luck and skill, and it's quite easy to ascribe such importance to luck in order to conclude that skill development is not very worthwhile.

The fine art of being managed by objectives is simple enough; to set objectives which are appealing because they represent an improvement over what has been done and which, in addition, have certain very special qualities which greatly moderate the risk of failure. Ideally, the objectives should not tax one's self-estimate of what is readily possible; they should offer plausible opportunities for explaining failures, and they should not draw too heavily on one's ultimate potential which must be reserved for next year's repetition of the goals-setting process. If achievement is what counts, then it is difficult to say that the manager on the golf course is not being productive, nor can one assert that those who are busiest are the most productive. Yet if the gentle heresy that there is room for productivity growth among managers is to find any believers, it would appear likely that the place to test it is in the world of middle managers.

HOW TO PROCEED

All of this not too pleasant commentary demands something constructive in return, and we have several hypotheses to suggest. There is little use in trying to summarize or to rewrite the essence of the vast literature on how to be a good manager. This body of ideas is plausible and makes interesting reading, but is of unknown effect. There is little evidence that telling people how to manage, how to use their time efficiently, how to get along with people, and how to make decisions has any noticeable influence on their behavior. It may well be useful, but it has not been really demonstrated to be so. It would seem more productive to take a fundamental look at the nature of managers and their working styles in the hope that the concept of management productivity may be found to have some relevance that is not now widely suspected.

The basic problem, quite clearly, is how to measure management productivity. If we go at this problem directly, trying to define in a reasonable way the functions of management and trying to relate the behavior of managers to the execution of these functions, we will surely fail. We would bog down in a mire of subtlety, ambiguity, uncertainty, and instability. If we are to accomplish anything, we must approach management productivity indirectly, dodging the problem of definition and measurement, and seeking ways to improve it which do not require a logical, explicit, head-on attack.

Why It's Impossible

There is no shortage of reasons why the definition, measurement, and possible improvement of management productivity are impossible, efforts in this direction are at least futile, if not tinged with idiocy. The basic argument, of course, is that, in general, managers are already about as productive as they can be. One can attempt to meet this objection by citing the reports to which we have earlier alluded—of the time spent in meetings, office politics, and long lunch hours. But, of course, these may in actuality be productive activities. One may suggest that there is a great variation in the number of managers among organizations of essentially the same size and character. One may show that there are "tall" organizations and "flat" organizations, and that perhaps one is more conducive to management productivity than the other. Some organizations seem heavily managed with many layers, and others have dramatically few managers and few layers; yet, it is difficult to relate these characteristics to productivity. This, of course, can be interpreted as simply indicating, by the very presence of such variation, some potential for productivity growth. One may suggest that managers are always busy, and that is all the outside observer can hope to determine. The work of management is diffuse, abstract, and impossible to precisely define; as long as they are doing something, one cannot expect to understand more.

We can speculate about interesting hypotheses for detecting productivity improvement potential among managers. Can one say there is a useful relationship among the results, the bottom line, and the productivity of the management group? Efforts to establish this relationship fail because there is just no demonstrable connection between the effectiveness of the creative and executive functions in an organization and the number of people or number of man-hours that go into its management. The results achieved seem to depend far more strongly on the special qualities of the individuals involved—on their differences rather than their similarities. How much effort goes into management can be measured only in terms which are interesting for record-keeping purposes. We do not understand the job well enough to make anything much in the way of analytical measurements.

We can raise hypotheses which suggest that the older an organization, the greater its potential for productivity improvement among management; the larger the organization, the greater the potential; the greater the difficulty in giving operational definition to the goals of the organization, the greater the possibilities for improving the productivity of management. It may be that the greater the emphasis on results alone, the greater the potential. It may even be that the rate of management innovation and of management productivity growth, may be inversely proportional to the size of the management group. We may raise these hypotheses, but there is little chance of demonstrating their validity at this time.

Some will argue that one of the necessary ingredients of management is a freedom from the kind of stultifying productivity judgments which are freely applied to the behavior of working people. It may well be suggested that getting interested in management productivity will have seriously dysfunctional consequences. Managers must be left alone to create and define their own jobs, and to make judgments that only they themselves can make about the effectiveness of what they are doing at any given moment. Management, at best, is an imperfectly understood activity, and the differences between good management and not so good management are matters of great uncertainty.

It may well be that the really important things which managers do, by their own estimates, are not the things which are printed in the management literature, but rather the activities of selling, persuading, giving convictions, and inspiring. Their most productive functions may be their highly intuitive evaluation of people and their inspirational responses to crucial decision-making situations. These really important things may occupy a very small portion of a manager's time, and there may be some justification for this allocation of his attention. The basic aspect of all these activities may well be that there are a great variety of personal styles which are used in carrying them out and many different personal styles may be effective.

Perhaps there is little opportunity to measure productivity in these great areas where individual style evolves from experience and from a career of successes and failures. The best thing to do may be simply to try and make a manager more effective in the way he does these things. However this is to be done, there is no evidence that it can be accomplished by lecturing managers or by having them read books. If their behavior is to be modified, they must modify it themselves. We seem, then, to be confronted with the primacy of individual differences among management styles, the possibility that many such styles are almost equally effective, and the possibility that there is little which can really be done to alter the behavior of experienced managers in any direction which we might define as more productive. There can be no general definitions, no general methods of measurement, and no general willingness to respond by modifying one's management style toward abstractly defined models.

Self-Definition

Suppose we accept all of these premises, but refuse to give up. There is a way of proceeding which can accommodate these restrictions, and yet also lead to the enhancement of management productivity. The early experiments with this method have already been performed, and the first data strongly suggests that it is worth developing further. Suppose, in particular, that we accept the propositions that:

* individual management styles are strong determinants of management effectiveness
* no individual management style is clearly more effective than another over a rather wide range of variations
* managers can be most effective when permitted wide latitude in the definition of their own jobs and the regulation of their own activities
* while it is difficult to decide when a manager is being productive, he himself, with a little practice, will be able to decide for himself
* managers are sufficiently well motivated that when they are shown how to evaluate their own productivity by their own definitions, the results will lead to self-directed behavior changes
* these behavior changes will be, by their own definitions, in the direction of productivity growth.

How can all of this be done? Perhaps very simply.

Self-Perception

Suppose one could get a manager to become sufficiently self-perceptive to establish three broad categories of his own activities. One category would cover those activities which he clearly saw as productive according to his own definition of his job and his own personal style of working. The second category would include those activities which he saw quite clearly as being nonproductive, the time wasters, the frustrating demands which accomplish little or nothing. The third category would include those activities about which he was uncertain. In his present state of self-perception and self-understanding, he was not quite clear about whether or not these activities were productive. This may well be a difficult assignment for managers not accustomed to high levels of self-awareness, and at the outset the third category may include a large number of things. But the results alone might motivate the manager to think more clearly about what he really ought to be doing and the way in which his style is evolving.

Suppose, then, at several randomly selected times each day

a simple device on his desk or on his person would give him a signal which prompted him to notice what he was doing and record it in the proper category. He might well be impatient with this nonsense; he might well exaggerate in categorizing the activities in which he found himself involved, but the evidence indicates that this would pass. Nobody but the manager will ever see the data and it may well occur to him that he could do something useful with it. There is good reason to suspect that the manager may be sufficiently motivated to realize that this bit of self-knowledge might become the basis for some important self-directed change. He may be surprised to discover, on the basis of estimates produced by his random observations of his own activities, how much time he is spending in meetings, or dictating courtesy letters, or hunting for information, or following up and expediting, or worrying about things he can do little about. He may be quite surprised to find how little time he devotes to actually making decisions about the central activities of his production system, to long range planning, to innovating, and to evaluating his own effectiveness.

This simple system is based on the premises that managers will be able to decide for themselves when they are being productive, and that a little data will be highly suggestive of changes they might make in their own personal styles toward becoming more productive.

Self-awareness, the system suggests, is not a natural attribute of the busy executive, and a little help in seeing what he is doing is needed. Just trying to remember what he has done with his time is not likely to be effective. The manager must be encouraged to be enough of a scientist to actually record the data that emerges from his study of himself. The method suggests that outsiders are not likely to be able to modify his style, but that he himself, when he really sees what he is doing, will be motivated to do so.

If the manager engages in this method, it may well lead to other benefits. He may refine his classification of activities into those which are very productive, those which are moderately productive, and so on. He may begin to appreciate the need to clarify his own goals and those of the production system which he manages. The result may be a gradual decline in the number of activities about which he is uncertain about their productiv-

ity. He may well come to appreciate the notion that the allocation of his effort might benefit from a little reflection, and the
notion that the central activities of information collection and
decision making may well be the locus of the greatest opportunities for improving his self-defined productivity. We will look
more carefully at each of these notions in subsequent sections.

MANAGEMENT EFFORT ALLOCATION

If a manager persists in this experiment in self-examina-
tion he may well discover that, although the wrong approach is
to try to provide an external definition of his productivity, the
right approach is to let him experimentally refine his own definition. His definition will not be in neatly turned verbal formulations, but rather in the progressively refined categorization
he makes of his own activities. Once this far, it seems very likely
that he will be his own stimulus for change, change which will
involve redirecting his efforts from those activities he sees as
unproductive toward those which seem clearly the most productive.

The categorization he makes of his activities and the proportion of time he devotes to each is an excellent operational
definition of his management style. As he goes about modifying
this style, as only he can do, he may make some rough judgments about the payoffs from efforts devoted to various categories of activities. Spending time with customers may be seen
as productive, but spending too much time with a single customer begins to be subject to diminishing marginal returns.
Spending time training his people may also be seen as productive, but this too is subject to diminishing marginal returns. And
so on. He begins to make, as a result of his increased level of
self-objectification, some rough judgments about the marginal
gains from efforts devoted to various things. He begins to develop what may really be a highly sophisticated system for allocating his energies in the most productive way.

He may even go on to develop some assists in allocating
his attention. Exception reporting systems are instituted, reflecting his judgment that it only makes sense to pay attention
to certain things if particular contingencies occur. He wants to

hear about something only in certain cases, or at certain times. He develops sampling systems, deliberately not attending to all that is going on in some part of his production system, but looking at things only on a sampling basis. He examines production reports and absence reports—not every day, but only two or three days a week. He can, in short, develop the simple kinds of effort allocating aids that many managers use anyway. The fact that these are common may mean that there is, after all, nothing much new about this proposal for the improvement of management productivity. It may also mean, however, that since it is already a part of the style of some managers, it has a realistic chance of becoming a part of the style of others. The existence of these aids at least suggests that the results of this proposal are not patently ridiculous.

Information Gathering, Uncertainty Reduction, and Decision Making

In an attempt to foresee the possible results of this process of self-exploration of management style for at least some individuals, we will suggest some plausible hypotheses. It seems likely on the basis of what is known to date that there will be a large number of managers who find that they are devoting a very important portion of their time and energy to gathering information, tracking down data, and seeking answers to their questions. The process of information collection, uncertainty reduction, and prediction are very likely to make formidable claims on their attention. Similarly, it would appear that there will be an interesting number of managers who spend a relatively small portion of their time in activities they would classify as decision making; in fact, these activities are of an importance far out of proportion to the time they occupy. If these hypotheses are correct for at least some individuals, then it would follow that the processes of uncertainty reduction and decision making are among the most fertile for possible productivity enhancement. Indeed, it may well be the case that information management and decision making hold more leverage for productivity growth than any other aspects of management activity. It follows as well that many managers arriving at this conclusion, like many managers who arrived at the same point by other routes, will look to the concept of a management information system as a productivity improving assist. So important is the concept of a management information system and so misunderstood and oversold is it among many managers, that it will be useful to look at the process of creating management information systems rather closely.

THE COMPUTER AND MANAGEMENT PRODUCTIVITY

For perspective, it may help to reflect on the way in which many of us developed our acquaintance with the computer. For some, the first exposure to its works and wonders comes through the "wisdom machine" theory of the popular press. Computers will select a mate for you, manage your investment portfolio, plan a production schedule for your plant, and so on. The wisdom machine which these superficial reports tend to create collapses when we are reminded that there must be a programmer to tell the machine what to do. Somewhat later perhaps, we begin to think of the computer as a giant system for capturing and delivering lots and lots of data. The problems at this stage include how to avoid being overwhelmed, starved, or misled by the computer as a source of information. The computer-programmer complex is still very much an external system which supplies us. Supply problems are supposed to be ironed out by adding to the complex a management information systems analyst who tries to get the right information to the right people at the right time. The third stage in our acquaintance may come when we begin to delegate parts of some decisions to the computer-programmer-analyst complex. This is somewhat disturbing because we see the computer making the decisions the way it is told to make them and worry if it agrees with the way we would make them. The computer is typically being asked to make the decision which the analyst sees rather than the one which we ourselves see. This may even lead to a little concern about technological unemployment as a personal threat, a tendency to rejoice when we catch the computer in a blunder, and frequent reminders to ourselves that there are some things which the computer certainly cannot do.

He cannot hire a secretary, recognize a face, or hit a home run. At least, not yet. We are certainly not friends with the computer; he remains at arms length, and he contributes nothing beyond additional external inputs to our own decisions. It is perhaps a reasonable hypothesis that what is happening to many of us today is a gradual realization that the computer might become usefully involved in our own decision-making activities, but it is not yet clear how to do this at all, to say nothing of how to do it well.

Just as the advent of the computer taking over the payroll and accounts receivable functions caused many firms to look very carefully at their procedures in these areas, so the advent of the "responsive executive environment" will doubtless cause many managers to take a hard look at their decision-making systems. Indeed, there are those, as there were before, who feel that the real payoff is in the hard look and not the hardware.

Some Critical Incidents

The clearest way to envision the sort of productivity problems we will be discussing is to consider some actual incidents in the evolution of real information-decision systems. Each of these incidents contains data about decision makers and their information resources which may be of basic significance to management productivity.

JOB SHOP A: The manager of a very large job shop has a young engineer who sits in a small office just outside his own. The duties of the young engineer consist exclusively of knowing at all times the exact status of every project in the shop, the current estimate of its completion time, and what difficulties are being encountered. Several times each day, the manager walks into the young engineer's office, barks a project number, and expects to be given an immediate, complete, verbal status report on the project. The engineer has various graphical devices on his office wall on which he stores some of this information. The majority of it, however, is in the form of hastily written rough notes resulting from a very large number of telephone calls to the shop foremen. Production planning and scheduling is done by a separate department down in the shop. The manager uses the information in two basic ways. He is primarily concerned with furnishing quick answers to customers and higher management about project progress. In addition, he decides from time to time that it is necessary to bring pressure to one certain foreman in order to expedite a lagging project.

UNIVERSITY B: The president of a major educational institution accepted without much enthusiasm the installation of a computer terminal in his office. The terminal, which could be operated with very little instruction, permitted him to interrogate the institution's computer-based information system. He could call up a great variety of information about the resources and activities of his university. All of the basic information about funds, students, faculty, research, and instructional activities was available. After a few weeks, the president directed that the terminal be moved to another office several doors down the hall. Whenever he needs information that he thinks is available through the terminal, he asks his executive assistant for it, as he has always done. The assistant walks down the hall, uses the terminal to obtain the information, and then presents it verbally to the president.

TRUCKING COMPANY C: A trucking firm operating among twelve terminals in major cities decided to decentralize the management of its operations by making each of the terminals a profit center. The anticipated effect of decentralization was to reduce the amount of information transmitted between the terminals and the main office by delegating many of the routine operating decisions to the terminal managers. The terminal managers were given major responsibility for the operation of their facilities and considerable freedom in making operating decisions. Their performance was to be measured by computing the profit "earned" by each terminal in a fairly conventional way. A portion of the revenues for all shipments handled by a terminal was allocated to that terminal. From this revenue was subtracted a portion of the firm's fixed costs and the variable costs which could be directly controlled by the terminal manager. The managers understood that they were to operate in order to maximize their terminal profit, and that they would receive a monthly profit and loss statement. After a very few months, it was noticed that direct labor costs for the firm as a whole were increasing and that the terminal managers were spending a good deal of time communicating with each other and with the main office.

Investigation revealed that a few of the terminal managers had quickly discovered that they could reduce their own direct labor costs by not sorting the freight as it was loaded. Instead, they instructed the dock people to get the freight loaded as quickly as possible, without any attempt to arrange it according to destination. The problem of sorting it out could be handled by the receiving terminal. The result was that the reduction in direct labor costs at the shipping terminal was more than outweighed by the increase in direct labor costs at the receiving terminal. Any manager who received this kind of shipment felt quite justified in responding in kind.

DESIGN GROUP D: A group of information system designers approached the management of one of their clients to determine their information requirements as the first step in a major redesign project. Each manager was simply asked to indicate what information he would like to have. After a very long and unexpectedly expensive effort, the design group brought on line a computer based system which supplied the managers with a substantial portion of the information they had expressed a desire for. Several months later, the cost of operating the system and the emergence of other demands for computer capacity caused the firm to reappraise the information system. The first step was to ask the managers what management reports they would be willing to do without. None could be found that were not felt to be of major importance. The second step was simply to stop producing a number of the reports without any indication to the management group that this was being done. In a small proportion of the cases, complaints were received and the reports were apologetically reinstated, accompanied by an explanation referring to the difficulties caused by computer center overloading. In the majority of cases, however, no complaints were received and the reports were permanently discontinued. Apparently no notice was taken of the missing reports. This process was continued somewhat judiciously until the system approached something near the real information needs of management. The final design was achieved by a process of "shrink fitting."

COMPUTER FACILITY E: A large computing facility had grown over the years by simply offering its service on a first-come-first-served basis to anyone in the organization which it served. Eventually, however, it reached a period when the demand for its services grew more rapidly than the management was willing to expand its capacity. The facility became saturated, turnaround times grew long, tensions developed, and in some cases serious and costly delays were experienced. The director of the computing facility proposed an elaborate system of priorities and some staff additions to assign the priorities and administer the scheduling of work. An industrial engineer, whose projects frequently involved the services of the computing facility, proposed an alternative mechanism.

Each subunit of the organization was allocated a budget for computing services. The budget was started at a level sufficient to permit the unit to buy the services of the computing facility at about the same level of its past usage. The computing facility was free to raise the prices of its services at time of excessive demand, and to lower them when it seemed to have excess capacity. This policy had the desirable side effects of giving management a view of who was using computing services and to what extent, as well as providing the computer facility director with a basis for justifying expansionary expenditures. It would, the industrial engineer argued, provide a way of avoiding much of the administrative cost and frustration of the priority system by using a miniature market mechanism to coordinate supply and demand.

Some Basic Issues

These incidents raise some basic questions which are the central concern of the designer who undertakes to create or modify information-decision systems.

* How can one design systems that will actually be used by managers?
* What role should be played by people and what role by machines, in gathering, storing and processing information for managers?
* Can patterns of delegation be devised which will reduce information-handling costs without incurring other penalties more severe?
* How can designers discover and distinguish between the information decision makers "want" and the information they "need"?

* How do information systems influence, for better or for worse, the effectiveness of coordination and control in organizations?

These are but limited examples of the sort of situations with which we will be working, and the type of problem we will consider as we develop an approach to information system design. Another way to attempt to be clear about our concern is to propose a definition of a management information-decision system.

Definition

An information-decision system captures, stores, processes, and transmits information in ways that seek to enhance management productivity.

Usually these systems are computer-based or arise as perceived design problems when the possibility of introducing a new computer emerges. It is important to recognize that the system includes complex arrangements of machines, people, and information storage media. The definition makes the special point that the designer's aim is the enhancing of management productivity. One of the key aspects of management activity is decision making, and much of the designer's concern will be with enhancing the management decision process. The system will thus include models, information structures, decision aids, and opportunities for interaction with decision makers. Our notion of a system of this sort is that it is essentially management decision-oriented, and that it may include planning decisions, operating decisions, and performance assessment decisions. It raises the troublesome question of the ways in which one can measure management productivity, a question we will ultimately sidestep by equating the effectiveness of management with the effectiveness of the organization as a whole.

Implicit in the definition is the notion of a system which is seen one level of observation above that of a single manager. We will be much concerned with groups of managers and the problems of coordination in such groups. We will suppose that in many management decisions, one of the significant sources of uncertainty is about what other managers are going to do. Although our design strategy involves looking at individual decisions when they are of real significance, we will devote most of our efforts to networks of decision makers whose choices are mutually influential.

The notion of the design process which is implicit in this opening definition must be understood to include both those rare occasions when an entire system is created, and those more frequent opportunities to modify some aspects of a system in being.

The objectives of a management information system, out of which come the criteria for choosing among alternative designs, are to:

* enhance the management decision process;
* assist in the achievement of higher standards of reasonableness;
* achieve a reasonably tolerable level of uncertainty in the major decisions;
* produce a reasonable degree of coordination among decision makers.

IMPLEMENTATION

The work of the designer, beyond the creation of the system, involves its implementation and its actual sustained use by the clients. The principal method by which he achieves this is not by selling the end product or by convincing managers that they like his design, but by involvement of the potential users in the design process. The designer must see the client as a participant in the creation of basic concepts as a data source, as an interpreter of data, as an evaluator of proposals at every level of development, as a decision aid creator, and as an experimenter who ultimately tests parts of the design through actual use. This strategy means that the designer will not be able to take all of the credit for whatever occurs, that the client will have to invest effort in creating the system, and that both will be quite familiar with what is finally selected for implementation.

A part of the designer's efforts toward implementation begin with a deliberate attempt to give the client realistic expectations about the cost of the design effort, how long it will take, the amount of his own effort that will be needed, and the order of magnitude of benefits that may be expected. These things are matters of considerable uncertainty at the beginning of a project, and it is probably best to make this uncertainty quite explicit for the client. As the design progresses and the uncertainty is reduced, periodic reviews of what can ultimately be expected are likely to prevent unpleasant surprises.

Implementation is also influenced by the basic design choice between a system which seeks to enhance the personal style of particular individual decision makers, and a system which concentrates on the impersonal, more objective aspects of the decision situations involved. This compromise involves trading the cost and impermanence of attending to individual abilities and behaviors for the greater appeal and possibly greater short-term effectiveness which results. The choice between a "personalized" system and an impersonal one is a design problem which is less appreciated than its importance warrants.

Client acceptance and implementation are often a function of the skill with which the designer can subtly educate potential users. Particular attention is needed to create a climate of opinion which is realistic without undertaking direct contradiction or becoming argumentative. Designers often encounter points of view such as:

> "There's almost no limit to the information one can have if one has a big computer."
>
> "All that mathematical modeling is theoretical. What this project needs is something practical, something based on good common sense."
>
> "Making decisions is an art. It's intuitive and can only be learned through experience. It's foolish to suppose that a management information system can do anything more than deliver information."
>
> "No management information system can ever take into account the human element."
>
> "No management information system can ever take into account the politics which is what really determines how things go around here."

"No management information system can ever take into account the really important things such as customer satisfaction, what the competition might do next year, or that feel of the market you get after twenty years in the business."

Implementation is also related to the effectiveness of the designer in organizing the client's participation in the project. Many designers favor a task force of key decision makers from all of the subunits involved, who are specifically asked to devote a portion of their time to the project. The organization, leadership, and motivation of such a group is a special skill which can be seen in most experienced system designers.

THE KEY DECISIONS

Identifying the key decisions in an organization, with the active participation of the client, is not usually very difficult. The key decisions, those which have important consequences for the future development and effectiveness of an organization, are made by people in visible positions. They occur where information flows come together. They are made by people who are compensated to take major responsibility, by people who call meetings and appoint committees, and by people to whom staff recommendations must be justified and defended. There are, of course, exceptions to these truisms, but one can only try to be sensitive to the possibility of such unusual circumstances.

It is helpful to look at the conventional decision-making categories, making sure one has identified the key decisions in the areas of: long-range planning; policy formulation; research and development programming operations (procurement, production, marketing, personnel, finance); budgeting; resource allocation; performance evaluation and control.

A key decision is one which, because of its potential impact on the performance of the organization or because of the frequency with which it is made, appears to warrant the primary effort in the design project. Decisions such as the addition of a new product line may be made rather seldom, but they have a potentially very significant effect on the future profits of a firm. Decisions on whether or not to grant credit to a new customer may be of small consequence individually, but may be made so frequently as to have an important consequence when taken collectively. Typically, the infrequent but consequential decisions occur at the higher levels of an organization, while the repetitive and individually less consequential ones occur at the lower levels.

It is often useful to consider the possibility that those decisions which will warrant primary attention in the design program may be those which are characterized by: high uncertainty; high intuitive content, lack of structure; lack of readily available measures of effectiveness; high ambiguity, poorly defined, artistic.

Having made, in cooperation with the client, a tentative identification of the key decisions, the designer may turn to the next phase — the development of some rough qualitative models. Note that, here again, the designer is called upon to make some project management judgments about how many decisions will be studied and what degree of detail will characterize the models produced.

Rough, Qualitative Models

In developing some first models of the key decisions, we are looking ahead toward enhancing management productivity both by providing assistance in each key decision and by creating more effective coordinating relationships among decisions. A rough model of a key decision will typically not be mathematical, but will more likely be a combination of graphical and narrative representation. Here again, the important thing is not that the decisions be modeled in some conventional form, but that the designer and the client share in the creation of the method of modeling.

It is useful to begin by classifying these key decisions as long-range planning decisions, operating decisions, and so on. One should also have available some rough estimates of the frequency with which they are made and the order of magnitude of their potential impact. These estimates provide the bases for deciding how much effort should be expended to understand and improve them. The decision model, in whatever form, should summarize the available information concerning:

* the alternatives or options
* the measures of effectiveness
* the information inputs available
* the major sources of uncertainty
* the constraints on choice
* the requirements for justification or selling choices
* the available evidence on past choices
* the relevant policies, doctrines
* the requirements for coordination
* those aspects which are intuitive, artistic, and implicit.

Models which represent these sorts of considerations tend toward impersonality, objectivity, and independence of particular decision makers. These models, which we will call Type 1 models, tend to suppress individual differences among decision makers. One can imagine a continuum of decision models; at the other end are those models which are highly personal — reflecting the perceptions, decision-making style, and special behavioral characteristics of particular decision-making individuals. The latter, or Type 2, models are basic to the ultimate design choices concerning the degree to which the information-decision system is to reflect the personal aspects of the incumbent managers, and the degree to which it is to suppress these individual differences. We will simply observe at this point that the tendency to develop Type 2 models usually increases as:

* one moves to higher levels of management
* the intuitive, implicit content of the decision increases
* the experience of the decision maker increases
* the frequency with which the decision is made decreases

The development of models which tend to be of Type 2 obviously involve the fullest participation on the part of the decision maker. One seeks to find out such things as:

* how he sees the decision
* whom he talks to
* what special experiences he finds relevant
* what the political considerations are
* how and to whom he justifies the decision
* how long he takes to make the decision
* what he regards as the difficult value judgments involved

* how he perceives uncertainty
* what risks he is willing to take
* the ways in which the decision is intuitive and implicit
* his level of satisfaction with the way he makes the decision
* what additional information he would most like to have
* what sorts of assistance he would find most useful
* the degree to which he relies on guesses
* his tolerance for ambiguity
* his need to rely on policy
* his tolerance for uncertainty
* his willingness to delegate parts of the decision

From these questions can come a useful basis for models of Type 2. It is generally important, however, whether one is emphasizing the impersonal aspects of a decision or the special characteristics of a decision maker, to keep in mind a series of basic hypotheses about the ways in which people think about and talk about their decision. Each of these reflects some of the data accumulated in the experimental literature on decision analysis.

Hypotheses for the Modeling of Decisions

People are seldom able to express uncertainty with any degree of ease. Often they deliberately suppress uncertainty and are reluctant to admit that they are in any degree uncertain. They believe that they have all the facts before they decide.

They are often not very clear about their objectives, particularly about the kind of trade-offs they are willing to make between objectives that cannot be simultaneously achieved. One should be well prepared to find superficial expressions of goals.

People are generally not very self-aware when it comes to their own decision-making style or behavior. Decision making is typically a highly over-learned task which is not a matter of self-consciousness.

People tend to give overly rationalistic explanations of their decision making, attempting to justify as they describe.

They tend to see decision making as an art which involves much that cannot be made explicit.

They see decision making as being dominated by implicit experience, judgments, hunches, guesses, politics, and the "human element."

They tend to view all general statements about decision making as inapplicable to their own situation.

They regard their decisions as subtle blends of many, highly complex facts and considerations which can only be achieved by the highly developed human intellect.

They tend to see themselves as operating more closely in consonance with prescribed doctrines and policies than, in fact, is the case.

They tend to see their decision making in repetitive situations as more consistent than is likely to be actually the case.

They tend to include non-operational concepts in their explanations of their decisions—that is, concepts which can be readily measured, identified, or demonstrated.

They usually regard as the sole opportunity to enhance their decisions, the obtaining of more facts, data, or information.

They find it difficult to distinguish between the choice and the outcome, the decision and the result. They are heavily conditioned to judging the quality of a decision by the goodness of the results.

People tend to be largely unaware of the degree to which their needs, tensions, anxieties, and psychological stresses influence their perception, their thinking, and their decision-making behavior.

These kinds of hypotheses, although all supported by published data, are clearly not universally true. They are useful, however, in sensitizing one to what he is likely to consider when he sets out to construct a rough model of a decision. He should:

* develop decision aids
* reduce some of the uncertainty
* clarify objectives
* filter out unused information
* search for additional alternatives
* delegate parts of the decision
* give meaningful structure to the available information

The person who notices possibilities will tend to be guided in his data gathering and modeling along particularly productive lines.

DECISION AIDING STRATEGIES

With some rough models of the key decisions in hand, the designer may now turn directly to the basic question of how an information system may be designed which will enhance the effectiveness with which these decisions are made. One useful way to look at the problem of enhancing decision making is to view the designer's task as one of finding a good division of labor. How can the work of making a decision be best divided between the human decision maker on the one hand and the information-decision system on the other? What is it that man can do more effectively than the system, what can the system do more effectively than man? It is important here to think of the system as more than just a computer system. In this context, it should include all the resources that can be brought to the assistance of the decision maker — including the computer, staff assistants, other managers, files, mathematical models, simulations, and all sorts of information storage media. It has always been clear, for example, that where decisions depended on the remembering of large quantities of explicit data, the system could usually do this more effectively than the decision maker himself. Where extensive, routine, and explicit calculations are involved, it is usually more effective to turn these over to the system. Beyond this, good generalizations are difficult to come by. However, we will suggest a series of hypotheses whose function may usefully be to give the designer some directions to explore as he considers possibilities for decision aiding through altering the division of labor.

Specific Methods

It may be useful at this point to catalog the main sorts of decision aiding strategies among which the designer may choose. Our catalog can only include a few brief comments on each, for many of these methods are the subjects of extensive discussion and research.

ENHANCE INTUITIVE FUNCTIONING: To a greater or lesser extent, there will be aspects of many important decisions which appear better left to the intuitive, experiential, and implicit behavior of the decision maker. To attempt to make them explicit does not appear to promise a favorable cost-benefit relationship. The basic decision aiding strategy is then to seek ways of permitting the intuition of the manager to function most effectively. It is well known that intuitive effectiveness is degraded by psychological stresses such as anxiety, frustration, and conflict. Physical stresses such as fatigue, time pressure, and distraction also have a deleterious effect. It is possible for the system designer to help the decision maker become aware of the conditions under which he is not likely to be intuitively effective and to help him compensate for or avoid these conditions. Some systems have a private terminal room or communication center where the decision maker can, among other things, free himself from the pressures and distractions of his regular affairs.

It is important, at very least, to recognize the substantial intuitive content of many decisions, to recognize that things are often best left that way, and to be alert for opportunities to increase the effectiveness of the decision makers involved.

STRUCTURE GIVING, EXPLICITNESS: The underlying premise of almost all decision analysis is that decision making effectiveness can be increased by making the decision explicit and by organizing the data, the alternatives, the predictions, and the evaluations into some orderly structure. Matrix structures and decision trees are familiar conventions for doing this. It is extremely useful, however, for the designer to consider whether or not the benefits of making the decision explicit are likely to warrant the costs of doing so. Having already undertaken the development of rough, qualitative models for the key decisions, the designer will have some approximate basis for judging how much effort might be required to proceed further in this direction.

The benefits of explicitness are well known and include all sorts of opportunities to check for consistency, for completeness, for agreement with others, and for logical deduction and inferences. Explicit decisions may be delegated in whole or in part to other people or to machines. Explicitness permits teaching, record keeping, learning from experience, and group decision making to become more effective. Hardly anything is as important to the work of the information-decision system designer as the degree to which he is able to make the key decisions explicit.

MODELING, ANALYSIS, AND SIMULATION: The whole field of systems analysis is concerned with the development of mathematically explicit representations of decisions. From these models, either by analysis or by simulation, all sorts of questions can be answered. The goodness of the answer is, of course, a key question for the creator of mathematical models. Nevertheless, a great variety of useful decision aiding is possible through the production of optimal solutions, sensitivity analysis, and the prediction of the consequences of all sorts of possible courses of action. A simulation which permits the decision maker to learn about what he manages by asking the simulation lots of "what if . . ." questions is a valuable part of many systems. The cost of mathematical analysis and simulation development is such, however, that it should not be undertaken without some careful judgments about the benefits which are likely to accrue.

REDUCE UNCERTAINTY BY PROVIDING MORE INFORMATION: This is, of course, the basic decision aiding method which is associated with the design of information systems. Decision making, it is supposed, will be enhanced by providing managers with more information, more reliable information, and more timely information. In many cases the benefits of doing this are so obvious that the designer will hardly concern himself with the question of whether or not to go ahead.

Again, however, a few words of caution. It is easy to swamp the decision maker with more information than he can use and to actually inhibit his effectiveness by doing so. This is not only easy, but actually achieved in what appears to be a rather large number of information decision systems. What the decision maker wants is not always equivalent to what he uses in the way of information. Our purpose in creating decision models is to try to make clear this basic distinction. Finally, information is never free and sometimes very expensive. The value of information for decision making purposes is almost always subject to diminishing marginal returns. The more information a decision maker has, the less the marginal value of additional information. Thus, there is a reasonable amount of information beyond which it is not sensible to go, or, in other words, there is a reasonable amount of uncertainty to tolerate.

ADD MEMORY CAPACITY: Providing greater capacity for the storage of information and greater ease in retrieving stored information is closely akin to providing more information. Many of the same cautions about balancing costs and benefits apply here as well. The notion of the "central data bank" which will remember "everything" is hardly a reasonable objective for systems design at this stage of our development. There are, however, a great variety of media and methods for storing and recalling information which occupy a central place in the decision aiding contributions of most systems.

REDUCE THE INFORMATION LOAD: Filtering out or eliminating some of the information coming to a decision maker is the opposite but often equally effective strategy. The classic management-by-exception reporting scheme is a persistently useful instance of this strategy. One of the purposes of modeling the key decisions is to examine the hypotheses that some information can be eliminated because it is not, in fact, useful, and that it might be reasonable to tolerate a somewhat higher level of uncertainty in some situations. It is rather commonly discovered that people obtain more information, pay more for information, or use information less effectively than is reasonable. Those interested in Bayesian decision analysis will recognize here the possible occurrence of this "conservatism effect."

PERSONAL STYLE ANALYSIS: Personal style is an expression of individuality. One might quickly develop a host of dimensions for describing it, and this may be well worth doing for at least two reasons. First and most important is the development of self-consciousness, self-awareness, or self-knowledge. One reading of a great deal of the evidence turned up by modern psychology reveals that the key to the improvement of intuitive, implicit decision processes is self-awareness, and this self-awareness must begin by motivating the subject to explore the various dimensions of his own style of deciding. Second, it seems clear that by exploring the dimensions of personal decision making styles, we will be able to suggest more or less specific ways of enhancing those styles. We would thus like to find ways of looking at styles, which are useful in the sense that they lead us to such enhancements.

COMPLEX UNCERTAINTIES FROM SIMPLE ONES: The principal use of probability theory in modern decision analysis is to deduce complex, unfamiliar, novel uncertainties that lie beyond the decision maker's experience from simple, habitual, familiar ones which are well within his experience. The principal motivation for expressing uncertainty in probabilistic terms is to take advantage of this possibility. Once uncertainties have been made explicit then all of the possibilities associated with explicitness generally become relevant.

PREDICTION MODELS: Significant reductions in uncertainty are sometimes possible by using prediction models with existing or readily available data. Regression models, exponential smoothing techniques and time series analysis as an on-line, continuously updated part of a system have often proven very useful.

EXPERT CONSULTATION: Routine, occasional, or exception-triggered consultation with experts is one of the most widely used ways of coping with difficult decision problems.

GROUP CONSULTATION: Committees, panel of experts, task forces, special project teams, and Delphi panels supplement the decision making resources of the individual by bringing to bear additional information, differing backgrounds, alternative value systems, and stimulation to creative insight. Group consultation also provides a valuable opportunity for a decision maker to clarify his own thinking by expressing his views to the group.

As our design experience grows, other ways of enhancing decision making behavior will emerge and other decision aiding techniques will be developed. The most difficult judgment, which at present can only be a judgment, is the degree to which the cost of these techniques will be returned by their results in improving management productivity.

THE EXPERIMENTAL PHILOSOPHY

Emerson, in one of his essays, offered some advice that might be interestingly appropriate for management. "All life is an experiment. The more experiments you make, the better."

If Emerson was serious, he expected a far more heroic detachment from our own affairs than most of us can manage. If, however, we invite a mature, professional manager to regard each instance of a decision, an action, and some results, as an experimental trial leading to further experiments, he may not find it so unreasonable. If Emerson was not only serious but right, then perhaps this notion is of some consequence in understanding management productivity.

To suggest the ongoing operations of a business be regarded as a series of experiments is to suggest a rather important management concept. This is the proposition that a firm should be run so as not only to produce its products or services at a profit but also to produce information on how to improve its own operations. Organizations ought deliberately to produce among their various outputs information relevant for moving further toward their objectives. In less general terms, a production manager should seek to produce not only the products, but also information on how the products and the production operations themselves may be improved. Each management action should be treated as a test of the decision concept upon which it is based, and as a test of a hypothesis which has been produced out of assumptions and simplifications — the truth of which is necessarily a matter of doubt and uncertainty. Ideally, the setting in which managers decide and act should be something like that of a laboratory.

One must stipulate and manage affairs conditionally in the face of the residue of uncertainty necessarily present when one confronts practical affairs. The ongoing operations which result should provide some kind of test of the "as if . . ." statements. Each decision becomes an experiment which benefits from the results of the previous one. This is the essential, self-correcting nature of science in general, and perhaps the basic contribution management science will make to management. Managers certainly learn from experience and are self-correcting, but the aim of productivity improvement is to make these corrections quickly and economically, perhaps more quickly and more economically than by any other casual procedures.

It is thus our central hypothesis that the ongoing operations of any enterprise be viewed as experiments, and that the idea of experiment here be interpreted much in the way it is in all of science. Indeed, this attitude is the meaning of scientific management, and considerable confusion about what can be scientific in management may be cleared up by exploring the implications of these data. It is important to note that the term "experiment" here stands in sharp distinction to casual or naive experience. It will be further argued that the function of the management scientist is to make experience into experiment, or to turn casual experience into "designed" experience.

This idea should not be entirely foreign to the thinking of managers ready to recognize that the results of their actions can not be perfectly predicted in advance. Thus any action is, in a crude sense, an attempt at experimentation. What has often been missing, however, are those aspects of experimentation which make it scientific rather than casual, trial-and-error conduct of affairs.

The kinds of experiments conducted with very little more prior consideration than "I wonder what would happen if we tried this?" or "let's just try a lot of different things to see if they work" are not particularly suggested. Usually in the conduct of the affairs of business there is the desire to take actions believed to be effective, however limited the notion of effectiveness may be. At least the desire to "look before you leap" is presupposed.

PRODUCTIVITY

The work of the management in productivity development is to refine the continuing sequence of consideration, choice, action, and the monitoring of results in order to make it an effective process not only for applying knowledge but also for producing more knowledge. The tasks involved include:

1. Raising good hypotheses and developing fruitful logical structures. It is most important to note, however, that raising hypotheses is not exclusively the task of either the operations designer or the manager. If the world were perfect the vast weight of the manager's experience and intuition would be coupled with the "objective" output of the designer to produce hypotheses consistent (insofar as possible) with both kinds of knowledge. Thus nobody is asked to worship at the shrine of any particular doctrinaire approach to management problems. Hypotheses may come from anywhere.

2. Making explicit a conceptualization of the management decision problem which provides the occasion for the inquiry. The most obvious, and widely neglected, pre-

condition for an experiment is an explicit statement of the hypotheses being tested.

3. Designing experiments, both in the "laboratory" setting and in the operations of the firm itself. The designer must consider sample size, controls, and the economics of experimentation. He must work as well as he can toward an answer to the basic question of when to stop gathering data and stipulate. He must formulate explicit policies for deciding how the experimental results are related to future experiments. He must try to design experiments which will show not merely that something went wrong but also what went wrong and what might be done about it.

4. Deciding what is meant by "under control" in connection with the operations of the firm. (Management control systems are simply routinized experiments.) This implies the staff man must help the manager distinguish between controllable and uncontrollable variations in his operations. Some variations are not economically explainable and thus are best regarded as inherent variations, while others can be economically explained and thus linked with causes which in principle could be removed. In short, if managers are to manage "by exception," some considerable effort may be required to decide what the exceptions are.

5. Interpreting the results of the experiment in terms of future management actions. (This is the same as saying "in terms of subsequent experiments.")

6. Showing as clearly as possible what aspects of each decision problem must depend on experience rather than experiment, thus emphasizing the competence of management science.

THE NEED FOR CERTAINTY

Managers experience in common with all of us a need to be certain about the decisions they are making. The scientist who argues that the only scientifically tenable attitude toward management is that of experimentation clearly defies this need rashly. In fact, one would suppose this view of the benefits of science would be something of a disappointment to managers, who may well have expected something more in the way of assurances about the conduct of their affairs. It seems that what science does is to display our ignorance more than it adds to our knowledge. This view is bound to be disappointing until one looks at alternate ways of doing things.

Overconfidence, strong predispositions, and the refusal to expect a variety of results from one's action are hardly compatible with the experimental attitude. Much of what passes for fact must indeed be regarded as hypothesis. For example, even the objectives of the decision maker or of his firm may turn out to be simply statements one stipulates and then puts to the empirical test. The tendency to make decisions and then refuse to look back on them or re-examine them in the light of emerging evidence will be challenged. The decisions managers make while they are planning and elaborating programs of action are seldom re-examined as the programs are executed.

Common Sense

On the other hand, managers may well find that much of what seems common sense to them is in general agreement with the view here suggested. For example, when a new policy is proposed the hypothesis is that the rate with which it is implemented is proportional to the increase in profits it promises. New policies in uncertain environments must be tried out gradually (experimentally), and the greater the difference between two policies, the less experience required to demonstrate this difference. This concept at least roughly agrees with the basic principles of experimental design in science.

There are important differences between experience, which all managers have, and experiment, which is the business of the scientifically trained. Experience may be regarded as loosely organized familiarity with the happenings of the past, out of which judgments and intuitions are produced. How these are produced from the vast complexity of past perceptions is hard to say. The process is personal, subjective, partially subconscious, and not easily explained. By contrast, experiments try to place what seems reasonable, plausible or intuitive against the facts so that one may modify his judgments.

If one produces a product or service at a profit he may

regard these happenings as business experience. If, at the same time, he can produce information on how his operations might be improved, then he has done something close to an experiment. Experiments are purposeful tests of explicitly stated hypotheses. It is very important indeed that the hypotheses be made explicit, as well as the data collected, the experimental controls provided, and the rules for moving from the data to the conclusions set. Experience may be one source of hypotheses, but experiment is the means by which these are tested, and experience must be rendered explicitly for this to be done. Although it would be foolish to attempt to draw a hard and fast line between these two, the sad feature of much management experience is that most of the knowledge that might be wrung from it is wasted.

Unless we have an explicit hypothesis and submit it to a deliberate test with expected results, we will not be alert to the unexpected. Incurious experience, making no effort to produce information, may lead one to miss even the obvious. Perhaps good advice to an inexperienced manager would be this: "Formulate a policy to guide your decision making, even if you can't think of one you regard as very good. If you have an explicit hypothesis or policy then your experience becomes an experimental evaluation of it. If you change it, at least you know what you are changing from. This is the only way to learn without unnecessary waste of experience."

Notes

In the voluminous literature on management, there is little which directly addresses the question of management productivity. The most useful exception is Gold, Bela. *Explorations in Managerial Economics: Productivity, Costs, Technology and Growth,* New York: Basic Books, Inc., 1971.

The AMA Survey and The Research Institute of America Survey were reported in the *National Observer,* April 13, 1974.

In a survey of nearly 3,000 U.S. businessmen, the American Management Association found:

1. "Fifty-two per cent of all respondents—including 58 per cent of all middle managers, 69 per cent of all supervisory-level managers, and 71 per cent of all technical employees in managerial positions—believe that advancement and promotion . . . are most often based on 'a largely subjective and arbitrary decision on the part of corporate superiors in the position to decide who gets promoted and who doesn't.'
2. "Eighty-eight per cent of all respondents say that 'a dynamic personality and the ability to sell yourself and your ideas' is more of an attribute to the manager on the move today than is 'a reputation for honesty, or firm adherence to principles.'
3. "Eighty-two per cent of all respondents believe that 'pleasing the boss' is the critical factor in determining 'promotability' in today's organizational environment."

A Research Institute of American study reported "Today, when business can least afford a dissipation of effort, 'office politics' is on the rise within many companies. As a menace to individuals and organizations alike, it deserves more concentrated study than anyone has given it. The price of office politics is tremendous, both to management and the individual."

The first experiment is having managers define and measure their own productivity in ways similar, but not identical to, those outlined as reported in *Business Week,* December 1, 1973. "Managers have long imposed time and motion studies upon hapless workers, but, until recently at least, they have generally been immune from clinical examination of their own routine. Now, with the help of an ingenious new electronic device, hundreds of executives in Europe are subjecting their own workday to analysis, and U.S. managers may soon be doing so as well. The results are often disturbing, as executives see how ineffectually they are using their time."

The literature on management information systems is almost exclusively concerned with the application of computers, computer programming, and computer systems designed. We have taken the view that this is a minor aspect of the problem of management productivity enhancement. The problem is the concepts and the "software" necessary for management information systems, not the hardware. This is consistent with Ackoff, Russell. "Management Misinformation Systems," *Management Science,* 14, 9, 1968.

The concept of the experimental philosophy of management has been mentioned but not extensively developed by Salveson and is closely related to the ideas of Churchman and Littauer. See Sebastian B. Littauer. "Social Aspects of Scientific Method in Industrial Production," *Philosophy of Science,* Vol. 21, No. 93, 1945.

C. West Churchman. "A Pragmatic Theory of Induction," in Philipp G. Frank, *The Validation of Scientific Theories,* Boston: The Beacon Press, 1954.

C. West Churchman, *Prediction and Optimal Decision,* Englewood Cliffs, N.J.: Prentice-Hall, Inc., 1961.

W. W. Cooper, "A Proposal for Extending the Theory of the Firm," *Quarterly Journal of Economics,* February, 1951.

Mention of this idea is also made in Melville Dalton. *Men Who Manage.* New York: John Wiley & Sons, Inc., 1959, p. 252.

Also, M. E. Salveson. "A Problem in Optimal Machine Loading," *Management Science,* Vol. 2, No. 3, 1956; and Roger Hilsman, *Strategic Intelligence and National Decision.* Glencoe, Ill.: The Free Press, 1956, p. 160.

It is consistent with the view of induction given by Reichenbach as well as the excellent practical discussion of Miller and Starr. See Hans Reichenbach. *The Rise of Scientific Philosophy.* Berkeley: University of California Press, 1959; and David W. Miller and Martin K. Starr. *Executive Decisions and Operations Research.* Englewood Cliffs, N.J.: Prentice-Hall, Inc., 1960, pp. 415–34.

8

New Targets: The Services

FIDDLING FASTER

The problem of the service sector is well illustrated by the ancient economic law: a fiddler cannot improve his productivity by fiddling faster. The possibilities which lie ahead in the service sector are illustrated by the classic rejoinder: no, but think what we can do if we put him on radio and television.

In 1800 nearly 80 percent of our work force was employed in agricultural pursuits, and the remainder were producing goods and services. Today less than eight percent remain in agriculture because the productivity of agriculture is very high. Today over two thirds of the work force are involved in the production of services, partly as well we shall see, because the productivity of the service sector is not very high. Sometime in the last few years we passed the point where more than half of the private, non-governmental working people were at work producing services. At this point the service portion of our economy started to get a lot of professional attention. As we began to run into difficulties with productivity growth it was natural to look closely at the major portion of our economic system. These are the people who work in transportation, wholesale and retail distribution, finance, insurance, real estate, repair services, hotels, restaurants, barber shops, recreation, health care, and of course one of the fastest growing undertakings of all, government.

Our impressions of what is going on in the services are various, but generally probably indicative of the underlying situation. Some services seem to be growing expensive beyond all reasonable expectations such as health care, TV repair, and domestic help. The first we cannot do without, the last, we can, TV repair, maybe. Nothing much seems to be happening to productivity in such areas, and they are likely culprits when we think about what "causes" inflation. We are a little proud but a little concerned when we are told that our increasing affluence has led us to spend more on services. We are a little concerned because there are those who see this as the first sign of our on-coming decadence. We marvel as the marketing of ever more complete, personal, and exotic services is announced. There are firms which will wake a person up, care for his house plants, find guests for his next cocktail party, and supply temporary corporate vice-presidents. Almost anything for a price is becoming a reality.

Services, we are becoming very aware, often cannot be inventoried. They are consumed as they are produced. No quality control inspector stands between us and the producer. We are the first to know if our luggage is lost, our reservation is not honored, or the car is repaired in a way which produces no noticeable improvement in the curious noises it makes. We are both consumer and inspector, and our only resort is often the complaint. The complaint is beyond question the least satisfying of all our consumption activities.

SERVICE PRODUCTIVITY

While two thirds of our working people are in the services, they produce only about one half of the gross national product. This rough indication of the low productivity of this sector seems to be confirmed almost every time we buy services. From 1950 to 1970, the productivity increment in services was generally lower than that in industry. The only exceptions were transportation, communications, and utilities where productivity increased faster than the industry average. Wage levels are generally lower in the services than in industry, but wage increases in the services tend to match those in industry. This seems to foretell the coming of still higher prices for services as the result of wage increases without matching productivity increases. In the service sector, wages represent something like

70 percent of the cost of the output, and thus a 10 percent increase in wages would be passed on in the form of a 7 percent price increase. In industry a 10 percent wage increase would translate into a 3 percent increase in prices.

Firms in the service sector, however conveniently they may be lumped by economists, have little in common. Some rely heavily on people (the restaurant, the corner store), yet some do not (the vending machine). While service firms are often small, some, like Sears, are giants. They are engaged in a vast variety of activities, which, when one is interested in productivity, are particularly resistant to general statements. From the point of view of productivity incrementing, we have a large collection of specific, individual problems it would appear.

It is often very easy for the consumer to conclude that he is not only the sole person concerned with the quality of a service, but also the sole person concerned with the productivity of those producing it. Once he has contracted for it, he can do little but sit back and await the bill. In fact, in many services it is difficult to even be clear about what one means by productivity, let alone measure it and do something about it. Information, for example, may be the greatest service of them all. The doctor, the lawyer, the broker, the teacher, the consultant, the pastor, and the librarian all produce information. But the problems of saying something about the quality of the information and the productivity of those who work at producing it are very serious indeed.

Now all of these impressions are not perfect generalities, but they do have a useful ring of validity. It will be important for us, however, to make a brief excursion from impressions into the economic data about the service sector to somewhat refine these notions.

THE ECONOMICS OF THE SERVICES

To look briefly at the data on the service sector, we will include wholesale and retail trade, finance, insurance, real estate, government, as well as professional, personal, business and repair services. The shift to a service dominated economy is indeed dramatic. Between 1947 and 1965 there were 13 million new service jobs, as compared to 4 million in manufacturing and 3 million in agriculture. The shift away from making things is even greater if we include the tremendous growth of the white collar group in the industrial sector. It turns out that the relative growth in service employment has not been primarily the result of our growing income and any resulting growth in the demand for services. Some of the growth is due to the emergence of new firms which provide services to the manufacturing sector that manufacturers formerly provided for themselves "in house" or simply did not have at all.

The major explanation of the employment growth is, unfortunately, the relatively slow growth in productivity, in output per man-hour. Productivity did not grow as rapidly in the service sector as it did in either manufacturing or agriculture. This turns out to be true even if we take government as a special case and remove it from consideration. The data shows, however, that productivity does grow in the service sector, but not very fast. Millions of people work as waiters, as janitors, as sales clerks, and so on; in fact some 35 million are in these occupations, and their productivity has not been growing very much at all.

The slower growth in output per man-hour appears to be importantly explained by a more rapid increase in the "quality of labor" in industry than in the services. Quality here means the proportion of working people in the prime working age groups, the amount of education and training, and the proportion of working people who are male. (One wonders how long economists will cling to this unpopular dimension of quality.) A somewhat less important source of the lower productivity growth is the slower growth in machines and equipment in the services than in manufacturing. The amount of physical capital per working person has not risen as fast in the services. Finally, perhaps the least important explanation is the greater utilization of the techniques of "working smarter" in industry, and the greater benefits to be realized there from economies of scale.

These explanations as we will shortly see correlate rather well with the efforts that are just beginning in the service sector toward the improvement of productivity—the upgrading of working people through training, the use of machines and technology more widely and more intensively, and the introduction of the techniques of operations design.

In the services, as in manufacturing, there is a synergistic relationship which is readily evident from the data. Growth stimulates productivity and productivity in turn stimulates growth. Productivity improvements tend to be translated into lower prices and better quality. These in turn stimulate greater demand for services. This greater demand provides the opportunity to introduce machines where technically possible, to increase the average size of the transaction which occurs, to decrease idle time, and to use the services of the operations designer. All of these serve to further increase productivity and reinforce the cycle. The "lump of labor" hypothesis is no more true in the service sector than it is in industry.

Generally speaking, hourly earnings are lower in the services than in industry. This is importantly related to the degree of unionization—only 10 percent in the service sector as opposed to 50 percent in industry. It is clear that unions will move into the service sector when they see an opportunity to form a bargaining unit of reasonable size.

Over the business cycle, output and employment in the services are more stable than in industry. Since the services cannot be stored, this sector avoids the amplified fluctuations that are due to inventory building and inventory drawing down. Employment is more stable because there are many self-employed, many salaried people, and many people like brokers, insurance agents, barbers, and capital equipment salesmen whose incomes are strongly determined by their output. Their earnings are more sensitive to fluctuations than are their hours of work. But, unfortunately, this factor results in greater productivity fluctuations in the service sector.

Growth Implications

The growth of the service sector presents us with some interesting implications. Large corporations today are producing a smaller percentage of the gross national product than in 1956. Hospitals, universities, and governments are producing more of it. We are moving, in this sense, from activities in which

productivity was relatively easy to measure to activities in which
it often appears virtually impossible to measure. We are moving
from activities in which there has been a strong incentive and a
strong tradition in favor of productivity toward activities where
these have not been present. Many services are being produced
by non-profit institutions such as the non-profit hospitals which
have been experiencing sharply rising costs.

Employment in the service sector is of a basically different
character. Women find it easier to compete with men and thus
dominate employment here. Older people are more prevalent,
especially in those kinds of service jobs which provide part-
time employment. Many people in the services are self-employed. All these considerations, according to some views, will
make it inherently more difficult to achieve productivity increases which will match those of industry.

On the plus side, it is supposed at least, that there is greater
personalization of work in the services, greater variety and rich-
ness in the jobs, greater contact with customers, less domination
by machines, less submergence in large organizations, greater
scope for the exercise of skill and craftsmanship, and greater
visibility of accomplishment. There are, as we have seen, those
who would argue that all of these things mean greater job satisfaction, and that greater job satisfaction will result in greater
productivity. There would appear, however, to be no reason
why this generalization should be any weaker or any more powerful than the data from industry has indicated. It is very likely
that in the services as well, all of this is very much a matter of
individual differences.

APPLYING THE INDUSTRIAL MODEL

The most obvious proposal for the greater productivity
growth of the service sector is to do what industry has been
doing for so long—to take the manufacturing attitude. The
productivity enhancing strategies that have found some success in industry ought to be transferred to the government, the
hospitals, and the barber shop. Industry has been effective in
using machines to increase the productivity of people, in using
operations design to produce systems which "work smarter,"

and to a degree, industry has been effective in using wage incentive systems to get people to work harder. Industry has made great productivity progress through product standardization and very high volumes of output. Why not do these things in the service producing sector?

From a macroscopic point of view, this proposal seems unlikely to have much effect. In fact, the proposal may seem a little ridiculous. There appear to be very good reasons why the services cannot be like industry. Everyone agrees that it is difficult to measure productivity in government, in a hospital, or in a law firm. And, of course, what cannot be measured does not exist, and therefore certainly cannot be improved. The recent attempts, in this view, to measure the quantity and quality of health care rendered by hospital are destined to yield only technical reports and nothing useful. The Bureau of Labor Statistics has little if anything in the way of productivity measures for two thirds of our economy. They have nothing at all for state and local governments, trade, construction, finance, medical services. Thus it is argued we don't even know where we stand in these areas.

The small size of most service enterprises, the small volume of output, and the individual nature of many service producers will prevent productivity growth through economies of scale. The lack of standardization of output, the scarcity of repetitive operations, the personal, individual nature of the work—all of these combine to prevent the application of the basic strategy of industry. It will just not be possible to standardize and mass produce most services.

There is also a cultural bias that seems to assert that services are services and by their very nature not proper subjects for questions about productivity. The concept of productivity is meaningless for a police department, a law firm, or a school. To become interested in productivity is to challenge the essential nature of what is being produced.

Furthermore, the services are intrinsically labor intensive. Services by and large are produced by people, will always have to be produced by people, and beyond a few trivial examples, machines and technology will have little impact.

If one accepts these highly plausible arguments, nothing could be more foolish than to attempt to increase the productivity of the service sector by applying the industrial model. Yet as so often happens, if one looks behind these generalities to things that are happening in specific situations, one finds that the industrial model is beginning to be applied rather vigorously. Not only is it being applied, but it appears to be succeeding to an interesting degree. Generalizations about the service sector are weaker than generalizations about the manufacturing sector. Productivity strategies that may have broad application in industry will be effective in some places in the services and ridiculous in others. The service sector is highly situation specific, importantly a matter of individual differences. The university, the airline, the doctor's office, and the barber shop are not very much alike. Once we take a look at them individually, there begins to be some sense to the application of some of the things which are widely used in industry.

Too Much Too Soon

The growth of employment that the services have experienced in recent years would probably have caused considerable productivity difficulties in industry as well had it occurred there. In those services where employment and output have grown rapidly, everyone has been too busy satisfying the demand to worry very much about productivity. Things were too new, there was too little experience, too little background on which to draw.

Aside from perhaps being strongly dependent on people to achieve their output, there is little that is common among the organizations in the service sector. They are distributed over the full range from single person businesses to corporate giants; they include a bewildering array of activities ranging from beauty shops to equipment leasing. If there are things in common among these units which are important from the viewpoint of productivity strategy, we have not yet discovered what they are. The service sector is too new an object of such attention to expect such insights.

In those services where this rapid growth has taken place, there is now a kind of maturation occurring, and they are beginning to pass through the same experiments which industry passed through in the 19th and early 20th centuries. Indeed, there may be a kind of universal growth process that many organizations go through as they seek to improve their own productivity. If this is the case, it would be a matter of some importance in developing productivity, and we will subsequently look further into this. What is going on in many of the services are things that industry has considerable experience with already. The important thing, however, is that very selectively and very particularly the industrial model is being applied.

Enter the Machines

Most obvious and most dramatic is the entrance of technology into service production in certain fields. The computer, the machine of the century, is every bit as powerful in these fields as it is in manufacturing generally. The examples are legion: the airline reservation systems, banking services, retail store inventorying and check out. Less visible are the applications of the computer in hospitals, for example, where it is being used to handle patient records, schedules, admissions, and even assist in diagnoisis. No one needs to write yet another essay on the wonders of this class of machines. Yet machines are improving productivity in far simpler and far more prosaic ways. In cleaning and pressing shops for example, two operators working with the latest equipment can do ninety shirts per hour as opposed to sixty-five with the old machines. There is little point in proliferating examples. There is some point, however, in pointing out that there are probably a very large number of specific production systems in the service sector where machines can be creatively applied to increase productivity. The point is that we don't yet understand very well how to do this, but all the evidence accumulated so far is positive, not negative.

Where information is captured, stored, and processed into decision making inputs, the computer and its array of related devices has a strong potential for increasing productivity. In the service sector it can become not just a supporting element of a production system, but the very essence of the production system itself. To the degree that the services are centrally involved in providing information, the computer is *the* productivity enhancing possibility.

Computers also have the possibility of adding a measure of trust at points in the service sector where trust has sometimes been in short supply. When one's car is connected to a computer and the machine performs the diagnosis, it has at least a consistency which we have sometimes suspected the service manager of lacking. Similarly, the computer may diagnose the difficulties with your TV or any other major appliance in a way which promises substantial increases in the productivity of repair operations.

Machines for the service industries provide the same sort of mixed blessing as they do for manufacturing. A big, fixed, inflexible investment in equipment makes it difficult to respond to the fluctuations in demand which have characterized many types of services. The airlines, for example, have a massive investment in planes which are designed to make them more productive. When demand levels off or declines, it becomes that much more difficult to respond with compensating adjustments in service.

Economies of Scale

In similar fashion, we are seeing the introduction of standardization and mass production. Every operation involved in distribution and marketing will benefit from the ultimate standardization of packages, cartons, and pallets. The fast food service operation and the credit card bank loan are classic examples of what for a long time had been seen as highly individualized operations. Standardization involves some tradeoffs that everyone may not wish to make, but the real point is, once again, that there are likely to be further opportunities to standardize and mass produce services.

In the distribution of food one encounters the kind of possibility which illustrates the tremendous potential of standardization. Manufacturers of packaged foods and major food retailers use a 48 by 40 inch pallet. Many wholesalers use a 40 by 32 inch pallet in their warehouse operations. When a truckload of merchandise moves through this distribution channel it must be repalletized by hand, an operation which requires about four hours. If everyone used a standard pallet, the time to handle a truckload could be cut to about thirty minutes. The

National Productivity Commission has suggested that standardization of pallets might bring productivity increases of the same order as those produced by the computer.

Closely linked with standardization is mass production. This may be as simple as the lawn care service which offers a special price if most of the homes on a block buy its services. It may be as old a strategy as the doctor who maintains several examining rooms and overschedules his appointments in order to reduce his idle time to virtually zero.

The service sector is seeing the advent of strategies aimed at taking advantage of economies of scale. Like the other industrial productivity strategies, the occurrence of this is spotty; it is not a general trend, but a strategy which works in some situations. Construction companies offer bigger packages of services. Airlines move into hotels. Chains and franchises in many kinds of services are deliberately designed to maximize economies of scale. Advertising, management skills, service design, and associated products are available to a single franchise operator in quantity and quality which could only be supported by a very large organization.

The services are moving into the "working smarter" strategies of industry as well. They are using the classical industrial engineering techniques of work measurement, job design and wage incentives in clerical operations, for example, and where repetitive operations occur. It is, unfortunately, quite likely that they will live through the same history of short run success and long run disappointment with this approach to productivity which has been experienced in industry. Operations design is being used to plan and schedule service operations, to eliminate useless activities, to cope with uncertainties, to establish management controls, to do, in short, all of the things that operations design has been doing in industry.

What is happening in the service sector in terms or productivity growth is exactly what has happened in the past in industry. The industrial model is being applied with some considerable success. The services are not, it is beginning to appear, essentially resistant to the sort of productivity enhancing strategies which are used in manufacturing. The problem is simply that the variety of the production systems one encounters in the service sector makes it necessary to look more carefully at very particular situations. Some things make sense in retailing which do not make much sense in government, or in education.

BEYOND THE INDUSTRIAL MODEL

Suppose, however, that one wanted to look at productivity in the services to see if there were possibilities which went beyond doing what has already been done in manufacturing. Applying the industrial model appears promising on the basis of the data we now have, but are there other approaches which are based upon some special characteristics, some special kinds of production systems which are found in the production of services? Perhaps we do not yet understand this sector well enough, but still it may be useful to propose a few hypotheses.

Measurement of productivity in general and quantification of output in particular are challenges which seem to occur rather generally in this area. In retailing, for example, the customer does not simply get the goods he purchased. He also gets to greatly varying degrees credit, delivery, service, repairs free of charge, return privileges, air conditioning, music, rest-rooms, parking facilities, the convenience of store location and hours, the advice of sales personnel, and so on. Just how to measure the output of a retail operation is thus far from clear. To judge whether or not a particular activity is productive presents serious practical as well as philosophical problems.

Similar problems occur widely throughout the services—in health care, in government, and even in construction and transportation. It is not clear at all, for example, that the productivity of a transportation system is well understood by measuring its output in passenger miles per day. Perhaps productivity should include some consideration of what people do when they get where they are going, what they do with the time they save or lose, what the system does toward creating or eliminating jobs, what influence the system has on land use and the development of neighborhoods, and so on.

These problems of measurement are unquestionably serious. It may perhaps be worth repeating once again, however, that their existence should not lead one to the conclusion that productivity growth cannot begin until they are solved. The prevalence of super-scientism continues to inhibit productivity improvement by the pseudo-logical assertion that surely we cannot improve what we cannot measure. It would appear that the measurement revolution will have its greatest impact on the productivity in the service sector. It appears also that the sort of strategy we have outlined for approaching management productivity may have extensive applications in law firms, hospitals, government, and a variety of other service systems. Let those who produce the service make their own systematic determinations of which of their activities are productive and which are not. Let them, by studying how they actually use their energies, begin to develop their working styles in more productive directions. This may not maximize social welfare, it may not increase productivity according to everyone's definition of it, but it will constitute a series of experiments which will not be all bad in their results. They will give us a good deal more understanding of the production of services than we now have.

CLIENT PARTICIPATION

One of the dramatic changes that has been taking place in retailing since 1920 is the growth of self-service, the growth of customer participation in the production process, and the transfer of some of the functions from the retailer to the client. This is common enough in our experience, but the opportunities for client participation in the production of services are far wider than retailing alone and have some interesting implications for the growth of productivity.

As clients, we can participate in all sorts of do-it-yourself activities such as assembling manufactured products, painting our own homes, repairing our own appliances, participating in our own educations, and so on. Client participation has the interesting effect of seeming to increase the productivity of those who render the service, but it has, of course, some kind of an effect on the productivity of the clients themselves. We will shortly be examining the problem of personal productivity and the problem of productivity of the household unit, and we will need then to consider the implications of client participation for the client. All shades of participation are often possible.

One can do without the service, do it entirely for one's self or participate with those whose work it is to provide part of the service. During times of economic uncertainty there is a tendency to increase our participation as clients, to buy fewer services. But client participation often has its own rewards. It may be fun, satisfying, convenient, sparing of embarrassment, or even relieve us from having to trust and rely upon those in whom we lack confidence.

New dimensions of participation are constantly emerging. Successful experiments have been conducted in which patients take their own medical histories by sitting at a computer terminal and typing in answers to questions that appear on the screen before them. Patients report that this relieves them of some anxiety and embarrassment, and physicians report that the results are wholly satisfactory. Garages are appearing which furnish tools and instructions for elaborate and complex car repairs. The fine art of wine making is practiced in more and more basements. When police protection is found to be inadequate, citizens' groups still emerge to undertake their own crime prevention programs.

The basic problem, of course, is to discover and to motivate that degree of client participation which is in some sense most productive for society. While it is unlikely that we can solve this problem in the near future, it is important that options be available so that we can choose highly varying degrees of participation. By experimenting with such options, and only by this means, we can learn something about what degrees of participation are good from the viewpoint of those who furnish the services, from those who are clients, and from those who only experience the secondary effects of such transactions.

Consider the case of health care, for example. The medical profession has, deliberately or not, acted to severely limit our participation in the maintenance of our own physical condition. Medical care is in short supply in many areas of our country and is very expensive everywhere. If we participated more fully in the process, more people would have access to the available professionals and the available facilities. If we participated more fully, then presumably the price of the services received would come down, further increasing the accessibility of care. To do this, aside from meeting a very great deal of institutionalized resistance, we must determine the willingness of people to participate in training which would increase their competence for self-care, their willingness to trade time and effort in order to cut the cost of health services or to increase their use of services formerly done without. We would have to find ways of making self-care reliable and give it some fail-safe protection in order to reduce the risks to a point which clients would find acceptable. The potential, however, is probably as great as it is in retailing or in home maintenance, but we will need to make experiments which will help us to understand how to do it.

Producer Convenience

Another form of client participation which has great potential involves the client's acceptance of the service at the convenience of the server. This is motivated by price reductions which reflect, at least in part, the resulting increase in productivity from the server's point of view. Stand-by fares for airline travel, special telephone rates for evenings and weekends, and off-season hotel rates are part of this tradition. The problem of fluctuating demand, uncertainty about service loads, and the alternation of idleness with more demand than can be met, are as close to general problems as we are likely to find in the service sector. The use of price incentives to motivate client participation in the better matching of demand with capacity probably has far greater application than we have so far imagined.

The doctor's office is the classic example of this pervasive problem of matching demand with capacity when the extent and timing of the demand are uncertain and largely in the hands of clients. The basic trade-offs are reasonably clear. If we increase the rate at which patients flow into the doctor's office, we increase the utilization of the doctor, reducing his idle time at the expense of increasing the waiting time of the patients. We can reduce the waiting time of the patients, which presumably increases their productivity, by reducing the rate at which they arrive at the office, but this will increase the idle time experienced by the physician. We can try to reduce the uncertainty associated with the process by carefully scheduling appointments, but this is subject to diminishing marginal returns because the times the doctor spends with patients are uncertain and variable, and the times at which patients will actually arrive, if at all, for a specified appointment time are also uncertain. A part of the problem is that these effects are non-linear and thus somewhat non-intuitive. If we double the rate at which patients arrive, we more than double the waiting time they experience. If we halve the rate at which patients arrive, we more than double the idle time which the doctor experiences. A part of the problem is the means of motivation which will be effective in eliciting the participation of the client. Physicians have generally experienced sufficient demand for their services so that arrangements can strongly favor their convenience and the reduction of their idle time at the expense of the patients. The same cannot be said for restaurants, taxis, or government agencies. The basic problem of matching demand with capacity can be met in part by the operations designer who can develop schedules and influence flow rates, in part by clients who can consider the degree to which they wish to participate in accepting services at other than their convenience, and in part by those who offer services by the use of price adjustments and similar incentives to regulate to a degree the timing of demand. The diffusion of these productivity enhancing techniques appears at the moment to be slow, but their potential throughout the service sector is considerable.

Labor Intensity

The third general feature which has some power in explaining productivity in the service sector is the high labor content of the output, the strong reliance on people, the importance of humans and the relative unimportance, at present at least, of machines. There is a long standing hypothesis that machines are easier to manage than people. Machines, it is supposed, are not absent, not tardy, not variable in the quantity and quality of their output, not given to generating grievances, and not in need of a lot of "human relations." As we have seen, machines do not live up to this supposition fully, nor do they possess the wonderful flexibility and versatility of people. Nonetheless, what some managers like to call "people problems" are magnified in their importance in the service sector. The influence of individual differences among working people on the quantity and quality of output is especially great. This will surely mean that what the economist likes to call "labor embodied technical change" will be of outstanding importance in the service sector. Training, education, health, and working style will be significant factors in productivity, but the ways in which individual working styles can be developed and given fuller freedom to influence productivity will be even more important here than we have suggested they may be in manufacturing. Fortunately, it is very likely to be true that in the service sector jobs can be designed with far less interdependence, far greater scope, far more opportunity for the development of personal working styles than is generally the case in manufacturing. The strategy which we anticipated in Chapter 4 and which we will develop more fully in subsequent chapters, appears to be especially appropriate and important in the services. The nature of services may well be that there is significant opportunity to define jobs in order to provide maximum freedom for the development of individual work styles, and this strategy may well be a strong candidate of a general productivity enhancing approach for the service sector.

While we cannot manage here a detailed survey of the great variety of productivity initiatives that are taking place in the service sector, perhaps we can supply one or two hypotheses in a few of the major areas. The function of these hypotheses may be to stimulate the reader to his own critical analysis of the routes toward productivity growth which are the subjects of these experiments, and those which, for one reason or another, are not.

WHERE THE ACTION IS

It may be useful to take a brief look at where some of the productivity improving action is taking place. In doing so, it might be possible to make a very casual test of some of our basic hypotheses about the service sector. It is highly varied in the size of its units and in the nature of its operations. The industrial model is being applied, not generally, but in specific places to specific degrees. There are, furthermore, some areas where we seem to be "hung up" on the problem of measuring output, and productivity growth is being slowed by this seemingly logical preoccupation.

Government

One in every six American workers is a government employee. The government is the giant of the service sector. At the local level, the industrial model is being applied with vigor, stimulated by ample grants from the Federal Government to help solve the problems of the cities. Garbage collection, police operations, and metropolitan transportation are all being subjected to the manufacturing attitude, led by the New York City project in municipal operations design of former Mayor Lindsay and the Rand Corporation. City to city variations of 300 percent to 500 percent in the productivity of garbage handling, known professionally as solid waste management, suggest the immense potential for improvement. In law enforcement, similar variability is being uncovered. In one city with 3,700 index crimes per 100,000 people, law enforcement expenditures amounted to less than $10 per capita. In a city of similar size with a nearly identical crime rate, expenditures amounted to $42 per person. Generally speaking, it would appear that in municipal services, people are not waiting for fine definitions of productivity and are moving ahead in an attempt to stamp out some of the worst situations by vigorous application of the industrial model.

Where to go beyond the services is not as clear, but there are some encouraging indications. There is a tendency not to worry obsessively about how to define the productivity of a court of law, but rather to look at the juvenile justice system or the criminal justice system as a whole. We are beginning to agree that recidivism rates are useful indicators of the productivity of many elements of these systems, and that perhaps it is a step toward productivity to close all of the juvenile institutions in the state of Massachusetts.

At the federal level, things are more difficult. There are indications that the current flurry of interest in measuring the productivity of the federal sector will be but another fad in a long sequence of such management ploys. Many career federal executives clearly say so in private conversations. The National

Productivity Commission gave great emphasis to measuring productivity in the federal sector, but its survival is seriously in question, and its present reduction to an Office of Productivity does not suggest a lot of interest in this effort. This is perhaps a classic case of the principle that one cannot do anything about productivity until it is measured, and it is unlikely to be measured here in any very widely acceptable way.

Education

Productivity in education was first stimulated by the rising student populations of the sixties which taxed the capacity of the system. As student populations are leveling off and declining, the twin forces of inflation and the refusal of taxpayers to widely support further funds for education have maintained the interest at a high level. On one hand the administrative and support aspects of education have been subjected strongly if belatedly to the working smarter strategies of the industrial model. "Sound business practices," work measurement, and computers have had their modest effect here — modest, because educational administrators are constantly distracted by the central function which they see themselves as providing, the enhancement of learning. The application of the industrial model here, in the form of performance contracting — so much money for so much learning as demonstrated by test results — has largely failed and passed into history. The use of machines in the classroom has also had a very limited success. There seems to be a persistent effectiveness associated with the personal presence of a good teacher and a moderate-sized group of students. Teachers especially, would like to encourage the notion that good teaching cannot be defined, and thus productivity cannot be discussed. There is a considerable body of research which is being interpreted very roughly as saying that the success of people in our society is almost independent of anything the schools may do, and thus the schools themselves are very questionable institutions. At least it is not very useful to worry about their productivity. Education, for all the effort that has been devoted to its study and analysis, is still very much a field for continuous experimentation. One thing, however, that may be clear is that people who participate most fully in their own education seem to learn most effectively—a good example of the productivity enhancing effects of client participation. The classic problem, of course, is how to motivate this participation.

Health Care

From 1960 to 1971 health care expenditures rose from 5.9 percent of the GNP to 7.4 percent. Hospital costs rose from $16.46 per patient day in 1960 to $53.95 in 1970 and are continuing to rise at an annual rate of over 13 percent. Health care is a huge industry which affects all of us and which has tremendous political impact. The productivity increasing efforts in this sector have been vigorous so far as the "business and support" side of things are concerned, but slow and heavily resisted on the side of the actual provision of professional care. Hospital administration has been operating for some time on an increasingly professional basis, and it is no longer necessary for an administrator to be a physician. The full range of "working smarter" strategies are gradually making their way into hospital operations. Considerable attention is being devoted to improving the productivity of hospital manpower, the use of disposable supplies, centralized purchasing, and so on. More recently the advanced techniques of the operations designer have found experimental application in scheduling admissions, scheduling surgery, increasing the utilization of beds and radiology equipment, examining productivity in clinical laboratories, and so on. Operations designers are being well received and seem generally successful as long as they do not become involved in the professional provision of care or in anything that could conceivably influence unfavorably the quality of care. Fortunately, the measurement of the quality of medical care is still of great interest, and sophisticated approaches are being taken, but productivity improvements are not held up until the measurement problem is somehow solved.

Interesting things are happening on the professional side of health care, but not to the delight of the professionals. Nursing care is a very large factor in hospital productivity, and successful experiments have now been concluded in well over one hundred hospitals which do three rather amazing things. Working very closely with nurses themselves, standards have been established for the quality of nursing care. Work measurement has been possible to produce a very good idea of how much time is required for various nursing tasks. These measurements are very sophisticated in the sense that they take into account the number of patients being cared for, the kinds and severities of illness, the extent of support assistance in the form of aids, and so on. From this it has been possible to develop standards for staffing which have in many cases reduced the numbers of nurses which were thought necessary to maintain the quality of care. To a degree, the once serious nursing shortage has been alleviated by these staffing standards. It is of special importance to note that these things were achieved in cooperation with the nurses themselves; otherwise, serious difficulties would certainly have appeared in attempting to apply the standards. In at least one professional area, productivity has been successfully faced.

Machines are being proposed to help physicians, mostly in the form of computers to handle patient data, but also in the use of TV equipment to permit the physicians to examine X-rays or look at blood smears at a distance. These sorts of things are rather readily accepted, but when the computer is used as a diagnostic decision making aid, serious difficulties are encountered. Such innovations which have their impact at the very core of professional activity are likely to be slow indeed in their rate of diffusion. The current major topic in the area of professional care is the Health Maintenance Organization which will furnish prepaid care to a membership group. There seems to be general agreement that HMO's will improve the quality of health care actually received by members, will perhaps reduce its cost slightly below current commercial insurance rates, and will provide real opportunities for productivity increases through more sophisticated management and scheduling of professional support functions such as laboratories. The principal objectors are, of course, the physicians who are not yet clear about what this form of practice would do to their incomes. Fortunately, it appears that we will study the possibilities of HMO's on an experimental basis and have an opportunity to explore their productivity implications before deciding how far to go.

Distribution

Selling and distribution represent seriously expensive aspects of getting products to users. These functions have periodically undergone attempts to make salesmen more productive, to find out if advertising really pays, to determine how fast delivery must be to keep a customer, and so on. Here is an area where a very great deal is known about productivity growth, but the knowledge has been extremely slow to diffuse. There are well developed examples of how to improve the productivity of a sales force, partly by the use of audio-visual equipment, by making calls on the phone, and partly by studying the optimum number of calls to make on a customer, the kinds of calls to make on big customers and little ones, and so on. The crucial question of what inventory levels to maintain is perhaps one of the best developed aspects of the sophisticated methods of modern operations design. Yet these things have received only the most limited application.

The exception to this observation, however, is the use of sophisticated materials handling and storing equipment. Used in conjunction with computers, the physical handling equipment which is employed in modern distribution systems is truly remarkable in its productivity. Dramatic increases in output per man-hour have been achieved in warehousing, order picking, packaging, sorting, and delivery of all sorts of merchandise. The soft side of the distribution sector has, however, a great potential for improvement.

STAMPING OUT THE HORROR STORIES

There is an old principle often used by operations designers to guide their efforts in improving the productivity of a production system. There is a greater marginal return from efforts devoted to making the worst elements of a system more productive than there is from efforts devoted to further increasing the productivity of those elements which are already among the best parts of the system. Look at the worst problems, the bottlenecks, and the horror stories first. In the service sector the period of rapid growth, high demand, and the absence of either the skill or the tradition of productivity has produced an expected quota of horror stories. Laundries lose our shirts, parking lots lose our cars, airlines lose our luggage. Repairs are made which are ineffective in restoring the performance of the car or the appliance. Teachers fail to meet their classes, instructional methods leave students hopelessly lost, the lack of guidance puts students in courses they neither want nor need. Computers scramble one's charge accounts, one's magazine subscriptions, and add a significant element of uncertainty to all of one's relations with big firms and big government. Vending machines, rapid transit systems, and welfare agencies just don't work very well. Each of us has his own list of horror stories arising from his adventures with the service sector. In manufacturing there is a tradition of feasibility before optimality. Let's first find out how to get the product out the door at all before we worry about the best possible way of getting it out of the door. Let's find out how to make it at all, before we get too involved in maximizing the productivity of the system.

The fact that the service sector tends to be often found in the stage of feasibility problems, doing it at all, rather than optimality problems, doing it the best way, is not really surprising. With the service sector's generally lower level of management sophistication, the existence of the customer complaint from the lonely individual as the prevalent mechanism for stimulating improvement, and its early attempts at standardization and mass production—these horror stories are to be expected. It seems worth saying, even though obvious, that the first steps in many parts of the service sector toward improving productivity will not require sophisticated output measures nor advanced methods of operations design. The first steps should simply be aimed at stamping out the horror stories. This may not create perfection, since it may be quite reasonable from everybody's point of view not to pay the price of a baggage handling system which would never lose a bag. What is important, however, is that simply obtained measures of the frequency of horror stories be obtained, that the working people involved be kept aware of the frequency with which horrors are being committed, and the just-paying-attention effect be allowed to operate. For the present at least, productivity in many parts of the service sector may not be a very subtle problem.

Notes

The work of Victor Fuchs is the outstanding source of data on productivity in the service sector.

Fuchs, Victor R. "Statistical Analysis of Productivity in Selected Service Industries in the United States, 1939–1963," *Review of Income and Wealth*. Vol. 12, No. 3, September, 1966.

Fuchs, Victor R., and Jean Alexander Wilburn. *Productivity Differences within the Service Sector.* Occasional Paper 102. New York: National Bureau of Economic Research, 1967.

Fuchs, Victor R., ed. *Production and Productivity in the Service Industries.* Studies in Income and Wealth, Vol. 34. New York: National Bureau of Economic Research, 1969.

The Second Annual Report of the National Commission on Productivity has expressed considerable concern about the service economy's productivity. For example, the following comments on productivity in government appear in the report's summary section:

> "The demands on government at all levels are large and growing larger. But the quality of government services do not appear to be keeping pace with these demands or these increased costs. The financial resources available to government are being squeezed between multiplying public needs and the rising costs of meeting those needs, on the one hand, and a growing and understandable resistance on the part of the public to provide more tax resources, on the other. One answer to this dilemma is improved productivity. The Commission, therefore, is devoting a major portion of its resources to projects in the area of state and local government productivity.
>
> The difficulty is that there exists in the public sector no price competition and thus no market discipline to induce efficiency. Governments that consistently provide poor services are not subject to the same risks that the market system imposes on inefficient or unproductive enterprises in the private sector. The only risk governments face comes at the ballot box. But the nearly total absence of objective performance yardsticks for measuring gov-

ernment productivity has left the voter with little basis for a sound judgment. It is not without political significance, however, that the public has substantial doubts about the productivity of the government worker. For example, in a public opinion study for the Commission, Louis Harris found that a greater percentage of those questioned (39 percent) attributed lower than average productivity to government workers than to any other occupational group."

9

New Targets:

Private Productivity

INVASION OF PRIVACY

Private productivity has usually been an exclusively private concern. Our productivity as individuals, as family units, as household units, not as members of some other producing system, has not been much discussed. How we spend our money, our time, and our cognitive energies have been concerns which have come close to the very essence of freedom and privacy. We have always been more or less casually concerned with getting the most for our money, consuming intelligently, using our time wisely, and getting the most fun and relaxation from our leisure. How seriously we attended to these things was, however, very much our own business. It becomes a little less our own business when we experience a gasoline shortage, when we are asked to conserve energy, or when we are invited to join a meat boycott. Inflation and shortages make us think about the productivity of our consumption activities, although we don't use the word "productivity." The question is still what we are getting out in relation to what we are putting in. In some sense we all want more for less. There is, however, a great array of differences among the energy expenditures we make to get more for less and the methods we use in going about it. Nobody much cares about these things beyond his own concerns until it becomes dramatically clear that one person's consumption patterns influence those of another. The productivity of one household unit has an influence on the productivity of others. What I consume, you cannot. What I buy helps reduce the availability and increase the price of what you want to buy. My consumption patterns can actually result, to a degree, in your giving up more for things you want less. Private productivity is the same sort of crucial variable as industrial or government productivity in the determination of rates of inflation, levels of real wealth, levels of unemployment, and so on. The basic motivation for whatever attention we choose to pay to private productivity is still getting more of what we want for less, but we are all in this together. The decision to have children, we are beginning to understand, is no longer a decision that we can sensibly make on strictly private grounds.

We are discovering also that the data we need to make productivity enhancing decisions, the data that will increase the rationality of our consumption decisions, we are not likely to obtain as individuals. It takes a consumer movement to bring forth the data on miles per gallon which we have never reliably had in the past and which represents only a first small step in obtaining the information necessary to rationalize the decision to buy a car.

It may well be that thinking about private productivity will at least raise some radical hypotheses. If, for example, we are in a period of sharply rising prices, the almost universal reaction is to seek higher wages to compensate for the rising "cost of living." But higher wages are to a degree self-defeating because they will only contribute to further inflation. It makes much more sense to reduce one's consumption, to contribute to a reduction in demand by either doing without or raising one's personal productivity to reduce the necessity for doing without. This would, in turn, tend to restore prices to lower or more stable levels, rather than aggravating inflation still further. This idea is, however, sufficiently radical as to be un-American.

THE MEANING OF
PRIVATE PRODUCTIVITY

Getting more money is almost always seen as a better choice than getting more for your money. Although there are doubtless great individual differences, getting more free time is almost always seen as better than being more productive with the available free time—productive in the sense of whatever it is we happen to wish to achieve with our free time. Being more productive not only in consumption, but in education, recreation, travel, and community services are hardly ever thought of as ways of increasing one's real wealth—real wealth in the sense of realizing whatever it is one's goals may be and of going on to create new goals. We consider here not only what the economist refers to as final consumption of the goods and services coming out of the economy, but one's personal production of time, energy, and thought.

The counter culture movement is an excellent example of some creative experiments in personal productivity. Stop coveting the material output of our economy. Stop being a consumer, stop being a person whose social role is largely to buy things. The consumer, say the counter culture philosophers, is a kind of servant or victim of industrial society, who, if he could free himself long enough to think about his real desires, would live quite differently. Many of us, they suggest, would stop being consumers and become producers—producers of ideas, friendships, and the things that we regard as real necessities. The key is to organize one's own life according to one's own standards, desires, and needs, not according to those suggested and imposed by our society. Doing this, the philosophers say, will lead one to some conclusions about what necessities really are; a person may discover that buying may not be the best way of getting what he needs. By redirecting our energies we can buy far less and make far more.

These suggestions will not appeal to all of us, but they represent an instance of the application of some very basic insights about personal productivity growth. A central problem is knowing what one wants; the key ingredient is to be sufficiently clear about one's goals in order to choose wisely. Second, it is important to choose deliberately, to plan, to organize one's life thoughtfully and reasonably. These, as we shall see, are insights perhaps worth attending to in the study of private productivity.

One of the wonderful, yet troubling, things about trying to be analytical about personal productivity is that it leads one almost immediately into rather deep philosophical water. One encounters immediately the questions of the meaning of freedom, of the formulation of life goals, about the selection and modification of life styles, and about what may be the meaning to each of us of the notion of the good life. In what follows, we have tried very hard not to conduct an amateur adventure into philosophy, to avoid proposals which imply or assume answers to these great questions, and to consider productivity always in terms of maximizing the freedom of the individual to achieve whatever he seeks to achieve, as well as he is able to understand this.

THE INDUSTRIAL MODEL

Why not run one's affairs and one's household along the lines of the industrial way of doing things? Industry, after all, has professionalized the skill of getting more with less, and it would seem perfectly sensible to transfer this skill and technology to the sphere of getting more of what one wants personally with less. The most obvious field for application of the concepts of goals, budgets, allocations, records, feedback, control and all the basic features of the industrial model is consumption. How can one be more productive as a consumer?

On the average, and there are great individual differences, we spend 25 percent of our personal disposable income for food, 14 percent for household operations, 13 percent for housing itself, 13 percent for transportation, and 10 percent for clothing. These five top categories account for 75 percent of our disposable income. If we could become more productive in the way we make these expenditures, we could make a significant impact on the degree to which we get what we want with the money we have. There are direct analogies, of course, between the consumption decisions of a household and those of industry. Should we make it or buy it? Should we do it ourselves or hire someone to do it? Should we participate more or less in production? What are the economic quantities we should purchase? How much inventory is it sensible to carry? How can we make the trade-offs between quality and price? At what price will an electric pencil sharpener or an electric can opener provide enough time saved, enough prestige, pleasure, or fascination to represent a good investment?

As with industry, there are basic problems associated with all of our major tools—the home, the car, and the appliances. When one buys a major tool, one wants to consider its initial cost, its anticipated service life, its maintenance costs, the benefits of preventive maintenance over emergency repairs, the rate of obsolescence as new models appear, the ultimate resale value, and so on. There are perfectly well developed methods at work in industry for considering these things. One needs only to get a little self-instruction in these methods and then be in a position to get the necessary input data at a reasonable cost. A very important aspect of the application of the industrial model must be emphatically noted. Just as in industry these decisions are not made on the basis of costs alone, so in personal decisions they would not and should not be. To apply the industrial model is not to assert that cost is the only consideration, or should be the only consideration. Our objectives include pleasure, status, pride of ownership, beauty, convenience, the courtesy and reliability of those who sell and service our tools, and so on. Just as these things are considered in industry, so should they be in personal decisions. To apply the industrial model is not to exclude them, but rather to try considering them as clearly and explicitly as possible. The industrial approach, roughly speaking, is to get the data and do the analysis which will permit those things to be expressed in dollars which can most readily be expressed in dollars. Those things about which we can only make qualitative judgments should at least have the judgments expressed explicitly, say in the form of a ranking among alternatives. There will always be those aspects of any decision, personal or industrial, which cannot readily be made explicit, but the hypothesis of this approach is that the more clear one is about one's decision, the more productive the results are likely to be.

Similarly, there are direct analogies in the area of personal financial planning. How much to save out of current income, how much life insurance is enough, how to plan for retirement, what combinations of risk and return are consistent with one's financial goals? All of these things are in industry the subject of data collection, analysis, and efforts to push the decisions toward greater and greater explicitness.

Explicitness

Applying the industrial model means in the first instance, the selection of the major decisions influencing one's operations and the decisions where the application of some effort toward productivity enhancement is likely to be rewarding to a degree which will warrant the cost of the effort. It means becoming somewhat explicit about goals, objectives, or targets, and formulating long-range plans for moving toward these. It means being to some degree explicit about the uncertainties which lie ahead, and the formulation of alternate plans to meet such contingencies as may appear most serious. It means translating long-range plans into decisions, and decisions into data collection programs, analyses, and explicit judgments. It means the establishment, as one executes the decisions, of budgets, controls, allocation programs, records, feedback, review, and finally reformulation of plans and the making of new decisions on the basis of what has been learned.

Beyond consumption, the industrial model has the same potential for application to the areas of education and personal development, leisure and recreation time allocation, community service and giving, health management, and so on. How often are educational programs chosen and vast investments of personal time committed on the flimsiest of career guidance information, the total absence of any forecast of future employment opportunities, and an almost infantile perception of what the works of various jobs and professions are actually like? How much of our planning of our own recreational activities is highly equipment oriented? We get a boat because it's the thing to get, and we find that we are then locked into boating for a considerable future period. This may be just fine in terms of our personal desires, but on the other hand, it may represent a loss of flexibility which we may regret as time passes. How much of our charitable giving is in response to a plan formulated on the basis of what we have to give and what causes we would like to support? How much of it is simply in response to being asked to give at the office and asked to give by someone who rings the doorbell on Sunday afternoon? How much of our eating, drinking, smoking and exercising is consistent with any sort of reasonable plan for the maintenance of our own physical health? How much is an error which we vaguely regret but never quite do anything about?

THE FAILURE OF THE INDUSTRIAL MODEL

Once again it is important to dwell on individual differences. There are those who go quite far in the application of the industrial model to personal productivity growth. There are those, the poor, the handicapped, and the unemployed, for whom the whole discussion is totally beside the point. But there are, in our economy, a great majority for whom an approximation of the industrial model would make some sense. If they were to apply it to some degree to the important aspects of their lives, they would find the results satisfying. It would take some time and effort to do this but the results would turn out to be rewarding in that they achieved more with less—more of what they wanted in life within the constraints of the time, energy, and money they had available. The obvious fact, is however, that the industrial model simply is not used by this great majority. It does not work. The ideas are too obvious to suppose they are not widely understood; it is simply that they are not used and quite deliberately not used. The industrial model is a contemporary phrase for the examined, the reflective life. The ancient wisdom, "The unexamined life is not worth living," is the imperative to apply the industrial model, an imperative which is widely ignored. How can one explain the failure of the industrial model as a key strategy for personal productivity growth? Where can we turn next if it cannot, as is quite obvious, provide a realistically useful productivity strategy?

There are three basic reasons for the failure of the industrial model: it requires data, evidence, and facts which are not readily available to the individual; it requires an investment of time and of cognitive energy which is not consistent with our personal styles of life; and finally, it requires a degree of clarity about what we want out of life which few of us possess or can readily develop. We will examine each of these in turn.

Data Requirements

The amount of data which most of us have in hand when we buy a car, a life insurance policy, invest in a stock, or pay our tuition at a university is really very modest indeed. In most of these major decisions, we are willing to rely on the most casual advice from acquaintances who have had some fragmentary experience, from those who make the goods and sell the services, whose advice is hardly disinterested, and on a faith in some minimal government regulation to protect us against the grossest forms of fraud and personal danger. We have become willing participants in a system of production and distribution which almost totally fails to produce the data on which consumers can make decisions approaching the most modest degree of reasonableness. Industrial consumption involves readily met demands for data of all sorts — guarantees, tests, cost analyses, and so on — which are largely absent in the stages of final consumption.

The consumer movement, as we have said, is moving in this direction. But based on the histories of similar attempts, it is not likely to enlist the massive support and power of consumers themselves. The home economics education movement, the agricultural extension services, the consumer research services, all have made efforts in this direction, but none of these has enlisted the broad enthusiasm of consumers, nor achieved a marked impact on their behavior.

The explanations for this lack of data are not hard to suggest. The cost of getting the data is beyond the means of any individual, and there is no social pressure to join with others in moving rapidly toward the collective gathering of it. Those who manufacture and serve have been permitted to stimulate demand with a form of advertising which is almost totally lacking in decision making information, permitted by consumers who have responded with full enthusiasm to this form of persuasion. The socially acceptable way of making consumption decisions is in the absence of facts. A part of keeping up with the Joneses is keeping up with the casual nature of their personal decision making.

One of the basic reasons that any proposal to apply the industrial model to personal productivity is met with little reaction but disdain is simply that the necessary input data doesn't seem to be available. Although things may be slowly moving in the right direction, there seems little possibility that the individual's private efforts to get the data would be worth the time required. It is a pretty reasonable decision, balancing the effort that it would take to get this sort of information against the benefits one might expect from it. We may welcome a Ralph Nader who presents us with the data at his expense, but we are unlikely to get personally involved in going much beyond the reaches of Naderism.

The Hard Work of Thinking

The second reason for the failure of the industrial model is the perceived effort that would be required for its use. Thinking, planning, analysis, and deliberate decision making are hard work. They require a lot of cognitive effort, a lot of mental strain. The investment of effort just doesn't look as if it would pay off. Our well developed styles of personal management are adequate, at least as long as shortages or inflation do not press too hard. Why make the effort to alter a satisfactory set of habits and comfortable style, and take on a lot of tough mental work? The benefits just don't seem to be great enough to be worth it.

It may be that one of the first things we have wanted to buy with our increasing real wealth is a freedom from the rational way of life, a freedom from concern with personal productivity growth. It may be very pleasant, and worth some sacrifice, not to have to do at home the sort of thing we are paid to do at the office in the interests of the organization. Exemption from the rational, relentless ways of business may be an important and deliberate choice of our life styles. The price, after all, of being more productive is examination of our styles, self-consciousness, and calculation, all of which are things we may wish quite deliberately to avoid. We may be quite willing to trade a lot of physical effort and a lot of money for the freedom from having to plan and calculate.

We could think about making relevant data readily available for consumption decisions. We could think about computers linked to our telephones and programmed with all sorts of decision aiding schemes which would make rational styles almost effortless. Yet there would very likely remain a significant number of us who would attach more importance to our styles than to rationality. There would be many who would find the minimal effort involved in getting more from life, having a greater freedom of choice, not a sensible expenditure for them. There may well be significant numbers who simply do not accept the hypothesis that satisfaction is likely to increase with an increase in the clarity, the reasonableness, and the self-awareness with which we make decisions.

Knowing What We Want

To those who are really poor, to those who are unemployed, to the sick, to the troubled, what one wants is pretty obvious and the question of one's personal goals is not a matter of great uncertainty. To those who permit it, advertising will create for them a set of goals. Advertising is known by actual experiment to be effective in doing this. It contains little information on alternative goals, but rather focuses on the comparison of color TV's—not on the question of whether it makes personal and individual sense to own a color TV. Advertising is deliberately manipulative in the sense that it creates goals which are in someone else's interests, not necessarily in ours.

What this means in practice is that most of us find life's trade-offs unclear, uncertain, difficult to resolve, and avoidable if possible. How much present income should we sacrifice for future income? How much risk should we accept for how much expected return? How much should we spend for life insurance and recreation? How much should we pay over and above basic transportation costs to have a car with prestige, beauty, comfort, and reliability? How much displeasure on the part of the children should we endure before trading the black and white TV for a color set? On and on, the basic, troublesome trade-offs occur which are the very essence of life's consumption decisions. How much of one good thing should we sacrifice for another good thing? How much of one bad thing should we accept in order to be relieved of another? If we were perfectly clear about our goals, then these things would not be a problem. Nor would it be a problem to formulate some personal or family long-range plans aimed at the attainment of our objectives. We would begin to talk about optimal decisions, optimal allocation of our resources, and doing things in order to maximize the expected achievement of our clearly understood goals. Yet, this is not so for most of us. Trading off is hard work, sometimes impossible work. All of the ancient wisdom about the importance of knowing what we want, the importance of developing a sense of life's purpose is just so much ancient wisdom as far as our own behavior is concerned—similarly for the industrial model.

The route to goal clarification probably begins with the realization we have already noted, that it doesn't make sense to try to be perfectly clear about one's goals, but it may make sense to move in that direction. Goals, as best we can understand them, are emergent. As one achieves one thing, another arises to take its place. Goals change as we experience, as we mature, as we grow. Goal clarification is thus not a one-shot effort, but rather a process that must sensibly be worked at more or less continuously.

Goal clarification is likely to be hard work, because for most of us it is an essentially experimental process. We can think about our objectives, imagine alternative possible futures, and formulate hypotheses about what the things are that we want to achieve. But as we decide and act and experience, we learn that some of the things we thought we wanted are not so satisfying after all. We learn that there are things we want to achieve of which we had not previously been aware. Thus goal clarification involves more or less continuous analysis, hypothesis raising, experiencing, testing, and revising.

For most of us, the economist's assumption that people go through life behaving as if they were trying to maximize something may be fine for other people, but it doesn't consciously characterize our own behavior. We are clear, generally speaking, that we are not very clear about what it is we are trying to maximize, if indeed we are trying to maximize anything at all. The industrial model seems to call for a great deal more self-perception than we are likely to achieve.

CASUAL CONSUMPTION

Thorstein Veblen wrote a marvelous book published in 1889 in which he held up a mirror to permit us to see something revealing about our consumption behavior. He showed us how much of our consumption was what he called "conspicuous." He helped us to see that much of our consuming was calculated to have its effect on others—to show others that we could waste time, waste things, and waste the efforts of those who provide goods and services. Veblen's work was valuable because he showed us something of our life styles and our life goals in a dramatic and interesting way. He held up the mirror to permit self-awareness and self-perception on which a change in consumption style might be based.

Conspicuous consumption has largely gone out of style today, perhaps at least indirectly as a result of people like Veblen. With the failure of the industrial model, the appropriate description of today's sterotypical consumption style is "casual." Casual consumption means consumption decision making on the basis of whims, inspiration, hunches, impulses, and minimal recourses to data, analysis, planning, and accounting. It is, in short, the very opposite of the industrial model. Casual consumption is itself a cultural norm, a cultural value, almost a cultural "good." In this way we buy and consume without spending more than the most modest effort on planning and analysis. We may spend a lot of time making a major consumption decision, but that time does not produce much in the way of data or decision analysis.

Although the industrial model may have a sort of pseudo-logical applicability, casual consumption has the advantages of being culturally accepted, educationally available, perceived as being reasonably satisfactory, and taken as an aspect of life competence and life style for most of us. Casual consumption is conspicuous in Veblen's sense in that it demonstrates a conspicuous lack of the need to take consumption decisions seriously, to be reasonable about them, to be concerned with private productivity.

What is meant by casual consumption can be put somewhat more precisely. Casual consumption decisions are those decisions which have a high probability of being seen upon later reflection and analysis as being inconsistent with one's goals. Casual consumption decisions are those which we have a high probability of regretting were we to review them against the tests of clarity, reasonableness, and consistency with our personal objectives. This does not mean that the review or the reflection actually takes place. If it did, we would probably not persist very long in our style of casual consumption. It does not mean that the analysis and reflection could take place very effectively for, as we have seen, a big part of the problem is our uncertainty about what our objectives are and what sort of actions are consistent with them.

Living and consuming, after all, must, to be at their best, have an element of spontaneity about them. If everything is carefully reasoned and carefully planned, it would take all or at least some of the joy out of life. The industrial model is not very much fun.

It would appear then that the industrial model is to fail in favor of the false competence of casual consumption. The industrial model may be all right in "theory," but it doesn't really fit in practice. It requires too much data, too much mental energy, and presumes too much clarity of objectives. People are unlikely to be lectured into using it, and are unlikely to be influenced to make such a basic alteration in their personal styles and their planning habits. To advocate the industrial model is to repeat a lot of very well-worn jewels of basic philosophy which have the common feature of not being very widely attended to nor very widely applied. We seem after all to live well enough and competently enough as casual consumers. Why change? Why not get busy earning more money instead of trying to be more effective in using the resources we already have?

Are there approaches to personal productivity growth which are non-manipulative, which require realistic investments of cognitive energy, which are socially acceptable within our culture, and which have self-reinforcing results? Probably not, but perhaps these questions define something of the problem with which we are faced.

HUMAN DEVELOPMENT

General knowledge of individual goals is a contradiction to a great extent, but the most widely accepted analysis of the ways in which we are alike in the emergence of our goals is that of Maslow. He saw goals in a series of levels describing a natural progression in human development from childhood to full psychological maturity.

Level 1: SURVIVAL AND SECURITY:

We have great concern with surviving, being protected, unthreatened, and safe. Concern extends through all levels from one's self through family, community, nation, and even the world. Similarly, threats are sensed at every level: physical, economic, emotional, intellectual, spiritual, and so forth.

Level 2: BELONGINGNESS:

The importance of being part of something bigger produces for the first time the ability to establish stable groups. This salient fact induces the dominant value pattern: that of conformity to the group norm, the sense that there is a "right" and a "wrong" way of looking at things, sometimes the conviction that only people who are like oneself are "good."

Level 3: ESTEEM:

The dominant value at this stage is that of achievement, frequently expressed as visible, even ostentatious, "success." Esteem needs and values are those of the "typical" American—materialistic, ambitious, power-oriented, status seeking, authoritarian, self-confident, high-pressured, entrepreneurial, possession-conscious, competitive, "better than" syndrome, winner/loser approach to things, upwardly mobile, measurement-oriented, active, planning, hardworking, driving, driven, manipulative, efficient, hard-nosed, fame- or money-oriented, effective.

Level 4: GROWTH:

The key value pattern is concern with living up to one's inner potential through full expression of what seems important. The self-actualizer is the emotionally mature person able to express himself fully, tapping the full range of his abilities, in the way that is peculiarly his. His attributes include:

Individualistic, expressive, acceptance of self and others, realistic, spontaneous, problem-centered, autonomous, unenculturated, inner driven, freshness of appreciation, tempered idealism, democratic, unhostile, creative, motivated by ends not means, self-reliant, flexible, willing to lead or follow, at peace with self, sense of mission, understands self, permissive, varied interests.

These kinds of general hypotheses may be extremely interesting, may provide some insights into our own emergent goals, and may help us to begin the work of goals clarification. They do not, however, automatically give us the clarity and perception that is needed for decision making purposes.

THE PROBLEM

The achievement of wide changes in styles of personal productivity growth appears at least very difficult, if not unrealistic, as an expectation. Although we have tried to think of personal productivity in such a way that it is similar to a universal good and that growth of personal productivity will mean we all are likely to get more of what we want with what we have, it is unlikely that great numbers of people will see it that way.

Under the presumption of freedom, the problem is a personal one and includes the freedom to personally ignore the problem. Yet those who have achieved some measure of personal productivity growth in their lives present a model which many of us will want to consider. If we choose to ignore it, we will want to do so knowingly and deliberately.

The conditions under which personal productivity growth seem most likely to occur are roughly these. Something motivates us to begin a process of developing self-awareness. We become interested in seeing what it is we are doing, what our life style looks like, how it is we go about making the important decisions. To develop self-perception we need help; we need models, hypotheses and possible dimensions with which to characterize our styles. But the more we succeed in seeing ourselves, the more interesting it becomes, and the process turns out to be self-reinforcing. One of the safest generalities of modern as well as ancient psychological knowledge is that self-perception leads reliably to self-directed change. As we see what it is we are doing, we change our behavior to make it more satisfying, more productive. Productivity growth is almost a natural consequence of coming to see our own behavior with some degree of objectivity. Life competence, it turns out repeatedly, is often a matter of recognizing the influences on our own behavior so that we can neutralize them and take charge ourselves. Once we have some understanding of what causes our behavior, we can compensate for those causes and become the chief managers of our own activities.

Productivity growth requires, for individuals as for organizations, a strategy of continuous experimentation. We do not know very well a priori, which directions to take in order to achieve greater productivity, and there is little in the way of available fact or theory to tell us. The only way is experimentation, to try new directions carefully and sensibly, to learn from these experiences, and to formulate new trials. In an atmosphere of continuous experimentation where we challenge old styles and old habits, we can become clearer about our goals; we can develop the habit of making the most of the experiences we have.

It is unlikely that this model provides *the* answer to personal productivity growth, or even an answer which many will find sufficiently riskless to try. For some it has been an answer and it may be for others. One of its virtues, if it has any, is that it doesn't simply rehearse the old platitudes about which we now have mountains of evidence. The evidence overwhelmingly supports the statement that the old platitudes are hardly ever used, and in that sense, they just don't work.

Notes

The work of A. H. Maslow on human goals has had an immense impact on the literature on decision making and productivity. His original paper is Maslow, A. H. "A Theory of Human Motivation," *Psychological Review*. 1943, 50, pp. 370–396.

The great classics which are probably most helpful in thinking about private productivity in the sense of this chapter include:

De Grazia, S. *Of Time, Work and Leisure*. New York: Twentieth Century Fund, 1962.

Riesman, D., and others. *The Lonely Crowd*. New Haven, Conn.: Yale University Press, 1950.

Veblen, Thorstein. *The Theory of the Leisure Class*. New York: Macmillan, 1889.

10

New Strategies

Our levels of productivity in all sorts of production situations can be explained in terms such as habit, not paying attention, lack of motivation, resistance, fear of change, job security needs, cultural norms, and aversion to the risk of innovation. All these explanations suggest that there are significant, unrealized potentials for productivity improvements in most situations. When we have gone about attempting to change our productivity levels more or less systematically, we have often been given to single-effect strategies, machines, working harder, or working smarter; we have restricted our attention to the traditional targets for productivity growth; we have been easily put off by uncertainty; we have been insufficiently sensitive to individual and organizational differences; and we have been overly manipulative in dealing with people. Can we design more productive ways for going about productivity improvement? It is idle to suppose that we could write a prescription which many people would find effective to follow. Things are just too complex. We might, however, be able to set down some notions which would help people develop their own strategies, their own experiments. At least this seems worth a try.

A strategy is a special kind of plan. It is rich with contingencies; if A happens, do X, if B happens, do Y. Each contingency is, in turn, related to prior contingencies. We find ourselves uncertain about whether A or B will happen, and so we make a plan for each eventuality. A strategy is essentially an experimental design. We begin by taking a look at some of the different kinds of productivity development strategies.

Viewpoints on Strategy

There are all sorts of interesting views about how productivity becomes improved; we will note only the essence of a few of them. These views, are, of course, not mutually exclusive, but overlap and intermingle with one another. They have the properties of being in some ways effective, in some ways ineffective, of being more or less reasonable, and of making greater or lesser sense in particular production situations.

1. Productivity is a lower level phenomenon which somehow just happens and is best left alone to take care of itself. The greatest leverage on productivity is through the very top managers and the entrepreneurial decisions they make. Getting into a business or out of one, launching a new product, building a new plant—these are the things which really have an influence on productivity. A somewhat lower order of leverage is in the hands of the research and development people, and a still lower order is in the hands of those who have charge of ongoing production operations. The least leverage is available at the level of production operations themselves, and thus it makes sense not to pay too much attention at this level. Productivity will somehow get improved, probably by the first line supervisor.

2. Productivity is a matter of the slow spread of innovations, of a sensibly modest rate of imitation. Someone else shoµld be the innovator, take the risks and develop the information. The expected gains from productivity innovations are not great enough to warrant a lot of disturbance of habitual methods and a strong possibility of disruption that may not pay off. Productivity improvements will happen in their own good time. When old machines break down, when people retire, when new products are introduced, when new plants are built, productivity improvements will accompany these events rather naturally.

3. Productivity is the result of a series of drives, programs or management initiatives which come along from time to time. One year there is a cost reduction program, the next, a program to introduce value engineering,

a "zero defects" program, and so on. Each of these efforts has some effect and produces some results, but eventually runs its course. Enthusiasm wanes, attention is distracted to other things, and the program rather naturally fades away, not, however, without some residual benefit. Each of these programs has an enthusiast or champion in the organization who provides the initiative and the motivating energy.

4. Productivity is essentially a contest between management and the working people. Management sees people as opposed to changes that might lead to productivity increases, ready to initiate grievances in response to the slightest attempt to change productivity, antagonistic to management interests, inherently devoted to restriction of output, and always pushing for more money in return for less effort. Working people see productivity in terms of speed-ups, threats to job security, attempts by management to get more out of them without due compensation, a set of games in which management makes the rules by which the workers must play if they are to increase their earnings, and an undertaking which is good for management but bad for working people.

5. Productivity is best improved by getting everybody at all levels interested in their own productivity. This involves giving people an incentive to make productivity improvements in their own jobs and operations. Tie their compensation to their own output, to the system's volume of production, or to company profits. Offer bonuses or savings shares for suggestions which lead to productivity gains. This requires an effort on the part of management to generate enthusiasm for everyone to get involved and to try to sustain this enthusiasm, and requires a minimal sort of training in how one might go about finding ways to improve one's own working style. The way to really achieve productivity growth is to get everyone working to achieve it.

6. Productivity is something which gets management attention when outside pressures force it upon them. When the organization is in trouble, we turn to pro-

ductivity improvement. Productivity gets attention when increasing costs can no longer be passed along in the form of price increases, when competition cuts into one's market share, when government agencies demand justification for price increases, when unions win wage increases. Productivity becomes an issue when some aspect of an operation "goes out of control," when strikes, absenteeism, low quality, and rapidly declining sales, make it clear that "something has got to be done." Productivity gets attention when management sees it as an opportunity to demonstrate accomplishment, to achieve some noticeable improvement.

7. Productivity is chiefly a function of exogenous variables, of things which happen outside the organization. Productivity depends strongly on whether or not the work ethic is disappearing, on the attitudes which working people bring to their jobs, on employee "commitment to organization goals," on levels of unemployment locally and nationally, on the phases of the business cycle, on the strength or weakness of the union, on current demand for output, and on the scale of operations. So much of what determines productivity is essentially beyond the control of people in the organization, that there is little justification for major efforts to influence it.

8. Productivity can be improved quite deliberately and quite reasonably by attending to the major source of all productivity gains. The way to improve productivity is to institutionalize a group of experts within the organization whose function is to work more or less continuously at developing productivity using a strategy based on the belief that major payoffs stem from this single source. What this source is differs from organization to organization and is an important part of the style and character of the organization. Some organizations behave as if productivity gains stemmed largely from strategies which emphasized research and development; others base their strategies essentially on machines, technology and equipment; still others see productivity as essentially a people problem and devote themselves almost exclusively to motivational

schemes. There are those organizations which strongly favor the "working smarter" approach and look primarily to industrial engineering or operations design groups. Finally, there are those of the sort already mentioned in item 1 above who see the basic strategy as high level management decision making. Each of these strategies sees productivity as the result of a single set of effects, as stemming from a single source, as being far easier to obtain one way than in another. These strategies are either primarily people centered, primarily capital centered, primarily management centered, or primarily research centered.

THE NEXT STEPS

All of these points of view on productivity strategy are to some degree valid, to some degree effective, and to some degree associated with demonstrable achievements in particular organizations. Yet our analysis so far suggests their weaknesses, their limitations, and the possibility that they may not be adequate responses to the living poorer-working harder scenario. Could one outline the next steps in productivity strategy development, outline the way in which one might sensibly respond to the complex, synergistic nature of productivity phenomena, the incompleteness and uncertainty of our knowledge of production systems, our hypothesis that individual and organizational differences have been given too little attention in efforts to promote productivity growth?

What is needed is a productivity development strategy which synthesizes some of the effective aspects of the various viewpoints we have examined and tries to avoid some of their shortcomings. It needs to make maximum use of what we think we know about productivity phenomena and to acknowledge clearly and frankly what we don't know. It needs to make a sensible allocation of staff time, of management time, and of the time of operating people in the production system.

It should account somehow for the complex, systematic nature of production systems and for the prominent differences among people and organizations as well as their similarities. In this chapter and the next we will outline the major features of such a strategy, such an attempt to take the next steps in productivity growth.

Our proposal, which follows from the analysis of the previous chapters, consists of two essential aspects based on two basic sets of considerations: adopting the systems perspective on the costs and benefits of productivity growth opportunities, and responding reasonably to uncertainty in an effort to make the best use of it.

The Systems Perspective

If, as it would strongly appear, productivity phenomena are interrelated in a complex and synergistic way, then it would seem appropriate to move away from the single variable strategies which emphasize one source of productivity improvement. The productivity of machines is intimately connected with the productivity of people, and both are related in terms of working styles and the methods by which operations are carried out. When new machines are installed, new opportunities appear to enhance productivity through new operations design. As one type of productivity gain is pressed forward, it suffers typically from diminishing marginal returns, and other sources begin to look relatively more favorable. The essence of the systems view is to avoid exclusive concentration on approaches which emphasize machines, or research and development, or working smarter or any other single source of gains. The systems view suggests that we should look broadly and systematically at a range of opportunities and a range of methods for enhancing productivity. The systems view suggests that we turn from single-fix approaches, from the search for "solutions" to the productivity problem, and broaden our horizon of choice.

A comprehensive strategy ought to consider together, simultaneously, and competitively, what can be done with machines, what can be done with people, what can be done with operations design, what can be achieved with research and development, and what can be accomplished at the entrepreneurial level. There is a basic design principle which suggests that the broader our horizon of choice, the greater the expected return. The systems perspective suggests that we quite deliberately take advantage of this principle.

The fundamental question continually asked is, of the broad range of productivity improvement opportunities which are available at any moment, which have the most favorable relationship between the cost of undertaking them and the benefits to be expected? Productivity enhancement is thus directed by estimates of marginal cost and marginal gain from the exploitation of the full spectrum of opportunities available. To consider the full range of opportunities is to consider not only strategies which involve combinations of machines, people, and operating methods, but also the full range to productivity enhancing tools from direct common sense to sophisticated modern methods of operations design. It means consideration of the full range of targets as well; in an industrial setting this includes production operations, indirect or overhead operations, management, distribution, staff services, and so on. It implies considering these targets not only singly, but in combination from an overall systems point of view.

It is essential to be realistic, sensible, and practical in advocating the systems perspective. Nobody can seriously hope to approach a deliberate consideration of anything near all of the opportunities that may be available to an organization at any moment. The opportunities one considers depend a great deal on one's cleverness, experience, imagination, and sensitivity to ways in which productivity might be increased. It is typical of the nature of things that there will be a small number of opportunities at any given time which clearly appear to have the most favorable relationship between the costs of exploiting them and the gains to be realized. What is important is that one be sensitive and creative, that one adopt a sufficiently broad perspective in order to achieve a reasonably high probability of considering these few best opportunities. Put another way, the more imaginative one's approach, the broader one's view, the greater the expected results of one's productivity improvement efforts.

Realism

It is essential to be realistic also in advocating the explicit consideration of the marginal costs and marginal gains associated with these opportunities. This is not to suppose that these estimates will be free of uncertainty. Indeed the burden of a great deal of our analysis so far is that such estimates are often matters of very considerable uncertainty. Yet the presence of uncertainty should not be taken as a cue to avoid estimating gains and costs. Instead, a comprehensive strategy should include some explicit recognition of the uncertainty associated with these estimates, at least in the cases of those opportunities which seem to have the most favorable cost-benefit relationships.

In many cases of the use of a single-effect strategy, these estimates are made more or less explicitly anyway. What we are now suggesting is simply that the horizon over which they are made be broadened, and that we proceed on the basis of a comparison of these estimates, choosing those opportunities which appear to be best. The second part of our comprehensive strategy will consider how to deal with this uncertainty, how to respond to it reasonably, and how to use it constructively. This strategy does not typically require more data than a single effect strategy, nor more in the way of judgment. It does require somewhat more in the way of explicitness and comparison.

The essence of the comprehensive strategy is an array of estimates of costs and benefits across a broad range of opportunities. The broader the range, the greater the expected pay off. The execution of productivity growth efforts then consists of examining these opportunities and allocating one's energies, one's efforts, and one's resources in order to assemble a portfolio of projects which maximizes the difference between the expected costs and the expected gains. Again, what is important is not that this portfolio selection be carried out with great precision or in the complete absence of uncertainty. What is important is the breadth of viewpoint it implies, the notion of an array of productivity growth projects, and the guiding principle that one made judgments aimed at assembling these projects in some good way.

THE SYSTEMS IDEA The underlying notion is that the productivity of people, machines, management, knowledge, and so on, cannot sensibly be discussed in terms of individual effects, nor can it be individually made the sensible basis of strategies for improvement. Each enhances or detracts from the productivity of the others. Each influences and is influenced by its membership as an element of a production system. If one uses knowledge which is fragmented and strategies which are compartmentalized, the results will be unreliable because the problems we are considering and the systems we are studying are not fragmented. To say that we are dealing with a systems problem is to say that the behavior of production systems is a strong function of the interactions among people, machines, and operating methods. Simple explanations and single cause strategies are likely to give weak predictions of system behavior and afford limited and undependable leverage for the improvement of productivity. The old measure of productivity per man-hour continues to disguise the synergistic nature of the elements which determine a man's productivity.

MAGIC SOLUTIONS The systems perspective also implies that we consider productivity phenomena as complex in the sense that there is a very low probability of discovering any single magic "solution" to the productivity problem. It implies a kind of recognition that neither wage incentives, nor management by objectives, nor transactional analysis are likely to provide anything near the final achievement of the productivity potential of a production system. Each of these things may be a candidate for inclusion in one's project portfolio, but not to the exclusion of other opportunities as well. Productivity is very likely not to be a solvable problem in any simple sense.

ALLOCATION OF MANAGEMENT EFFORT

The consideration of costs and benefits, however roughly, includes the costs of the management attention and the staff effort that would be required to execute various productivity improvement projects. It thus represents an effort toward a sensible allocation of management attention and a direction of management time and skill toward those activities which are likely to have the best pay off. If, instead of committing effort to a cost reduction program, one considers the options of committing it to either cost reduction, product redesign, or equipment modernization, the very consideration of this range of alternatives increases the probability that management and staff efforts will be used more effectively. Indeed, the essence of the systems perspective may be the development of a portfolio of productivity improvement projects which gives a more reasonable character to the allocation of the efforts which go into such projects. Productivity gets improved when people devote attention to it, and the direction of this attention is crucial to the degree of improvement to be expected. Recognizing that these efforts are subject to diminishing marginal returns, and that as organizations grow and change, new and more attractive opportunities continually appear, may be a major contribution of the comprehensive strategy.

ESTIMATING COST, BENEFITS, AND RISKS

In one of the leading manufacturing organizations of this country, a broad range of productivity improvement projects is carried forward by a large staff department. All sorts of strategies are employed, using all sorts of tools and techniques, aimed at all sorts of targets. Each project in the portfolio is requested by a line manager, an operating department, or some profit center in the organization which has a budget for its operations. The services of the staff department are charged against the budget of the profit center. The head of the staff department provides estimates to the heads of the profit centers of what it will cost to execute the various projects requested. The heads of the profit centers are presumably making their own estimates of what their payoff would be, because their compensation is tied to the profits realized at their centers. Thus both the estimates of costs and those of benefits are being made. One hopes that the projects which are actually executed, which are included in the company's portfolio, are roughly the best set of projects which could be accommodated within the constraint of the limited capacities of the staff group. This is a sort of prototype of the comprehensive strategy actually at work.

The difficulties associated with making the necessary estimates of costs and benefits, and of making more or less explicit assessments of the uncertainties involved should not be underestimated. To be realistic, it is important to look at these some-what more closely to see if any useful insights are available to help here. Suppose we consider, in a somewhat simplified way, that a productivity improvement project consists of a target, a method, and an implementation plan. The target is simply the set of operations to be studied in the hope of achieving some productivity growth. The method includes the equip-ment, the analysis, the design approach, and the common sense to be applied in an attempt to evolve an improved op-erations design. The implementation plan reflects the consid-eration of how the changes are to be actually put into practice, actually put on line. Each of these involves costs, contributes to the benefits, and may be the source of uncertainty about how the project will ultimately turn out. We will consider each in turn.

Targets

One sort of recommendation frequently heard for identi-fying potential targets for productivity improvement is to as-sume everything has some potential for improvement, to ques-tion everything, to let nothing escape. Perhaps more realistic is the notion that one might want to develop some targeting strategies which might be a little more efficient than trying to cope with everything. Some targeting is typically built into the management control system: when profits go down, when com-plaints go up, when output falls, when in-process inventory rises, when any of a whole vector of performance measures departs from satisfactory or standard levels, attention is in-dicated. Some targeting is based on rough but plausible principles which suggest, for example, that the most likely places to find favorable opportunities for productivity growth are:

* the operations which involve the most money, the most people, the highest volume of output;
* the operations which have been least profitable, have the slowest growth rate, or have the greatest incidence of "foul-ups";
* the operations which have been longest spared the at-tention of those interested in productivity improvement;

* the operations with the oldest equipment, the oldest methods of operation, the highest seniority people;
* the operations which are newest, about which we have the least experience, which have most recently emerged from their "start-up" period.

All of these have a certain plausibility as indicators of potential productivity gains, but none of them provides an uncertainty-free guide for all kinds of production systems. The efficient way to proceed in such circumstances is to raise some possible targeting hypotheses similar to these, to let one's behavior be systematically guided by these hypotheses, and to experimentally evaluate the effectiveness of each hypothesis as a systematic method for identifying opportunities. The objective of a reasonable approach to targeting is to develop experimentally a set of diagnostics for a particular production system which will increase the effectiveness of the process of identifying good projects. A residue of uncertainty will always remain to be dealt with.

Targeting is also partly a matter of one's level of observation. We may look at individual operations, groups of operations, manufacturing systems, manufacturing and distribution systems, and so on. The boundaries of what it may be useful to consider expand as we develop more sophisticated methods for designing large scale systems; they expand as it becomes important to consider what were once called externalities, pollution, energy consumption, customer liability, and so on. They expand as the size and responsiveness of one's system makes it more important to look further into the future. Generally speaking, the higher one's level of observation, the greater the potential for productivity improvement. But this, like most such effects, is subject to diminishing marginal returns.

Methods and Organizational Development

We have referred from time to time to a rough but very useful hypothesis which suggests that the payoff from any productivity enhancing method applied to any particular organization depends on where the organization has been, what its present state of development is, and what its style is. What we mean by methods runs all the way from unaided "common sense" to sophisticated, computer-based systems analysis. Methods include automating, mechanizing, and modernizing as well as changes in the scale of operations, changes in the quality of the inputs, changes in the way operations are scheduled and integrated, and changes in the nature of the product or service being produced. Our rough hypothesis, the Ontogenic Hypothesis, suggests that some methods are more likely to work than others, and that this depends on the history of the organization, on what it has already lived through. It suggests rather crudely that organizations grow up, mature, and live through stages which predispose them toward succeeding stages. It suggests that changes in the organization which are compatible with its maturation or consistent with its pattern of evolution are more likely to be effective than are changes for which it is not yet "ready." This kind of hypothesis is, of course, difficult to document, yet it has the support of at least some professional opinion and some anecdotal evidence.

This hypothesis suggests, for example, that an organization is not ready for sophisticated computerized production scheduling until it has first lived through putting billing and accounts receivable on the computer, then putting some inventory control on the computer, then putting purchasing and the customer order book on the computer. When the organization has lived through these experiences, then it is "ready" for sophisticated computerized production scheduling, and such a strategy has a greatly increased probability of success than it might have had previously.

In similar fashion, an organization is not ready for wage incentives until it has lived through the establishment of a stable and reasonably reliable technology, until it has gone through an extensive period of job design, operations design, and arrived at fairly explicit job descriptions and operation specifications. Having lived through all this, wage incentives have a somewhat higher probability of success. Once wage incentives have arrived and once work measurement has become a part of the life of the organization, other kinds of measurement and design become "natural." These events establish a kind of climate for the study and design of production operations, a climate of concern for productivity which make further steps easier to assimilate. The organization may then go on to job enrichment and work restructuring. It may go on to participative methods. It may go on to production planning and control, to quality control, and to the analysis of not only direct production operations but to the analysis of materials handling as well. From materials handling, it is natural to progress to inventorying and ultimately to distribution. Nobody yet knows enough about the Ontogenic Hypothesis to quantify how the probabilities of success for various methods change as an organization matures; but it is for many, a useful guide to sensitizing one's self to what an organization is likely to be ready to accommodate. An operations research group will have greater success if the organization has had a conventional industrial engineering department. Purchasing and marketing, as well as finance and personnel will be more readily studied if production has been looked at rather thoroughly first. Total management information systems are just not with us yet, because no organization has lived through the necessary stages of gradual evolution of management reporting and decision aiding stages which seem to be needed to give anything like a reasonable success for a total management information system. The function of the Ontogenic Hypothesis is to call our attention to the possibility that the costs, benefits, and uncertainties associated with any productivity development method depend strongly on the individual character of the organization. This, in turn, can be partially understood in terms of the development and maturation of the organization.

One of the consequences of the Ontogenic Hypothesis is the diagnostic question, "How long has it been since your operation was last improved?" The time since the last improvement is not only related to the general tendency of order and organization to degenerate toward disorder and disorganization, it is also a rough measure of the amount of maturation which has taken place. The greater the time since the last improvement, the greater the readiness of the organization to succeed with a new method.

Fads and Passing Fancies

A second thing that it is most helpful to be aware of in considering productivity enhancing methods is the almost fadlike nature of their comings and goings. To emphasize the faddish aspect of many productivity improvement methods is not to be unnecessarily cynical about them. It is simply a fact that many such methods seem to behave as do other sort of fads, and this is a very useful observation to have in mind when considering one of the currently popular methods for enhancing productivity. Consider, for example, automation, N/C machines, robots, dedicated mini-computers, PERT, operations research, management by objectives, job enrichment, participation, transactional analysis, T-groups, human relations, democratic management, and job stylizing. Consider the evolution, progress, application, and decline of these methods in relation to the following model. It may be clear that there is a kind of life cycle through which some of these have already passed, and to various stages of which others have just recently progressed.

We will take as an illustrative example, PERT—program evaluation and review technique—a graphical and analytical method of production planning and control. In the first stage there is a reformulation and renaming of some basic ideas. PERT had many direct ancestors including the Gantt chart, for example. These newly named ideas are then applied to a particular production situation. It is important to build atomic submarines in a hurry, and PERT is applied to help increase the productivity of this program. If the next stage and the specific program succeeds, then some of the credit and glory goes to the method. PERT gets some of the credit for the successful ship construction program. At this point, three types of persons enter the picture, stimulated by the publicity which the method has received. The academics enter, generalizing the method, making it more sophisticated, enriching it and publishing articles discussing their results. These are not articles about application, but about the sophistication of the technique itself, a sophistication which may even lead to a whole new body of applied mathematics—where the work "applied" refers only to imagined possibilities. The second group to enter are the consultants who see the favorable publicity as a sound basis for a marketing effort. They begin to market the technique, emphasizing its newness, the "revolutionary" character of the method, and its great and universal potential for productivity improvement. The third group consists of people in organizations whose careers are not progressing to their own satisfaction. They decide that it might be possible to build a career on the new method so they become resident advocates and local spokesmen for it. They become leaders and marketers of in-house programs to apply the method, hoping that its success will also result in their own advancement. At this point, extensive marketing effort has built up expectations which simply cannot all be realized. A lot of people, however, now have vested interests in the technique, so it is pushed to the point of actual application in a variety of situations. Its implementation produces mixed results, a few successes, but quite a few failures. The technique has been oversold; disappointments are inevitable; re-evaluations and "second thoughts" begin to appear in the management literature. The technique generally passes into decline, although it does remain and make a useful contribution in a few places where it turns out to be appropriate.

Now this model doesn't fit precisely all of the techniques which have been listed above, but it may perhaps be sufficiently suggestive to be useful. In looking at a technique which is "current," it may be helpful to ask rather closely about what stages of its life cycle it's in, what its actual record of accomplishment has been, how much real evidence there is of its effectiveness, and to what extent those who are marketing it might have an interest in or a tendency toward overselling it?

The fad model is interesting because it does after all describe one aspect of the diffusion of innovation. It contributes to one's formulation of the decision to innovate or not to innovate. It suggests a certain skepticism on the part of those who have participated in one or more cycles of the model and supports an attitude that whatever is being suggested as the solution to the problem of productivity is, in reality, nothing more than this year's passing fancy. To the extent that we keep living through these cycles, however, the model suggests that we are not very efficient in learning from experience—that we cherish the hope that what is new will turn out to be the long sought "solution" to the problem of productivity. It may just be the simple solution which has always just eluded us. These fads are an interesting example of an experimental approach to productivity enhancement, but an approach that doesn't make particularly efficient use of the information obtained in previous experiments.

Like the Ontogenic Hypothesis, the model is neither precise nor quantitative, but it does help one make a more objective estimate of the costs of using one of the current methods, of the possible benefits to be expected, and of the degree of uncertainty which surrounds both of these estimates. It is as yet a dimly recognized aspect of the sociology of productivity phenomena.

Implementation

Those with experience in the improvement of productivity are fond of telling those without experience that all the sophistication of targeting and all of the advanced methodology are useless if the improvements cannot actually be implemented, if behaviors cannot actually be changed, if new methods cannot be brought on-line. Clearly, the process of implementation is one that is both costly and the source of considerable uncertainty—a process which must be considered in estimating the costs and benefits of any productivity development method. We have already given considerable attention to the implementation problem, but it may be useful to summarize the major concepts in the context of a comprehensive strategy. We speak about the ease of implementation as meaning it is less costly, less demanding of resources, less disruptive, generating less antagonism, and it has a higher probability of actually resulting in an improvement.

The more a productivity changing method is the product of self-perception and self-directed change by those actually involved in operations, the greater its ease of implementation.

The greater the participation of those whose behavior is likely to be changed in the development, creation, and formulation of productivity improvement, the greater its ease of implementation.

The greater the compatibility of a productivity improving method with the style, the character, and the evolutionary development of an organization, the greater the ease of implementation.

The greater the compatibility of a productivity improving method with the personal working style and individual decision making styles of those whose behavior must be changed, the greater the ease of implementation.

The greater the evidence of previous effectiveness, the smaller the perceived uncertainty about the effectiveness, the greater the expected size of the productivity improvement, the greater the chances that the decision will be made to innovate, and thus the greater the ease of implementation.

The lower the perceived threat to job security, not only to those directly involved but to other jobs as well, the greater the ease of implementation.

In designing implementation plans, we have probably paid less attention to individual differences, to organizational differences, and to the specifics of particular production situations than is warranted by their potential impact on the ease of implementation.

While these tend to reflect something of a current consensus on the question of the costs and uncertainties associated with implementing productivity changes, they do not in any sense "solve" the problem. We are left with considerable uncertainty about just what is meant by such terms as participation, organizational character, and personal decision making style. We have only the roughest qualitative view about what these variables imply for the ease of implementation, itself a weakly defined notion. All of this represents another source of uncertainty in our comprehensive strategy which must be recognized, managed, and if possible, used for constructive purposes.

TOWARD COPING
WITH UNCERTAINTY

The first of the two basic aspects of our comprehensive productivity development strategy suggests that we progress toward a broad view of the opportunities which may exist in an organization at any given time. Productivity phenomena are complex, depend heavily on interactions, change with time, with organizational development, and are generally subject to diminishing marginal returns. In such a situation, devotion to single effect strategies is less effective than broadening one's horizon of choice. For each of the more promising opportunities identified in this wide range of targets and of methods, explicit estimates of costs, benefits, and uncertainties are necessary. These permit the formulation of a portfolio of productivity improvement projects which approaches some sort of optimality within the constraints of the organization's resources for such projects.

All of these steps, as we have seen, are sources of greater or lesser uncertainty. To neglect these uncertainties is to adopt a strategy which is simplistic and unrealistic. It is these uncertainties which must be faced, dealt with, and brought to tolerable levels; and it is this process which constitutes the second essential aspect of our comprehensive strategy. Uncertainty, neglected by most proposals for improving productivity, turns out to be of central importance in the development of methods which respond to what we know and acknowledge what we don't know. Uncertainty also turns out to have a useful and functional role in the enhancement of productivity, to which we will turn our attention in the next chapter.

11
Experimentation and Freedom

COPING WITH UNCERTAINTY

Uncertainty, in greater or lesser degrees, has turned out to be a prominent consideration whenever we have looked into the exploration of strategies for raising our annual productivity increment. The decision to innovate or the decision to imitate, whether they are involved options that emphasized people, or technology, or working smarter—all were decisions in which uncertainty could not reasonably be suppressed. The key to understanding these decisions was their uncertainty. Productivity phenomena were too little understood; there was only the most limited theory available; experience seemed subject to severe restrictions on its generality; things depended very strongly on the individual characteristics of people, or organizations, or on specific production systems. All of this uncertainty became focussed on the costs and the benefits of productivity improvement opportunities as we sought to develop a comprehensive strategy leading to a portfolio of productivity growth efforts.

In such a situation, experimentation is the logical response. A productivity initiative is most sensibly regarded as an experimental undertaking, a tentative but deliberate effort to produce not only growth in productivity, but information about the costs and benefits of the initiative. When uncertainty about the methods, the people, and the organization involved are high, the initiative will be a small, limited experiment with the objective of learning and producing information far more prominent than that of productivity growth itself. When the uncertainty about these things is low, the experiment may be much more extensive, involve much more of a commitment. With low uncertainty, the function of producing information becomes less important, and the major objective becomes the actual enhancement of productivity.

How does this differ from what one can see going on in organizations all the time? To regard a productivity initiative as an experiment is to acknowledge frankly, openly, and explicitly that there is some degree of uncertainty in how it will turn out. Most strategies, if they are not actually oversold, presume a lot more than we honestly know about productivity. To see a project as an experiment is to plan its extent according to one's uncertainty; high uncertainty suggests caution, low uncertainty suggests a stronger effort aimed at realizing the productivity pay off. Above all, the notion of an experiment implies some measurement of productivity change. It is remarkable how frequently efforts to improve productivity fail to produce useful information because they were simply not designed to capture some measure of the system's behavior before the effort and then to assess its behavior again afterwards. Experimentation is simply the good sense to admit we are not sure how things will turn out and to be clear about what it is we are testing. It is the good sense to think in advance about what data will be necessary to make some judgment about whether or not what happened was good, and to be very careful about collecting this data and using its message in moving foward to the next experiment. Experimentation done this way is good science, and what many people think is good management is pretty much like good science.

Thus the second basic element of our strategy is the coping with uncertainty about productivity phenomena by giving our actions the character and efficiency of experiments. The way to cope with uncertainty is to try to sensibly and deliberately produce information to reduce it.

EXPERIMENTAL PROGRAMS

A number of indications appeared in our analysis which seem to have a single message for the design of productivity growth experiments. If the Ontogenic Hypothesis is taken seriously, it suggests that people change and organizations develop and grow. The results of a given effort to improve productivity will not be the same at various points in the maturing process of the organization. Time, too, takes its toll on organizations. Order degenerates relentlessly into disorder. Well-designed systems, if simply left alone, seem to decay, to develop imperfections, and to grow less productive. Outside influences change attitudes, change the urgency of raising productivity, and change people's receptiveness to change itself. Productivity efforts that are undertaken are subject to diminishing marginal effectiveness. One needs to keep track of whether continuing an experiment which is under way will yield the same order of payoff with which it began. As the marginal payoff from one sort of effort declines, others may become more attractive. Finally, there appears to be evidence that productivity programs which involve people have a strong tendency to wear off. The initial enthusiasm, interest, and challenge dissipates, and what may seem in its early stages to be a success, gradually fades away. A great many productivity strategies which emphasize people seem to have this characteristic.

All of these indications seem to lead in the same direction. *Experimentation must be more or less continuous; it must be an ongoing process.* The phenomena we are studying are changing even as we study them. What didn't work today may work very well in the future, and what worked last year may not work next year. Continuous experimentation is thus the second major aspect of a policy which seeks to respond to what we have learned so far.

It is idle to suppose that having simply said this is enough to be convincing. We must look somewhat more closely at the implications of a policy of continuous experimentation and some of the very special advantages it holds, in addition to producing information about how to build productivity.

CONTINUOUS EXPERIMENTATION AS A POLICY

One of the discouraging arguments against a policy of continuous experimentation is that the long history of experiments which have been made have proved little. Even if this were true, there is little choice. No matter what our past experience, the only way to learn, to progress, and to enhance productivity is to experiment. If individual differences among people and among organizations are as important as they now appear to be, each person and each organization will have to do their own experimentation to some extent. The strategy of waiting for others to solve the problem of productivity will fail for the inability to generalize from other people's results. The difficulty with our past experiments is not that they have proved so little; we have, after all, become the most productive nation in the world. The difficulty, rather, is that our past attempts have had far more the character of casual experience that thoughtfully designed experiments. What we are suggesting are ways of making the process more effective, more efficient—in fact, of making it more productive. An experiment in productivity growth is likely to be expensive, time consuming, and a nontrivial matter in the life of an organization. We ought to give some attention to making its knowledge-producing function as cost-effective as is reasonably possible.

But the way to really understand this argument is to return to our distinction between fads and experiments. Many of the current solutions to the productivity problem which were tried in the past were fads in the sense that the trials were kinds of memoryless experiments. Little was learned from these trials except that whatever it was didn't work and was best quickly forgotten. The point that there may not be a simple "solution" to the productivity problem was largely missed. The point that the "current solutions" were oversold and presented as almost sure things, was largely missed. The point that many kinds of things will improve productivity a little bit for a short while was missed, as was the point that what little evidence there was in favor of the current fad was likely to be of the most limited generality.

A policy of continuous experimentation implies that if we are to make an experiment with management by objectives, or with transactional analysis, or with total management information systems, that we do so in an open, experimentally oriented atmosphere. We need frankness concerning our uncertainty about how it will work, openness to the possibility of failure, and heavy emphasis on the notion that what we learn from the experiment is at least as important as the success or failure of the effort itself. We should admit that some of the things which come along have a fad-like nature and are oversold by those with a vested interest in them, but they still represent the experiment as an effort to see what it will tell us about our people, our organization, and our production system. If it fails, we are sufficiently careful to collect the data and analyze the results. We know something about why it failed, something which may be useful in the next experiment. It is not just a matter of getting it out of sight as quickly as possible.

One wonders how many of the failures of productivity experiments in the past were the result of the actions of participants grown cynical by a series of "annual solutions" to the productivity problem. Participants, often in a position to influence success or failure, may fully realize that if they give only the semblance of cooperation, this fad will go away as the others always have. Things will return to their normal, relatively secure state. People must be informed about the nature of the experiment; they should be made a part of the experiment in the sense of being invited to share the uncertainty about how it will turn out, to share the results which are produced, and to share in what is learned about their working styles and their production system. People must see that an experiment is an honest venture into innovation, and they must come to appreciate that innovation is risky. Risk means that some things fail but that other experiments have a major impact, a permanent impact, on the operation of the production system. Fads always go away, but innovative experiments sometimes have real impacts. This kind of experience must build toward the point where the admission of uncertainty by management is not taken by people who participate in the experiments as an invitation to insure the failure of the undertaking. Experiments must be honest and open or they will not be taken seriously. The more honesty and openness, the less the tendency of people who participate to feel manipulated, "managed," or "motivated" by the staff and management elite.

Managers will be naturally hesitant to declare that what they are doing in the way of productivity innovation should be considered as a continuous series of experiments. Some effort must be devoted to dispelling the notion that whatever is experimental is temporary, trivial, or ill-considered. The point must be clear to everyone involved that to call a program experimental is not to identify it as reckless tinkering, risky adventuring, or irresponsible manipulation. Continuous experimentation as a policy must demonstrate that the higher the uncertainty and the higher the cost of the experiment, the more likely it is to be small, incremental, sequential, evolutionary, and non-radical. Experimentation must be clearly presented, by fully involving participants, as a highly reasonable and carefully considered approach to innovation.

Creating the Climate

Just as people resist change, so they respond to the notion of experimentation with uncertainty, insecurity, and a strong preference for the old and the familiar. The goal of a policy of continuous experimentation is to create a special kind of organizational climate—a climate which seems to be characteristic of many of our most successful organizations. Just as it is well known that successful people welcome change and enjoy the uncertainty and the learning that goes with experimenting, so it appears to be with organizations. Successful organizations have the confidence bred of this success. They welcome change, learning, and renewal. Successful organizations are very often described as being open to new ideas and given to continuous, nondisruptive change and experimentation. Experimentation, in turn, increases the probability of continuing to be successful, and the process is one of those that wonderfully reinforces itself. The practical beginnings of the creation of this non-threatening experimental climate are simple enough to state:

* honesty, clarity in keeping people informed, in making them full participants in the adventure of learning, of trying new things
* avoiding the overcommitment to productivity strategies—the personal stake, the established position, the overselling—which makes experimentation, change, and the possibility of failure a personally threatening process

* a gradual breaking down of the defensive, previously held positions, a gradual relaxation of the notion that the sources of ideas are more important than the ideas themselves
* a reinforcing of the relationship among openness to experimentation, success, confidence in the face of change, and further experimentation
* an honest guarantee of job security, the most basic ingredient of all in the development of the open, non-threatening experimental atmosphere
* the clear admission that we are uncertain about the outcomes of our experiments, that the admission of uncertainty is a basic ingredient of science, not an admission of weakness or incompetence
* a continuing demonstration that, although failure is not a trivial matter, the failure of a well-designed experiment does not itself demonstrate incompetence or inadequacy, that there is a kind of freedom to fail as long as it is done logically, reasonably, and responsibly

It is, of course, easy to say these things, yet difficult, time consuming and frustrating to actually create this kind of organizational climate. The existing organizations which have approached it, however, suggest strongly that it may well be worth the effort.

Maturity and Change

It will be immediately recognized that the kind of organizational climate we are describing is the organizational analog to Maslow's level four personality type outlined in Chapter 9. In this sense, it describes an individual or an organization which has made considerable progress toward psychological maturity. We should expect to find few such organizations in existence today, just as there are relatively few level four people. But we would expect that, to the extent Maslow's ideas will turn out to be valid, the atmosphere of open, non-threatening experimentation is the goal toward which organizations are growing. The policy of continuous experimentation seems very likely to be the route toward the psychological maturity for the organization as it is for the individual.

Experimentation, especially on a small scale, is itself a part of many strategies for encouraging people to be comfortable with change. While they may strongly resist wholesale, radical changes in their working styles, they are likely to be far more open to what is honestly billed as a small scale feasibility study. The conduct of the study itself, in addition to generating useful information, has the effect of acquainting people with what is being tried, removing much of its mystery and uncertainty, and permitting them time to grow accustomed to particular possibilities for change. Thus experimentation can be a kind of preparation for change and accommodation to it.

The Unions

Continuous experimentation is, after all, not the exclusive province of management. Unions have also seen its possibilities and have on occasion led the way. In 1971, the United Auto Workers negotiated an experiment in the feasibility of the four day, forty hour week as a part of their collective bargaining agreement with Chrysler. No such proposal had been written into contracts previously signed with Ford and GM, and it was a deliberate experimental trial balloon which originated with the union. The suggestion that the experiment be made in some of Chrysler's production and maintenance operations came from a UAW vice president. The UAW record with such experiments is a very good one. Their initiatives led to successful experiments in the provision of health insurance, cost-of-living increases, and a guaranteed annual wage.

Becoming Involved

If a policy of continuous experimentation can be executed in such a way that many people in the organization become partners in its design and interpreters of its results, they become involved in what may be a whole new dimension of education and commitment. They become involved in gathering knowledge about the systems within which they work; in doing so, they themselves become more knowledgeable. They participate and learn in a way which tends to reduce the gap among the working people, the staff people, and management. The distinctions between the managers and the managed tend to blur into a joint effort to find out how to do things more productively. The systematic involvement of as many people as reasonably possible provides the opportunity for a kind of participation which has seldom been available in the past. People are asked not just to be hired hands, not just to work for the organization, but to help the organization find out more about itself. They are asked to engage in activities which are frankly learning experiences for everyone. The implications of superior knowledge on the part of managers and staff specialists are weakened in favor of a joint venture into finding out more about the way our production system really works. As people learn through this policy of continuous experimentation, their potential as contributors goes up.

Organizations which have achieved an atmosphere of open, non-threatening, continuous experimentation will be continually learning about people, and the people will be learning about the organizations. They will tend to develop individuals who are mature in their working styles, who can function effectively in an atmosphere of change, and who see productivity growth as leading to general increases in real wealth and increases in their own job security. These organizations will tend to become explicit about their goals, and this explicitness will be widely shared. They will be conscious of their performance, not just in terms of a few tightly circulated management reports, but generally conscious at all levels. They will tend to systematically depersonalize failure and emphasize individual and organizational learning. Above all, they will be organizations in which the many are not motivated, manipulated, and managed by the few.

These will be the sort of organizations which represent the next stage beyond bureaucracy. Major organizational experiments are made with increasing frequency; the project group, the task force and experimental restructuring become the norm as the organization seeks to adapt to its environment and learn more about itself. Although the permanence of reorganization may be yet in the somewhat distant future, organizational redesign as a continuing experimental function is becoming increasingly common.

There remains to be noted, however, what may be the two

most important, most far reaching implications of a policy of continuous experimentation. The first of these is the inherent functional power of experimentation itself; the second is the strong possibility that continuous experimentation may provide the only realistic way of actually carrying forward productivity strategies which take reasonable account of the primacy of individual differences among people.

The Functional Character of Experimentation

As we saw in Chapter 4, one of the most appealing readings in the Hawthorne studies suggests that experimentation is in itself motivating. To be a participant is motivating simply because one is a participant. It seemed very likely that all sorts of productivity growth strategies had demonstrated some effectiveness, not because of their substantive nature so much as because they involved people in experiments. Almost any reasonable productivity strategy is likely to produce some results, simply because it is stimulating to be involved in testing it. The conclusion, we suggested, was that the Hawthorne effect was itself the basis for increasing productivity. A policy of continuous experimentation simply takes advantage of this effect and of the additional observation that experiments, when people become accustomed to them, tend to lose some of their force as stimulants to productivity. There is nothing cynical nor anything particularly manipulative about the open recognition that it is motivating to be involved in experiments, and that people who work as participants in systems which are continuously experimenting are very likely to be more productive than people who work in more traditionally stagnant systems. It is, after all, a highly motivating aspect of the working lives of many managers and professionals, that they are continually involved in the new, the uncertain, and the experimental. Their productivity is stimulated by a continuous learning from experience and learning from experiment.

The theory of emergent needs suggests that whenever one need is satisfied, another will soon emerge to take its place. Human beings are inherently needing, complaining, and desiring creatures. To satisfy one set of wants is to be pleased and delighted for a little while, but soon we forget about these pleasures and delights and think about how we might be yet more pleased and delighted. As soon as we get used to anything, it tends to lose its force for shaping our behavior and we look forward to other things. A policy of continuous experimentation would appear to be the only way to approach productivity growth which would be consistent with this sort of insight into human nature.

INDIVIDUAL DIFFERENCES FROM THE MANAGEMENT VIEWPOINT

Managers are quite properly skeptical when they are told that we are entering a new era in organizational design. The job is to be brought to the person, not the person to the job. No more setting up job descriptions and trying to find somebody who will fit. Individual differences in working styles, in decision making styles, in the functions that work performs for the individual, should be carefully studied and understood. Then the job should be created to match the style of the individual. It is hard to think of anything less practical, more expensive, and less appealing to one with an eye to costs and benefits. No organization could possibly afford to design a job to suit each individual. The cost, the time, and the detail would be prohibitive. Perhaps at the very highest levels one might abandon the ancient military tradition that the job is defined independent of any special characteristic of the incumbent; the job is an utterly "apersonal" concept. Maybe for the president and the vice presidents, it might pay to design jobs to suit individual styles. But how is this done at the higher levels of any organization? What is the strategy already in use for taking account of the individualities of top managers? The essence of the strategy is to presume that the individual understands the broad requirements of his position and then to permit an absolute maximum of freedom for him to create his own job within these requirements. It is, in fact, the basic feature of top level jobs that they are conceived quite deliberately in order to maximize the freedom of the incumbent to design the job himself. He is assumed to design the job, within wide limits, to suit his own style, his own decision making methods, and his own individual nature. It is assumed, that when a new incumbent appears, he, too, will redesign the job in order to maximize its compatibility with his personal style and thus maximize his productivity as an incumbent. Why not introduce the same strategy at other levels, perhaps even at all levels in the organization? Clearly the strategy would have to be applied at different places to different degrees. Yet, in spite of some severe limitations which may appear at the operating levels, it might have some exciting implications.

If individual differences in working style are strong determiners of productivity, then it follows that no single "treatment" or no single "strategy" such as job enrichment is likely to bring everyone equally far toward their productivity potential. If the only way to respond to what appears to be the single most reliable thread in all of our history of experimentation with productivity phenomena, is to deliberately design each job to suit each individual, then there appears to be little chance of early success. We do not presently understand enough of the relevant dimensions of individual working style to even begin the process on a systematic basis. We could only begin it on an *experimental* basis. If we were to undertake these experiments on a usefully broad scale with even a small group such as professional staff people, the whole process would be prohibitively expensive.

Suppose on the other hand, we make two assumptions.

1. People are already, to a useful degree, self-perceptive about their own personal working styles, about the working arrangements under which they tend to be more productive, and about the working arrangements under which they tend to be less productive.

2. Given the freedom to experiment with their own job designs, they will be motivated to discover more about themselves; they will be motivated to make experiments until they find the conditions which increase their productivity toward its potential and until they find the working arrangements which permit the job to reach a high degree of effectiveness in meeting their needs.

These two assumptions imply that experiments motivated by management and designed and executed by the staff are not the only sorts of experiments contemplated within our policy of continuous, non-threatening experimentation. People, given the freedom to do so, will, it is assumed, become interested in experimenting with their own ways of working, with their own working arrangements. These experiments which are conducted by nearly everyone in the organization, will not, it is supposed, be directionless. People will experimentally evolve the designs of their own jobs to match their own working personalities, and the result will be a movement toward their productivity potential. Work serves very different functions for different people, and to the degree they are able to understand these functions and have the freedom to arrange their work accordingly, they are assumed to be increasingly productive. This is, after all, the essential message of the productivity of the free professional, the top manager, and the university professor. It is the central effect explaining the productivity of the independent business man, the self-employed craftsman, the artist, the composer, and the writer.

While these hypotheses may not be too farfetched, while they may be perfectly consistent with such data as we have, they immediately conjure a picture of utter confusion. An organization in which everyone is very busy experimenting with alternate designs for his own job will immediately cease to function, grinding quickly to a halt in complete disorder born of lack of coordination. Clearly there must be limits, bounds, and constraints on what the individual may do to redesign his job, to experiment with his working arrangements. But it is these very limits which suggest a very different, and very practical approach to job design.

DESIGN OBJECTIVES

The goal of the designer of production systems now shifts toward the exact opposite of what it has been historically. The Taylor tradition of "the one best way," of the complete homogenization of work styles under the dominance of the operations sheet, is fully set aside. The notion of training for work competence is changed radically from the homogenization process. The goal of the designer now becomes the creation of job specifications, job constraints, which, while preserving the necessary coordination among jobs, serves to maximize the freedom of the individual within these constraints. The goal is to design a production system which will efficiently accommodate the widest possible diversity of behaviors and attitudes, rather than forcing as many individuals as possible to conform to rigidly specified work methods. This does not mean that anything goes. It does suggest that in many systems, work behavior has been homogenized far beyond anything that was useful or necessary. It means that the designer begins to experiment seriously with the basic notion that our historical mistake has been to seriously overestimate the costs and underestimate the benefits of attending to individual differences in the planning of production systems.

The objectives of systems design and job design now become the maximization of the degree to which jobs are self-contained, the minimizing of the interactive, interdependence among jobs, the maximization of the degrees of freedom which a person has to design his job himself, and the production of the minimum necessary list of output specifications for each job which will permit the production system to operate in a coordinated fashion. Jobs will be specified in terms of boundary conditions, coordination requirements, equipment constraints, time constraints, and balance requirements, with the goal being to maximize the freedom available within these constraints. In-process inventories tend to reduce the coordination requirements among jobs. Aggregation of tasks into complete and natural work units (job enrichment, but without the detailed task specification) brings the necessary coordination *within* jobs to a greater degree and *among* jobs to a lesser degree. The good designer is the one who achieves the maximum freedom for individual experimentation with work styles, while still meeting the conditions necessary for effective coordination among the jobs that form a system. Beyond this, into the details of job performance, it simply does not pay for the designer to get involved.

Jobs will come to be characterized by the degree of constraint necessary for system coordination. Clearly not all of the jobs we see today will permit very much freedom. Some are so constrained by the demands of machines and by the pace of mechanized assembly lines that only a little room for increased freedom exists. But one should also state clearly, as the evidence has shown us, that not everyone wants to be free to design his own job. Some people will continue to choose, as they do presently, the jobs in which tight specifications and constraints are found. On the other hand, there are a very great number and variety of jobs where much can be done.

If there are to be wage incentives, they will have to be based on output, rather than on the complexities of standard methods and the traditions of work measurement. Questions of equity, of equal pay for equal work will arise. Part of the new concept of job evaluation and of wage and salary planning, will become the amount of freedom or constraint which a job involves. Our great tradition of wage and salary determination has had the effect, if not the deliberate intention, of the greater the freedom, the greater the monetary rewards. Along with freedom went responsibility, greater education and training requirements, and so on. Ultimately, it may very well turn out that as general levels of psychological maturity rise, this effect may become reversed. It may become necessary to pay people more to take those jobs where there is minimal freedom to design the work themselves according to their own styles. But if this happens, it will be a great testament to the success of the new concept of job design. This freedom will have been proven to have motivational power.

Training

In the new concept of job design, the opposite of the "one best way," training will no longer be aimed at homogenization. Training must equip people to be interested in, and self-perceptive about, their own working personalities, their own decision making styles, the functions work may fulfill for them, and the needs which can be satisfied by experimenting with working arrangements. Training will help people understand that the objective of the climate of non-threatening, continuous experimentation is ultimately to bring about productivity growth. It will suggest to them that they may become both designers of productivity enhancing experiments and participants in such undertakings. Qualification for jobs will depend on the ability to design experiments and one's openness to change.

The essence of job design becomes the attempt to treat people as much like professionals as possible, maximizing their opportunity to experiment with optimum working arrangements from their individual points of view. To give people more freedom is as close as one can get to the opposite of manipulating them.

This concept of job design and systems design to accommodate the greatest possible diversity of human working styles sounds a little like job enrichment and work restructuring, but it is not. Job enrichment tends to mean a movement from small chunks of homogenized work to bigger chunks of homogenized work. The concept of restructuring tends to imply progress from tight specifications for little jobs to tight specifications for larger, more complex jobs. The new concept sounds like participation, but it is not. To the degree that participation means people are invited to participate in the homogenization of their own working styles, maximizing their freedom is to move in a different direction. This is not to say, however, that job enrichment and participation might not be useful steps in bringing an organization toward readiness for the new concept of production systems design. As the Ontogenic Hypothesis would suggest, these steps might well increase the ease with which the new concept could be introduced.

Giving people maximum freedom to design their own jobs within system oriented constraints may appear to be an attempt to return to the philosophy of work simplification. Everyone, so it went, should be interested in improving their own productivity. But this is not so. The work simplification philosophy, when it was actually applied below the supervisory levels, involved two difficulties which the maximization of job design freedom does not share. Work simplification was motivated solely by the interest of the company in increasing productivity. People were asked to be creative in the furthering of what were seen as rather strictly management objectives. In spite of bonuses, or the opportunity to share in productivity savings, people were being asked to act in the interests of management, to do things which they saw as potentially threatening to their own job security and that of their fellows. We are proposing that people be given freedom to design their own jobs, always within reasonable limitations, with an eye to their own interests and their own needs. Vary one's starting time, vary the job method, vary the tools and techniques used, vary the sequence of activities, anticipate future needs—all of these things may be possible in some jobs. But people should have these choices from the viewpoint of their own needs outside the work situation, their own needs for satisfaction or craftsmanship, their own needs for social contact, and even their own needs to have a completely routinized work style so that they can attend to other aspects of their lives. Clearly it is anticipated that this freedom will result in increased productivity. The essence of this anticipation is that productivity, like happiness, is more likely to be found if we go at it indirectly, rather than seeking it head on.

The second difficulty with the philosophy of work simplification was that working people who did make improvements in their work methods knew that all too often, the improved methods would simply be frozen into an operation sheet, a new time study taken, and a new rate set on the job. Thus there was every possibility that such a methods improvement would result in an increase in output which was only marginally to the benefit of the person who created it and produced it. Ever since the time of Taylor's great innovations, short-sighted managements, trying to keep rates "in line," trying to avoid being outplayed at the incentive game by working people, have cut themselves off from this source of productivity growth by cutting rates.

The notion of giving people freedom to design their own jobs is aimed at permitting the maximum adaptation of different interests, different attitudes, and different working personalities. The key to its success is the realization that the work situation can be recreated to fit into the needs and styles of a variety of people; it can be made more accommodating to their "off the job" goals and problems, and it can be made more accommodating to those of them whose work has some fulfilling potential. We do not wish to make the assumptions currently held by so many behavioral scientists that work can become a great, wonderful, satisfying, self-actualizing aspect of one's life. In many cases it cannot; many people have neither the skill nor the desire to make it so; in many cases the implications are grossly unrealistic. If self-actualizing work is to be achieved by doing away with line assembly systems, a lot of people who choose this type of work will be disappointed, and a lot of people who consume the outputs of these systems will find their real income declining. This is a choice that working people themselves should make on the basis of their own experiments, not a choice which should be made for them by experts of some sort.

We are proposing nothing more than a strategy which has long been in use at the higher levels of our organizations among managers and professionals. We are simply suggesting that we make the experiment of trying to move this strategy toward the operating levels of our production systems, trying to find ways of making these jobs more open, less rigid, more adaptable by people to their own lives and personalities. Just as the effectiveness of those at the management and professional levels is heavily determined by their attention to system objectives and coordination, so our experiments at the operating levels will have to proceed carefully with these things in mind. Freedom to design one's job is always to be bought at the expense of attending to the objectives and coordination requirements of the job. To neglect these is, after all, to fail in the performance of the job.

TOWARD PRODUCTIVITY GROWTH

Our reading of the data, the experience, and the history of attempts to understand productivity phenomena suggests that a consistent strategy should have several aspects:

1. A broad and comprehensive view of the targets, methods, and opportunities for productivity growth in a production system. The avoidance of single effect strategies and the search for sudden technical solutions to the problem of achieving productivity potentials.

2. An explicit attempt to make estimates of the costs of pursuing each of the several best opportunities for productivity growth that are available to a system at

any time. Explicit attempts to estimate the payoffs from these opportunities and explicit renderings of the uncertainties associated with them.

3. The formation of a portfolio of productivity improvement projects which are in some sense good or even "best" for the system.

4. The recognition that uncertainty is a prominent element of innovation decisions and that this uncertainty stems from our imperfect knowledge of the potential for productivity growth associated with various targets, the effectiveness of various productivity improvement methods, and the difficulties of actual implementation.

5. The conclusion that the sensible response to such uncertainty is to regard productivity improvement attempts as essentially experimental undertakings, designed not only to yield productivity growth but also to yield additional knowledge of productivity phenomena.

6. The acceptance of the current indications that individual differences among people, among organizations, and among opportunities to improve productivity through mechanizing, through motivating people and through working smarter, are significant. Knowledge of productivity phenomena is at present not readily generalizable.

7. The acceptance of the notion that productivity phenomena depend strongly on complex interactions among the elements of production systems.

8. The recognition of the experimentation as a basic productivity growth strategy must be continuous because people and organizations change significantly with time.

9. The recognition that continuous experimentation is itself functional in the sense that to be involved in experiments is strongly motivating.

10. The aim of achieving an organizational climate of non-threatening, non-disruptive, continuous experimentation. An organizational climate in which uncertainty is acknowledged, in which the participants co-

operate in the excitement of learning about their own behavior and that of their production system.

11. The realization that our past efforts have been very likely characterized by an underestimating of the significance of individual differences and a failure to appreciate the extent to which we could usefully attend to individual differences in the design of production systems.

12. An acceptance of the impossibility of designing each job to match the individual working styles of each individual. An acceptance of the impracticality of trying to understand the complex array of individual needs which work may be satisfying for each person.

13. A willingness to consider a philosophy of job design and system design which attempts to maximize the freedom of the individual to experimentally create his own working arrangements to match his own working personality and his own array of needs to be satisfied through work.

14. A willingness to test the hypothesis that some individuals will respond to this freedom to create their own work structure in ways which are consistent with the job constraints necessary to insure system wide coordination, and in ways which enhance productivity.

Taking Our Own Medicine

Whether or not this sort of strategy will work is, we should be quick to admit, a matter of uncertainty. What is to be hoped is that it will soon become the subject of some carefully designed experiments, some experiments which are not irresponsible and which are seen as having a reasonable chance of success and are able to contribute to our understanding of the curious nature of productivity. This sort of strategy represents one reading of the evidence and the experience which has been accumulated. It represents a direction in which things seem quite clearly to be moving. It seems to be consistent with innovations that are beginning to be tried, with insights that are being advanced by well-informed people, and with the foresight of at least a few managers who are looking ahead for a stronger understanding of the productivity of their systems. Yet it must remain a matter of uncertainty, a hypothesis which will be amply justified if it stimulates an experiment, regardless of how the experiment may turn out.

Productivity is, like most things, a limited virtue. One can have too much of it, make it an end in itself, make something of a religion out of it. But it is one of those rare concepts which, when one has a hold of it, one has a hold of a lot of important things.

We have tried to face the possibility that our traditional methods of enhancing our productivity may not have the force and the effectiveness to achieve what we will require of our economic system in the future. We have tried to read the message of the data, the experience we have in hand on productivity phenomena, and to look for its suggestions about new directions. We set ourselves the task of producing a strategy which meets some specifications of realism and practicality.

Whether or not we have succeeded is a matter of uncertainty—uncertainty which must be resolved through experimentation. All of which is neatly summarized in 1974 by the remark of Henry Ford II, Chairman of the Board of the Ford Motor Company: "Productivity is a measure not of how hard we work, but of how well we use our intelligence, our imagination, and our capital."

INDEX